Hollywood Propaganda

How TV, Movies, and Music Shape Our Culture

Mark Dice

Hollywood Propaganda: How TV, Movies, and Music Shape Our Culture
© 2020 by Mark Dice
All Rights Reserved
Published by The Resistance Manifesto
San Diego, CA

Printed in the United States of America

Visit www.MarkDice.com

ISBN: 978-1-943591-09-1

Cover images licensed from iStockPhoto

Table of Contents

Also by Mark Dice:

- *The True Story of Fake News*
- *Liberalism: Find a Cure*
- *The Liberal Media Industrial Complex*

Introduction

A lot of people say, "I don't follow politics," but the reality is that pop culture *is* politics. It's woven into the fabric of movies, television shows, music—and now even professional sports. Just as art imitates life, life imitates art, and what is often seen as mere "entertainment" actually functions as a container to deliver carefully crafted pieces of propaganda intended to influence the audience as much as it is to entertain them.

Millions of people practically worship celebrities and blindly follow their lead, imitating characters' hair styles, the way they dress, and even their attitudes and behaviors. People subconsciously absorb ideas and actions they see in the media and regurgitate them as part of their own personalities.

While many celebrities engage in political activism as a hobby during their off time, the more subtle power of Hollywood is using entertainment itself to influence. The ability to influence is a tool, and tools can do great things for humanity, but in the wrong hands easily turn into weapons.

In the 1980s, *The Cosby Show* brought a nice upper middle class Black family into the homes of millions of Americans, depicting the husband as a doctor and the wife as a lawyer, changing the way many looked at the possibility of Black people achieving higher education and making a better life for themselves.[1]

---

[1] The Los Angeles Times "'The Cosby Show' Was Profound, Influential--and Indispensable" by Bobby Crawford (May 11th 1992)

For Generation X kids who grew up during this time period we watched *He-Man* and *GI Joe* cartoons which always taught a valuable lesson, either through the plotline, or a brief PSA at the end. "So now you know, and knowing is half the battle!" Shows like *Family Ties* and *Growing Pains* often tackled serious issues kids and families sometimes faced, and as cheesy as those shows may seem today, by the end of the episode there was an obvious moral to the story that undoubtedly, however subtle, affected millions of people in a positive way.

And while there are still plenty of nice family shows on television today, they are surrounded by landmines consisting of the most degenerate characters and perverted plots one could imagine—shows so vile just a generation ago it would have been unthinkable that major networks would air such content.

A strategic and relentless campaign by LGBT activists has saturated television shows, movies, and even commercials with gay, lesbian, and transgender characters which is the sole reason they have become normalized in the minds of the masses. Despite denying there was a "gay agenda," you'll see that well-funded and highly organized groups have been lobbying Hollywood studios to promote and celebrate such characters.[2]

America went from having one television per household in the 1950s—prominently placed in the family room—to children as young as seven or eight years old carrying their own TV around in their pocket and being able to watch practically anything they want with virtually

---

[2] Bloomberg "Why Stop at 10%? Advocates Push for Even More LGBT Characters on TV" by Jeff Green (November 8th 2019)

no adult supervision.[3]   So not only has there been a stunning drop in the moral quality of content in recent years, the safeguards to prevent children from consuming it have all but vanished as well.

Joshua Meyrowitz, professor of Media Studies at the University of New Hampshire, points out, "Television dilutes the innocence of childhood and the authority of adults by undermining the system of information control that supported them.   Television bypasses the year-by-year slices of knowledge given to children.   It presents the same general experiences to adults and to children of all ages.   Children may not understand everything that they see on television, but they are exposed to many aspects of adult life from which their parents (and traditional children's books) would have once shielded them."[4]

He continues, "Television and its visitors take children across the globe before parents even give them permission to cross the street."[5]   How true is that?!   And he said this in a book I've had since college—a book published back in 1995 when the Internet was just in its infancy, and a decade before social media would begin to wrap its tentacles around an entire generation of children.

Today, kids have access to unlimited adult content in the palm of their hand thanks to YouTube, Netflix, Snapchat and the rest.   Parents don't know what to do, and trying to shield children from inappropriate content in

---

[3] The Guardian "Most children own mobile phone by age of seven, study finds" (January 29th 2020)

[4] *Questioning the Media* - Chapter 3, the Mediating Communication - What Happens? page 43 by Joshua Meyrowitz

[5] *Questioning the Media* - Chapter 3, the Mediating Communication - What Happens? page 44 by Joshua Meyrowitz

today's online age would require living like the Amish. Pandora's Box has been opened.

Meanwhile, celebrities continue to speak out of both sides of their mouths—saying entertainment inspires, encourages, and teaches viewers about life, while at the same time denying that it can influence anyone in a negative way. About 100 years ago a British film industry paper called *Bioscope* once wrote that movies were the Christian church's "legitimate competitor in moulding the character of the nation."[6] Since then, the Church has lost out, and it's no longer a question of which institution has more influence.

The majority of people don't even realize what has happened. Professional hypnotherapist Dr. Rachel Copelan warned, "Most people drift into a common, everyday trance when they gaze into the light of the TV tube. Indirect hypnosis manipulates the minds of millions of unsuspecting viewers every day. Surreptitiously, subliminal persuasion leaves its mark upon the collective subconscious. Ideas implanted by commercials affect the health and behavior of all of us. We eat, drink, dress, and make love based on what we see and hear. Television has the power to lull the mind into a state of exaggerated suggestibility, opening it up to behavior control from the outside."[7]

Singer Miley Cyrus popularized "twerking" in 2013, a form of "dance" (if you can call it that) where girls rapidly shake their butt—an act that was instantly mimicked by millions of teens who now regularly post twerking videos on TikTok and Snapchat, etc. In the early

---

[6] History of British Film (Volume 4): The History of the British Film 1918 - 1929 - edited by Rachael Low

[7] Dr. Rachel Copelan - *How to Hypnotize Yourself And Others* page 3

2000s we saw the "Jackass Effect"—where kids got hurt imitating the stunts they saw Johnny Knoxville and his friends doing on the popular MTV series.[8]

A college football-themed film in 1993 called *The Program* had a scene edited out when it was later released on DVD because at one point several of the players decided to lay down in the middle of a busy highway at night to show how "brave" they were. Of course, several groups of teenagers imitated the scene which resulted in at least one death and numerous others getting seriously injured when they were struck by a car.[9]

Edward Bernays, the man who is credited with being the father of public relations, was a 20th century genius who knew how to manipulate the media in order to shape public opinion around virtually any issue. He was hired by advertising agencies and even the U.S. government to deploy his methods for a variety of aims.[10] He's the man responsible for diamond engagement rings being the cultural standard and even convinced women that smoking cigarettes was an act of defiance against the patriarchy.[11]

The De Beers diamond monopoly and the tobacco industry paid him well for his ingenuity, and because of his knowledge of psychology and mass media he was able

---

[8] New York Times "Boy, 13, Is Critically Burned After Imitating Stunt on MTV" by Sherri Day (January 29th 2001)

[9] The New York Times "Disney Plans to Omit Film Scene After Teen-Ager Dies Imitating It" by The Associated Press (October 20th 1993)

[10] Encyclopedia Britannica online edition entry "Edward Bernays: American publicist" (July 20th 1998)

[11] New York Times "Edward Bernays, 'Father of Public Relations' And Leader in Opinion Making, Dies at 103" (March 10th 1995)

to play the public like a fiddle through a series of cleverly crafted press releases and ad campaigns.

In his 1928 book *Propaganda*, he admitted, "our minds are molded, our tastes formed, our ideas suggested, largely by men we have never heard of...in almost every act of our lives whether in the sphere of politics or business in our social conduct or our ethical thinking, we are dominated by the relatively small number of persons who understand the mental processes and social patterns of the masses. It is they who pull the wires that control the public mind, who harness old social forces and contrive new ways to bind and guide the world."[12]

He even went so far as to say that those in control of the media "constitute an invisible government which is the true ruling power of our country."[13]

Entertainment rules America. Charlie Sheen made it into the *Guinness Book of World Records* as the person to reach 1 million Twitter followers the fastest once joining.[14] Ellen DeGeneres set a world record for the most retweeted tweet after she posted a selfie taken with a group of other celebrities at the 2014 Oscars.[15] Music videos get more views than political speeches, and celebrities make more money while they sleep than police officers or fire fighters do risking their lives to keep their communities safe.

---

[12] Bernays, Edward – *Propaganda* page 37-38 (Ig Publishing 2005)

[13] Ibid.

[14] CBS News "Charlie Sheen Sets Guinness World Record: Fastest to a million Twitter followers" by Crimesider Staff (March 4th 2011)

[15] USA Today "Ellen DeGeneres nabs most retweeted tweet of the year" by Alison Maxwell (December 10th 2014)

The majority of media today functions as a modern-day equivalent of the "bread and circuses" of ancient Rome, where people were pacified by games and food at the Colosseum, so they weren't paying attention to the collapsing empire around them. Karl Marx famously said that religion was the "opiate of the masses," but really its entertainment. It's television sitcoms, sports, and anything that streams. It's the trending list on Twitter and the viral hashtags on Instagram.

Entertainment is such a powerful medium for influencing people's behavior that for several years the CIA actually secretly recruited and directed popular rappers in Cuba to write and perform "protest songs" denouncing their Communist leader Raul Castro in order to foment civil unrest and erode support for his regime.[16] It may seem like the plot out of a movie, but declassified documents obtained by the Associated Press years later show that's exactly what they did.[17]

The CIA had a budget of millions of dollars for this program and used a front company (which is commonplace) named Creative Associates International in order to conceal their activities.[18] They literally created a talent agency to mold the music and careers of artists they thought could be used to influence Cubans to rise up

---

[16] Billboard "How the U.S. Government Infiltrated Cuba's Hip-Hop Scene to Spark Change" via Associated Press (December 11th 2014)

[17] Reuters "U.S. defends program to fund anti-government hip-hop music in Cuba" by David Adams (December 11th 2014)

[18] CBS News "U.S. infiltrated Cuba's hip-hop scene to spark change" (December 11th 2014)

against Raul Castro.[19]   Similar operations have been run in America.

Shortly after President Trump's inauguration, the DJ Moby, who was fairly popular in the early 2000s, revealed that he had been in contact with "active and former CIA agents" who "confirmed" to him that Russia was "blackmailing" Trump and said they needed his help to get the word out. "So they passed on some information to me and they said, like, 'Look, you have more of a social media following than any of us do, can you please post some of these things just in a way that…sort of put it out there.'"[20]   Deep State operatives reaching out to celebrities hoping to use them to smear Donald Trump— and that's just the tip of the iceberg.

In this book you'll learn in detail how the Hollywood elite are using their media conglomerates to wage a war on President Trump and his supporters, and not just by celebrities "speaking out," but by incorporating countless anti-Trump themes into their projects. You'll see who is behind the coordinated effort to promote climate change hysteria, how the entertainment industry was instrumental in getting the public to accept gay "marriage," and how they are waging a war against traditional family values, American culture, and even against God Himself.

The late Andrew Breitbart famously said that politics is downstream from culture, meaning if you want to change the laws in a country, you have to first change the culture. This saying became known as the Breitbart Doctrine because it captures the essence of power,

---

[19] *The Guardian* "US agency infiltrated Cuban hip-hop scene to spark youth unrest" by Matthew Weaver (December 10th 2014)

[20] Pitchfork "Moby Says CIA Agents Asked Him to Spread the Word About Trump and Russia" by Noah Yoo (January 12th 2018)

propaganda, and politics and explains how many once fringe ideas and behaviors are now legally protected and any business, school, or landlord that dares to disagree can now be punished with the full force of the courts.

Within these pages you'll also learn that liberal Hollywood has some interesting bedfellows when it comes to promoting war, and you'll be shocked to find that the U.S. government often works hand in hand with major studios to produce what essentially amounts to propaganda films; and why there has been an explosion in plots promoting mass immigration, abortion, and socialism.

Not even sports coverage is immune from being turned into another mouthpiece for their agenda as the Left is now pulling out all of the stops hoping to succeed in their "cultural revolution." Let's now pull back the curtain and take a look around behind the scenes of *Hollywood Propaganda*.

The Politics of Entertainment

Television commercials try to sell you a product or a service despite the fact that most of the time the content of the commercials has nothing to do at all with what they're actually selling. Celebrities drink a soda and react as if it gives them an orgasm. "Ahhh! Pepsi, the choice of a new generation" they say with a huge fake smile. Samuel L. Jackson shouts "What's in your wallet!" as if it's a punchline from a sitcom while he's simply promoting a credit card. Ads for insurance featuring a caveman and a gecko are passed off as if they're characters from a recurring comedy series, and the list goes on.

But it's not just products or services that companies try to sell us through entertainment. It's ideas. Hollywood propaganda is carefully woven into movies and TV shows with the intent of influencing the audience rather than merely entertain them. Sometimes the central plot serves as the propaganda which is coated in a thin layer of entertainment, but the writers and producers know, and often openly admit, what their true intentions are.

Film critic James Combs wrote, "The term *propaganda* comes from the Latin *propagare*, denoting the ability to produce and spread fertile messages that, once sown, will germinate in large human cultures," adding, "Removed from its pejorative connotation,

11

propaganda may be viewed objectively as a form of communication that has practical and influential consequences," and can "sway relevant groups of people in order to achieve their purposes."[21]

In the late 1980s a man named Jay Winsten, who worked as an associate dean at Harvard's School of Public Health, launched a campaign to convince Hollywood producers to include messages about the dangers of drunk driving in TV shows along with the importance of using designated drivers.[22] It was called the Harvard Alcohol Project and soon the term "designated driver" was being used in shows like *Cheers*, *L.A. Law*, *The Cosby Show*, and countless others, catapulting it into the public lexicon.[23]

Before the 1980s there wasn't much of a social stigma against driving drunk, but with a persistent propaganda campaign from groups like the Harvard Alcohol Project and MADD [Mothers Against Drunk Driving], the country as a whole began thinking differently about the issue.

More recently, special interest groups use their power to promote abortion, the gay agenda, Obamacare, climate change hysteria, and literally every one of their social justice crusades in the same way. But in these cases, instead of raising awareness for a public good, like

[21] *Film Propaganda and American Politics: An Analysis and Filmography* by James Combs and Sara T. Combs page 6 (Routledge 2013)

[22] New York Observer "Hooray for Hollywood: How Charities Influence Your Favorite TV Shows" by Anne Easton (October 28th 2015)

[23] The Washington Post "This Harvard professor used TV sitcoms to fight drunk driving. Can he do the same for distracted driving?" by Fredrick Kunkie (April 26th 2017)

stigmatizing drunk driving, they're using their influence to push fringe political ideas into the mainstream and convince the masses to accept the most flagrant violations of morality and decency.

Social Impact Entertainment

Today there are over 100 organizations dedicated to using entertainment to further political and social causes, and there's even an Orwellian term for the propaganda they create—"Social Impact Entertainment." In 2014 UCLA opened the Skoll Center for Social Impact Entertainment (SIE) which boasts to be "the first of its kind dedicated solely to advancing the power of entertainment and performing arts to inspire social change."[24]

The department is committed to "exploring innovative approaches to curricular development for the emerging field of social impact entertainment, but also provide students and faculty with workshops, lectures, distinguished visiting artists programs and unique opportunities to focus their scholarly and creative work in this arena."[25]

"It will launch research initiatives that explore the development of a new field in social impact entertainment research and practice; inspire students and faculty to use the power of story to make a difference and inspire social change; galvanize the public to action to foster positive social change; develop meaningful partnerships between

---

[24] UCLA's official Theater, Film & Television department website. http://www.tft.ucla.edu/skoll-center-for-social-impact-entertainment/

[25] Ibid.

13

the public and private sectors to create new models to drive social change; and engage local, national and global communities about how the industry impacts global society through film, television, animation, digital media and theater."[26]

In 2019 they released a report titled "The State of SIE" [Social Impact Entertainment] where they said, "Given the magnitude of today's challenges—climate change, economic inequality, forced migrations and any number of other problems—it's easy for people to get discouraged about their capacity to make a difference in the world. But as the case studies in this report reveal, SIE can play a critical role in catalyzing significant change."[27]

The report cited Al Gore's documentary *An Inconvenient Truth*, which it said, "helped shift global opinions on climate change, one of the most contentious issues of our time, and mobilized a new generation of pioneering environmental activists."[28]

It appears that the Skoll Center for Social Impact grew out of another UCLA program which had the same goals called the Global Media Center for Social Impact (GMI) which was founded a year earlier in 2013. Sandra de Castro Buffington, who was the director of the program, said, "Topics that have been traditionally taboo are showing up on series television and they're being discussed, especially via social media, and because of this they don't seem so controversial anymore. When

26 Ibid.

27 https://thestateofsie.com/the-state-of-social-impact-entertainment-sie-report-introduction-peter-bisanz/

28 Ibid.

something goes from being taboo to being openly discussed, it's a predictor of mass behavior change."[29]

An industry publication called *Cinema of Change* noted, "[The Global Media Center for Social Impact] provides the entertainment industry with free, on-demand access to leading experts and cutting-edge resources on topics such as health, immigration, racial justice, America's prison crisis, the environment, LGBT/gender equality, learning and attention issues, youth sexuality, reproductive health and rights and more. From script reviews and writers' room consultations to off-site visits and special events, GMI facilitates experiences for industry professionals that inspire them to create stories that entertain, engage, and empower viewers to make change on issues that matter to them."[30]

Their website, GMImpact.org is now defunct, and it appears they morphed into UCLA's Skoll Center for Social Impact in 2014, which was created with a $10 million dollar donation by billionaire Jeffrey Skoll, who made his money as the first president of e-Bay.

The Center for Media & Social Impact

A similar SIE organization is located in Washington D.C. at American University called the Center for Media & Social Impact (CMSI). They describe themselves as "an innovation lab and research center that creates, studies and showcases media for social

29 New York Observer "Hooray for Hollywood: How Charities Influence Your Favorite TV Shows" by Anne Easton (October 28th 2015)

30 https://www.cinemaofchange.com/directory/listing/the-global-media-center-for-social-impact.

impact. Focusing on independent, documentary, entertainment, and public media, the Center bridges boundaries between scholars, producers and communication practitioners across media production, media impact and effects, public policy and audience engagement. The Center produces resources for the field and academic research; convenes conferences and events; and works collaboratively to understand and design media that matter."[31]

They receive funding through various grants and list some of those contributors on their website, including Bill Gates, the Rockefeller Foundation, the Ford Foundation, the National Endowment for the Arts, and Univision.

In 2019 the Center for Media & Social Impact launched "Comedy Think Tanks" which aims to use comedy to promote social justice issues. The following year they released a report titled *Comedy and Racial Justice in the Climate Crisis* that "analyzes the value and importance of comedy for local public mobilization in climate change."[32]

The report highlights "the unique potential of social justice comedy" and suggests it be used as a "mobilization strategy, and as disruptive creative expression inserted into a broader cultural conversation about climate change, centering communities of color and low-income people who are 'hit first and worst' by climate disasters."[33]

---

[31] https://cmsimpact.org/about-us/ (August 2020)

[32] Comedy for Racial Justice in the Climate Crisis by Caty Borum Chattoo page 5 (August 2020)

[33] Ibid.

It concludes, "Through the open-minded experience of co-creating with comedy professionals, social justice organizations can embrace the innovation and creativity that comedy can provide. Comedy can cut through cultural clutter, and it also entertains and invites feelings of play. This kind of light is needed in the climate movement, which can feel too complicated and difficult to engage disparate groups and communities beyond a stream of fatiguing outrage or clinical statistics."[34]

Propper Daley

Propper Daley is another "social impact agency" which was founded by Greg Propper and Mark Daley, who are close associates to Hillary Clinton. Before helping start the agency, Greg Propper actually worked for the Clinton Foundation, and when Hillary was running for president in 2016, Propper Daley helped organized fundraisers for her, bringing together stars like Leonardo DiCaprio, Tobey Maguire and others under the same roof.[35]

Previously they had organized meetings with writers from TV shows like *Parks and Recreation*, *How I Met Your Mother*, and *Glee*, to sit down with Chelsea Clinton to discuss how they could help promote some of the Clinton Foundation's initiatives.[36] Patti Miller, who worked for the foundation, admitted the meeting aimed to

---

[34] Comedy for Racial Justice in the Climate Crisis by Caty Borum Chattoo page 19 (August 2020).

[35] Hollywood Reporter "Hillary Clinton Woos Young Hollywood Democrats at Fundraisers in L.A." by Tina Daunt (June 19th 2015)

[36] Hollywood Reporter "Chelsea Clinton to Meet With Network TV Writers on Saturday" by Tina Daunt (June 13th 2014)

"bring together a cross section of the industry, with leading television comedy writers, hoping they can help us reach our audience with creative, funny content."[37]

In March 2019 Propper Daley held a private invite-only conference with 400 writers, producers and executives to discuss how they could use their positions to "think differently or with more nuance about certain characters or storylines and hopefully create a more empathetic public."[38] In other words, to lobby them to include more pro-gay and transgender storylines, and promote mass immigration, abortion, and other Leftist causes through their work.

GLAAD

GLAAD [the Gay and Lesbian Alliance Against Defamation] has been aggressively lobbying Hollywood for years to include gay and transgender characters in television series and films. One of their current aims is to pressure studios to include gay characters in 20% of films by the year 2021 and 50% of all films by the year 2024.[39]

Each year they release their *Studio Responsibility Index*, a report where they track their progress and complain that mainstream entertainment isn't gay enough. They even have what they call the "GLAAD Media

---

[37] Ibid.

[38] Forbes "The Power Of Purpose: How Propper Daley Is Driving 'Unreasonable Conversations'" by Afdhel Aziz (March 12th 2019)

[39] GLAAD.org "2018 Studio Responsibility Index" by Megan Townsend (May 22nd 2018)

Institute" that has drawn up a "roadmap for Hollywood to grow LGBTQ inclusion in film."[40]

Their 2018 *Studio Responsibility Index* says, "With wildly successful films like *Wonder Woman* and *Black Panther* proving that audiences want to see diverse stories that haven't been told before, there is simply no reason for major studios to have such low scores...At a time when the entertainment industry is holding much needed discussions about inclusion, now is the time to ensure the industry takes meaningful action and incorporates LGBTQ stories and creators as among priorities areas for growing diversity."[41]

It goes on, "Studios must do better to include more LGBTQ characters, and construct those stories in a way that is directly tied to the film's plot...Far too often LGBTQ characters and stories are relegated to subtext, and it is left up to the audience to interpret or read into a character as being LGBTQ. Audiences may not realize they are seeing an LGBTQ character unless they have outside knowledge of a real figure, have consumed source material for an adaptation, or have read external press confirmations. This is not enough...Our stories deserve to be seen on screen just as much as everyone else's, not hidden away or left to guess work, but boldly and fully shown."[42]

It's really an open secret in Hollywood, but few people outside the industry are familiar with the intense (and very successful) lobbying efforts the organization engages in. *Entertainment Weekly* recently admitted that

---

[40] Ibid.

[41] Ibid.

[42] Ibid.

"GLAAD is changing Hollywood's LGBTQ narrative—one script at a time," and CEO Sarah Kate Ellis confirmed that as far back as the mid-1980s, "we realized we needed Hollywood to be telling our stories to humanize LGBTQ people. So we opened a chapter very quickly in Los Angeles, in Hollywood, and really the main focus was lobbying Hollywood to tell our stories."[43]

I'll cover this topic in more detail in "The LGBT Agenda" chapter because it's one of the Left's most aggressive efforts, and in the last few years they have successfully caused an influx of LGBT characters in major television series, and even convinced Disney and Sesame Street to get on board with their plans.[44]

United Nations

The United Nations has a special program called the Creative Community Outreach Initiative to lobby producers and celebrities to help them promote various agendas as well. In 2009 they convinced producers of NBC's *Law and Order: Special Victims Unit* to make an episode about child soldiers who were brainwashed by the Lord's Resistance Army in Uganda.[45] The U.N. also convinced ABC's *Ugly Betty* to incorporate the use of mosquito nets over beds to prevent the spread of malaria in Africa by having the lead character promote the (real)

---

[43] Entertainment Weekly "How GLAAD is changing Hollywood's LGBTQ narrative — one script at a time" by Gerrad Hall (May 23rd 2020)

[44] The Advocate "Sesame Street Celebrates LGBTQ+ Pride With Rainbow Muppet Message" by Daniel Reynolds (June 12th 2020)

[45] CNN "U.N. hosts filming of 'Law & Order: SVU' episode" by Richard Roth and Even Buxbaum (March 30th 2009)

Nothing But Nets program which works to donate bed nets to people there.[46]

The United Nations has even launched a campaign called "The Unstereotype Alliance" which has been backed by consumer product giants Procter & Gamble and Unilever, along with the Big Tech companies like Google, Facebook and others to promote "social justice" through advertising campaigns for unrelated products.[47]

"Advertising is a reflection of culture and sometimes can be ahead of the curve and help effect change. We are proud to be a founding member of this UN sponsored initiative to 'unstereotype' through the power and breadth of our messaging. We are all in," said a Microsoft executive.[48]

It used to be that commercials promoted the benefits of their products and did their best to avoid getting political because Republicans and Democrats both drink beer, eat hamburgers, and buy cars; and companies didn't want to ostracize half of their potential customers by supporting any polarizing causes. But since the liberal pathogen has caused a zombie-like apocalypse in America recently, many large corporations have decided to take up the banner of "social justice," and when lobbyists from the "Unstereotype" campaign make demands, companies often oblige.

This goes far beyond companies trying to be environmentally friendly, introducing recyclable

---

[46] TV Guide "*Ugly Betty* Teams with United Nations to Fight Malaria" by Adam Bryant (October 9th 2009)

[47] AdAge "The UN Believes Ads Can Turn the Tide in Long-Losing War for Gender Equality" by Jack Neff (June 23rd 2017)

[48] Unilever Press Release "Launch of Unstereotype Alliance set to eradicate outdated stereotypes in advertising" (June 20th 2017)

packaging, or highlighting how they're using renewable energy to power their factories. Nobody could really disagree with those practices. I'm talking about companies that actually now insult half of their potential customers in the hopes of gaining the unwavering support of a smaller segment of society because of their "woke" campaigns.

They don't even see it as insulting people, they're just so arrogant that they feel they need to "educate" people about social justice causes, or think they need to virtue signal about how much "they care" by jumping on the bandwagon. The Unstereotype Alliance has boasted of "smashing" gender roles in commercials so now they don't depict cleaning as "women's work," and regularly feature interracial and homosexual couples to give them more "visibility."[49]

Promoting Obamacare

When President Obama was trying to get Obamacare passed into law, his administration was aided by a chorus of enthusiastic celebrities who used their voice to support the bill, but behind the scenes strings were being pulled to encourage them to speak up, and Hollywood studios were actually lobbied to include pro Obamacare messages in the plots of popular TV shows.[50]

One such lobbyist group called Hollywood, Health & Society works with studios to promote health based initiatives and were paid $500,000 to convince them to

---

[49] Unilever.com "12 Unilever Ads That Smash Stereotypes" (January 8th 2019)

[50] New York Post "Is there ObamaCare 'propaganda' on our favorite shows?" by Kyle Smith (October 19th 2013)

incorporate "the need for Obamacare" into storylines of network TV shows[51] An executive with the organization said, "Our experience has shown that the public gets just as much, if not more, information about current events and important issues from their favorite television shows and characters as they do from the news media...This grant will allow us to ensure that industry practitioners have up-to-date, relevant facts on health care reform to integrate into their storylines and projects."[52]

Hollywood, Health & Society has become the one-stop-shop for organizations that want to have their messages covertly inserted into entertainment. Executive Kate Folb, admitted, "There was a time when there were so many organizations lobbying the entertainment industry on just their one issue, that it was just too much. They were all calling the same writers and trying to get meetings with the same shows. What happened was the industry stopped taking all of those calls because they became so overwhelmed. That's part of the reason HH&S came into being: to help writers get what they need and keep them from getting overwhelmed with requests to include certain messages in their shows."[53]

Another PR firm called Ogilvy Public Relations Worldwide was paid $900,000 to pitch Obamacare plots to major networks. They even tried to get major networks

---

[51] The Washington Times "TV propaganda? $500K grant to sneak pro-Obamacare messages in shows" by Cheryl Chumley (October 11th 2013)

[52] The New York Post "Is there ObamaCare 'propaganda' on our favorite shows?" by Kyle Smith (October 19th 2013)

[53] New York Observer "Hooray for Hollywood: How Charities Influence Your Favorite TV Shows" by Anne Easton (October 28th 2015)

to shoot a reality show about "the trials and tribulations of families living without medical coverage."[54]

"I'd like to see 10 of the major TV shows, or telenovelas, have people talking about 'that health insurance thing,'" said Peter V. Lee, the California Health Benefit Exchange's executive director, which hired the PR firm. "There are good story lines here."[55]

President Obama brought a bunch of actors and producers to the White House to ask them for their help promoting Obamacare, and soon they started happily doing so.[56] In October 2013, Jennifer Hudson starred in a *Funny or Die* skit designed to promote Obamacare where she played a Washington D.C. "fixer" or a "scandal manager" in a parody of ABC's series *Scandal*.

The "funny part" was that everyone who tried to hire her to fix their problems (like a college student without any health insurance, and a guy who was changing insurance companies but was worried they were going to drop him because of preexisting conditions), learned that there was no problem at all because of Obamacare.[57] It was a pathetic attempt at humor and to do such a lame skit under the *Funny or Die* banner made it even more sad, but they wanted to do their part to help the cause.

President Obama also appeared on Zach Galifianakis' *Funny or Die* skit "Between Two Ferns" for a scripted

---

[54] The New York Times "California Tries to Guide the Way on Health Law" by Abby Goodnough (September 14th 2012)

[55] Ibid.

[56] The Los Angeles Times "Obama looks to Hollywood to help promote his healthcare law" by Maeve Reston (September 20th 2013)

[57] The Hollywood Reporter "Jennifer Hudson Pitches Obamacare in Will Ferrell's Funny or Die Clip" by Paul Bond (September 30th 2013)

interview meant to be funny but was just another stunt to promote Obamacare. It worked, however, and when the segment was posted online it became the number one source of traffic to the new HealthCare.gov website.[58]

The White House Entertainment Advisory Council admitted, "This is a perfect example of a great partnership with *Funny or Die* stepping up in a big way. The site has a very robust traffic base of young men and women who are on the edge of the cultural zeitgeist. It has an organic reach, and now the traditional media will be talking about it for days."[59]

Under the Obama administration all of Hollywood was more than willing to support anything the White House wanted, but once Donald Trump took over the Oval Office everything changed as I will detail in the next chapter, the "War on Trump."

Abortion

Planned Parenthood is America's largest abortion factory and most people have no idea they also have a special Arts & Entertainment Engagement department that reaches out to television studios and "feeds" them plot points they would like included in shows.[60] Few people outside of the industry know such a department exists and

---

[58] USA Today "Healthcare.gov gets traffic boost after Obama's 'Funny or Die' video" by Jolie Lee (March 12th 2014)

[59] Hollywood Reporter "ObamaCare Website Traffic Spikes After President's 'Funny or Die' Interview" by Tina Daunt (March 11th 2014)

[60] National Catholic Register "Planned Parenthood 'Secret Weapon' Script Doctor Feeds Abortion Line to Hollywood" by Lauretta Brown (September 23rd 2019)

most would probably have a hard time believing it, but it does. And for eight years now they've been hosting an annual "Sex, Politics, Film, & TV Reception" at the Sundance Film Festival to "celebrate" films and television shows that promote abortion.[61]

Little press coverage has been given to Planned Parenthood's Arts & Entertainment Engagement department, but *The Washington Post* did mention their work once, saying, "For nearly 50 years, it has been legal to have an abortion in America yet stubbornly taboo to show one on television or film. But both those things are now changing."[62] The article went on to admit the existence of the abortion A&E department and list some of their "successes." I'll cover their activities in more detail in the "War on America" chapter, but for now you should at least know that such an apparatus exists and has been working behind the scenes for years.

Easy abortions cause many women to ignore the use of simple precautions to reduce the risk of pregnancy, and by softening the social stigma that has historically been associated with abortions, many young girls now see them as a regular part of life.

---

[61] PlannedParenthood.org "Planned Parenthood Hosts 8th Annual Sex, Politics, Film, & TV Reception at Sundance Film Festival" Press Release (January 27th 2020)

[62] The Washington Post "Planned Parenthood's Secret Weapon" by Nora Caplain-Bricker (September 23rd 2019)

War on Trump

It's obvious that the "news" media has been waging a disinformation war against President Trump since the day he won the 2016 election—something I chronicled in my previous book *The True Story of Fake News*. But the entertainment industry has also dedicated much of their creative efforts to continuously casting him and everything he does in a negative light by weaving anti-Trump narratives into the plot lines of countless television dramas and sitcoms to ensure as many people as possible are inundated with the message. Stephen Colbert went so far as to produce an entire animated series for HBO called *Our Cartoon President* which is dedicated to mocking him.

Before becoming President, the media used to love Donald Trump. For decades he was a symbol of wealth and success, and throughout the 1980s and 90s made cameos in dozens of TV shows and movies like *The Fresh Prince of Bel-Air*, *Spin City*, *WrestleMania*, *Home Alone 2*, *Zoolander*, and more. But all that changed after winning the 2016 election, when the Liberal Media Industrial Complex launched a war against him hoping to derail his administration and prevent him from cleaning up the corruption in Washington D.C. and bringing the government gravy train to a halt.

ABC's sitcom *Black-ish* revolves around an African American family and the issues they face as a Black middle-class family in America today, and shortly after the 2016 election there was an episode about how "terrified" everyone was about Trump's victory and what it would mean for Black people.[63]

For his entire professional life Donald Trump has been a friend of the Black community and had been given awards for all he did.[64] Every leader in the Black community from Jesse Jackson and Al Sharpton to Muhammad Ali had sung praises of him for decades, but now the media started gaslighting that he was a racist, hoping to get Black people to turn against him.[65]

In an episode of *The Simpsons*, Lisa is seen reading *To Kill a Mockingbird* while seated on the couch next to Homer, when he tells her, "Now just remember, it's set in the South a long time ago. The terrible racism you're reading about is now *everywhere*."[66] Homer and Lisa then head off to the local mall and pass a TV news crew which is interviewing a group of men, one wearing a red hat. "Kent Brockman here interviewing three blue-collar men who voted for Trump. How do you feel now?" the reporter asks them. One of the men replies, "Please stop interviewing us," as if he's ashamed he voted for President Trump and realized he made a big mistake.

In an episode of the revived *Murphy Brown* series, a character (who is a reporter) was depicted as being attacked by rabid Trump supporters because of their

---

[63] Black-ish (Season 3, episode titled "Lemons") first aired January 11th 2017

[64] Snopes "Did Donald Trump Receive an Ellis Island Award in 1986?" Rating: True by Dan Evon (September 5th 2016)

[65] Patheos "FLASHBACK: Jesse Jackson Praises Donald Trump for 'Lifetime of Service' to Blacks" by Martin English (January 16th 2018)

[66] The Simpsons (Season 30, episode 9, title "Daddicus Finch")

hatred for the media.[67]   While promoting the show Candice Bergen (who plays Murphy Brown) said Donald Trump winning the 2016 election was the motivation to revive it.[68]   The original series which aired from 1988-1998 depicted Murphy Brown as an investigative journalist and news anchor, so producers thought with Trump's war on the media raging they could bring the show back and have Murphy Brown working to "expose" him.

Rolling Stone noted, "The season premiere climaxes with Murphy swapping insults with President Trump during a live broadcast (him via Twitter, her glaring at the camera). The second episode has her lecturing Sarah Huckabee Sanders about the fundamental dishonesty of her press briefings, while the third sees her verbally dismantling a barely-disguised version of Steve Bannon."[69]   Literally the entire reason for bringing the show back was to use the angle of Trump vs the media, with Murphy Brown and other reporters being the underdogs and the "victims" of President Trump's attacks.

When NBC brought back *Will & Grace* in 2017 after initially ending the series in 2006, one new episode depicted a character walking into a cake shop because she's hosting a birthday party for the president and wants a cake that says Make America Great Again on it. While ordering the cake she makes a comment about how she'll

67 Newsbusters "Reporter Beaten at Trump Rally on 'Murphy Brown,' Attacked by 'Sea of Red Hats'" by Karen Townsend (November 29th 2018)

68 CBS This Morning "Trump's election motivated 'Murphy Brown' reboot, Candice Bergen says" by Jessica Kegu (September 26th 2018)

69 Rolling Stone 'Murphy Brown' Review: A Crusty Comeback" by Alan Sepinwall (September 25th 2018)

be serving White Russians, a reference to the Democrats' obsession that the Trump campaign "conspired" with Russians to "steal" the 2016 election, adding, "But you don't need to know the guest list."[70]   The baker then refused to bake the cake saying that the phrase "Make America Great Again" is racist.[71]

Vice News had a whole series called *The Hunt for the Trump Tapes* starring comedian Tom Arnold where he traveled around the world looking for the rumored "Trump pee tape" or a supposed recording of him saying the n-word.   And just like the shows about people searching for Bigfoot that are somehow able to be drawn out for an hour each week despite never finding a shred of evidence, *The Hunt for the Trump Tapes* finally ended without uncovering a thing.[72]

Even the *X-Files* has included anti-Trump messages. The series, which originally ran from 1993-2002 was revived in 2016 for a few more seasons and in January 2018 the season premiere kicked off with the "Cigarette Smoking Man" narrating footage of President Trump's inauguration which then cuts to a montage of clips including Vladimir Putin, people at voting booths, a KKK rally, and police confronting Black Lives Matter protesters while he continues to talk about the state of the country.[73]   Robert Mueller is also depicted as the head of

---

[70] News Busters "Will & Grace Won't Bake MAGA Cake: Conservatives are 'Terrible People' with 'Horrible Beliefs'" by Dawn Slusher (March 16th 2018)

[71] Ibid.

[72] Vulture "The Hunt for the Trump Tapes Doesn't Seem Likely to Uncover Much" by Jen Chaney (September 14th 2018)

[73] The Verge "In a post-truth environment, The X-Files has gotten political" by Samantha Nelson (February 9th 2018)

the FBI in the series, but "the bureau's not in good standing with the White House."

In one episode Scully tells Mulder "Sometimes I think the world is going to hell and we're the only two people who can save it," to which he responds, "The world is going to hell, Scully. And the president is working to bring down the FBI along with it."[74]   After an assassination attempt on Mulder he later discovers the perpetrator is a Russian contractor with a special security clearance given to him by "the Executive branch" of our government, insinuating the President was trying to have him killed.[75]

But the anti-Trump snides in sitcoms and dramas get much darker than just obsessing about how "terrible" President Trump is, or promoting the conspiracy theory that he's a Russian agent. They're openly calling for violence against his supporters, and want him to be assassinated.

Endorsing Violence

The CBS legal drama *The Good Fight* posted a trailer on their official Twitter account which showed one of the main characters ranting about how "some speech" deserves "enforcement" and that it's time to physically attack American citizens "unprovoked" who are engaging

---

[74] Ibid.

[75] Newsbusters "'The X-Files' Wants to Believe in Trump-Russia Conspiracy" by Lindsay Kornick (January 10th 2018)

in speech that social justice warriors perceive as "racist."[76]

To the Left, supporting the border wall is considered "racist" and all Trump voters are Nazis and they want us all to be silenced, jailed, or dead. *The Good Fight* clip also referred to Alt-Right leader Richard Spencer getting sucker punched while giving an interview in Washington D.C. and insinuated that anyone wearing a MAGA hat in public should face the same fate.

The show's Twitter account also posted a picture showing a list of words stacked on top of each other reading, "Assassinate," "President," and "Trump."[77] In one episode a character was arrested for participating in a riot, and during his court appearance when he was talking with his lawyer he told her that the judge was a Trump appointee and so he is "fucked." She advises him not to say anything radical, and he responds in a quiet voice, "Oh, like 'we need to assassinate the president?'"

Later, when they're back at his house she says to him, "Tell me what you said today in court was a joke" to which he responds, "Why? You don't believe in regime change?"

"You're discussing a crime with your lawyer," she responds and then takes his pistol and unloads it. He looks at her, disappointed, and says, "This won't slow us down."[78]

---

[76] RedState "Is CBS Inciting Violence In The Latest Episode Of 'The Good Fight'" by Jennifer Van Laar (April 13th 2019)

[77] The Wrap "CBS All Access' 'The Good Fight' Deletes Tweet with List of Words That Included 'Assassinate' and 'Trump'" by Sean Burch (April 16th 2019)

[78] Newsbusters "'The Good Fight' Character: 'We Need to Assassinate the President' by Callista Ring (April 22nd 2018)

In another episode one of the lead characters (Diane) goes on a rant about needing to get rid of President Trump and when she proposes spreading fake news about him, some of her colleagues push back thinking she's gone too far. She then responds, "I have a Smith & Wesson 64 [handgun] in my desk, and I'm this close to taking to the streets."[79]

The series even depicted the lawyers obtaining the fabled "Trump golden showers video" after getting a flash drive sent to them by a Russian woman who claimed to have been one of the prostitutes in the video. *The Daily Beast*, a garbage online outlet and waste of cyberspace, was happy that such a grotesque plot line was aired on network television, saying, "It allows the show to channel our collective anxieties and outrage better than most other series that grapple with our new political reality."[80]

Amazon produced a show for their Prime streaming service titled *Hunters* which is about a "diverse" group of vigilantes led by Al Pacino who go around assassinating people they think are closet "Nazis" working in the United States to revive the Third Reich. In one of the trailers posted online a "Nazi" could be seen wearing a red baseball cap with some white writing on it, looking almost identical to a Make America Great Again hat.[81]

"The best revenge, is revenge," says Al Pacino's character, who tells the vigilantes they "have to find them

---

[79] Ibid.

[80] The Daily Beast "'The Good Fight' Imagines a Trump 'Pee Tape' as Impeachment Heads to Network TV" by Kevin Fallon (April 30th 2018)

[81] Summit News "New Amazon Show Features White People Wearing Red MAGA-Style Hats Being Hunted As 'Nazis'" by Paul Joseph Watson (November 25th 2019)

before they find us." The series could easily incite (and perhaps has incited) vigilantes to go out and attack supposed "Nazis" (meaning ordinary Trump supporters). The Left thinks free speech is "hate speech" and "hate speech" is "violence," so they justify physically attacking Trump supporters unprovoked because Antifa believes they're fighting actual Nazis.

The executive producer of *Hunters* is Jordan Peele, the Black director behind *Get Out* who has an axe to grind with White people, so it's not surprising he would be involved with a series that fetishizes torturing and killing them.

The Left always accuse others of exactly what they're guilty of themselves. It's a form psychological projection, as well as a gaslighting technique. They are so detached from reality that they lack the ability of introspection and can't see that *they* are the violent ones, while claiming that it's President Trump and his supporters. They're acting like fascists, while accusing President Trump of being one. They are the racists, spewing hatred of White people every day while claiming White people are conspiring to uphold the "systemic White supremacist system" in the United States simply because they exist.

Alec Baldwin says, "the near moral collapse of this country falls squarely in the lap of Trump's supporters," when in reality they are the immoral degenerates destroying the foundations of our Republic.[82]

Law and Order: SVU aired an episode about a character based on an amalgamation of Ann Coulter and Millie Weaver who was sexually assaulted by a suspected

---

[82] Washington Times "Alec Baldwin sees 'near moral collapse' in America, blames it on Trump 'supporters'" by Jessica Chasmar (January 14th 2020)

Antifa member, but because of her political views some of the police investigating the attack wrestled with sympathizing with her. The episode was titled "Info Wars."

At the end, the final twist was the attacker might not have been Antifa after all, but one of her own supporters (depicted as a vile White supremacist) because he got upset with her after she had turned down his advances the night before when they met at a bar. The "moral" of the story was Antifa are just peaceful protesters fighting against right-wing extremists, and while the victim was worried about them, thinking they were responsible for her assault, it was her own supporters who are the violent ones.

The series usually depicts White men as the criminals, often rapists, and avoids storylines about illegal aliens being the perpetrators or Latino gangs involved in sex trafficking even though the show is supposedly often inspired by actual events. And it is extra careful not to include very many Black people as perpetrators out of the usual concerns of supposedly perpetuating "stereotypes" about Black men and crime.

Actress Jessica Chastain once posted a link on Twitter to a *Time* magazine article denouncing Antifa, the Left's terrorist foot soldiers, adding "If we resort to violence as a way to combat hate, we become what we are fighting," but then later posted a video tearfully apologizing after being barraged by social justice warriors saying that she was helping "Nazis" (meaning Trump supporters) by denouncing the increasing violence being waged against them.

"I'm making a video because my heart is very heavy," the apology began. "I've learned so much the past few days about the trauma many people are experiencing in our country. I've had the opportunity to listen, more than to speak. And [dramatic pause] it's really hard for me to express my feelings, my thoughts, in 140 characters on Twitter so here's my first video. I wanted you guys to know that I hear you. I want you to know that I'm committed to creating transformative social change. That I'm committed to dismantling systems of oppression. I share in the sadness of what is happening in the country. I hear you and you may never have met me, but I love you."[83] She literally cried and apologized for denouncing violence against Trump supporters!

Teen Vogue magazine declared "Antifa grows out of a larger revolutionary politics that aspires toward creating a better world, but the primary motivation is to stop racists from organizing."[84] A better world? If Donald Trump wins reelection, Antifa may feel they have no other option to stop him than to become overt terrorists like the Weather Underground or the Symbionese Liberation Army since every attempt from the last four years to demonize him and remove him through impeachment and the ballot box have failed.

Daily Show host Trevor Noah, who is from South Africa, says that Trump's demeanor and style is like "many African dictators" or those from the Middle East.[85] And virtually every celebrity with a talk show from the

---

[83] Hollywood Reporter "Jessica Chastain Clarifies Comments About Non-Violent Protests" by THR Staff (September 1st 2017)

[84] https://twitter.com/TeenVogue/status/1250159551111929862

[85] Breitbart "Trevor Noah: Trump's 'Demeanor,' 'Style' Is Like 'Many African Dictators'" by Pam Key (July 10th 2018)

old bags on *The View* to Stephen Colbert and Jimmy Kimmel regularly paint the president as such.[86]

While everyone is familiar with Trump Derangement Syndrome—the irrational hatred and fear of President Trump, for the first time in modern history the chorus of Hollywood celebrities crossed the line far beyond their usual criticisms and hatred of a Republican president into openly calling for him to be assassinated.

Madonna famously said she "thought an awful lot about blowing up the White House."[87] Comedian Kathy Griffin did a photo shoot showing her holding Trump's bloody decapitated head which looked like an ISIS beheading. Griffin also said she wanted to beat down Donald Trump's then 11-year-old son Barron.[88]

At one of their shows in Mexico, Guns N' Roses brought a Donald Trump piñata on stage and invited their fans to beat on it.[89] At a Green Day concert in Oakland, California singer Billie Joe Armstrong shouted "Kill Donald Trump!" in the middle of a song.[90] Rapper Snoop Dogg "shot" Trump in the head in one of his music

[86] Newsbusters "'View' Attacks 'Menace' 'Dictator' Trump for Acosta Heckling" by Kristine Marsh (August 1st 2018)

[87] Washington Post "Madonna says she's thought about 'blowing up the White House'" by Coby Itkowitz (January 21st 2017)

[88] Washington Examiner "Kathy Griffin said in 2016 she wanted to 'beat down' Donald and Barron Trump" by Leah DePiero (June 2nd 2017)

[89] Time "Watch Guns N' Roses Invite Mexican Fans Onstage to Smash a Donald Trump Piñata" by Tessa Berenson (December 2nd 2016)

[90] Multiple people recorded video of the incident and posted it on YouTube the next day, although it went unnoticed by major media outlets unlike most of the other incidents of celebrities making similar threatening statements.

videos.[91]   Marylin Manson "beheaded" him with a large knife in one of his.[92]   Rapper Big Sean did a freestyle about murdering Donald Trump with an ice pick on a popular hip hop radio show.[93]   All with no consequences whatsoever.

Actor Adam Pally, who starred in a time traveling comedy series called *Making History*, told TMZ that if time travel were possible he would go back and kill Donald Trump.[94]   Johnny Depp went even further saying someone should assassinate him right now.   "When was the last time an actor assassinated a president?" he asked a crowd.   "It's been awhile, and maybe it's time," he concluded, referring to John Wilkes Booth (who was an actor) killing Abraham Lincoln.[95]

He faced no consequences whatsoever.   He wasn't dropped by his management company, none of his movies were pulled from the streaming services; nothing!

Before she dropped out of the 2020 Presidential race, Kamala Harris joked with Ellen DeGeneres about killing Trump if she was stuck in an elevator with him.[96]   Robert

[91] The Hill "Snoop Dogg shoots clown dressed as Trump in latest music video" by Judy Kurtz (March 13th 2017)

[92] Metro UK "Donald Trump brutally beheaded in new Marilyn Manson video" by Ann Lee (November 8th 2016)

[93] Rolling Stone "Hear Big Sean Threaten Donald Trump in New Freestyle" by Daniel Kreps (February 3rd 2017)

[94] TMZ "'Making History' Star Adam Pally 'I'd Have to Kill Trump or Hitler'.. If Time Travel Existed" (March 16th 2017)

[95] NBC News "Johnny Depp: 'When Was the Last Time an Actor Assassinated a President?'" (June 23rd 2017)

[96] San Francisco Chronicle "Sen. Kamala Harris ruffles feathers with 'Trump death joke' on 'Ellen' show" by Michelle Robertson (April 5th 2018)

De Niro has said numerous times that he wants to punch President Trump in the face. Jim Carrey said he had a dream of murdering him with a golf club, and now draws pictures almost daily and posts them on his Twitter account depicting Trump and those in his administration as madmen hell-bent on destroying the earth.

Mickey Rourke said that he wants to beat him with a baseball bat.[97] After the Iranian government put an $80 million bounty on President Trump's head, comedian George Lopez responded on Instagram saying, "We'll do it for half."[98]

While hosting *Saturday Night Live*, comedian John Mulaney urged people to assassinate President Trump like Julius Caesar. "It is a Leap Year, as I said. Leap Year began in 45 B.C. under Julius Caesar. This is true, he started the Leap Year in order to correct the calendar and we still do it to this day," he began.[99] "Another thing that happened under Julius Caesar, he was such a powerful maniac that all the senators grabbed knives and they stabbed him to death. That would be an interesting thing if we brought that back now."[100]

The atmosphere the media has created in the Trump era, where publicly wishing for his death has become commonplace, has incited numerous unhinged lunatics to attempt to storm the White House and Trump's Mar-a-

---

[97] Toronto Sun "Mickey Rourke goes on vicious anti-Trump rant" (April 7th 2016)

[98] Newsweek "Comedian George Lopez Under Fire for Instagram Joke About $80-Million Bounty for Trump's Head" by Tufayel Ahmed (January 6th 2020)

[99] Mediaite "SNL: John Mulaney Jokes That Senators Should Stab Trump Like Julius Caesar" by Sarah Rumpf (March 1st 2020)

[100] Ibid.

Lago resort in Florida where he often goes on holidays.[101] Yet with the exception of Kathy Griffin getting dropped by CNN as cohost of their New Year's Eve coverage, none of the celebrities calling for his assassination have faced any consequences. Not legally or professionally.

Imagine the outrage if anyone even remotely suggested that Barack Obama should be assassinated, or hung for treason. Their career would have been over by the end of the day and their "terrorist threats" would have dominated the news cycle for an entire week.

The 25th Amendment Fantasies

As you likely know, every few months throughout the Trump Administration the mainstream media repeats the same news cycle about the "possibility" that President Trump may be removed from office by enacting the 25th Amendment, which allows the expulsion of a president if the majority of his cabinet agree he is mentally unfit for office, which would result in the Vice President taking over.

Such pipe dreams have been fueled by gossip columnists like Michael Wolff in his tabloid trash books that are hailed by the media for his supposed "anonymous sources" inside the White House who say this possibility is "being discussed" every day.[102] The Left's desperate hope that the 25th Amendment could end their Trump

---

[101] CNBC "Trump's Mar-a-Lago security breach: Officials shoot Connecticut woman's SUV after she crashes through checkpoints" by Dan Mangan, Mike Calia, and Yelena Dzhanova (January 31st 2020)

[102] Newsweek "Michael Wolff Says Trump's White House Is 'That Bad' The 25th Amendment Mentioned Every Day" by Harriet Sinclair (January 7th 2018)

nightmare has caused the issue to get written into the plots of various political dramas on television, allowing those with Trump Derangement Syndrome to have the emotional satisfaction for a fleeting moment that it has actually happened. These plot lines also serve to plant seeds in people's minds hoping they'll grow and increase discussions and pressure about actually doing a such thing to President Trump.

The Showtime series *Homeland*, a spy thriller about the Department of Homeland Security investigating terrorist threats against the United States, is just one of numerous shows to include this plot point. "I am here to relieve you of your command," says the character playing the Vice President to a flabbergasted now former President standing in the Oval office as he is informed of the decision.[103]

Before President Trump, such a topic was never addressed in any political drama or thriller. The 25th Amendment was an obscure provision few people ever heard of, but it's included in the Constitution just in case the President becomes mentally incapacitated. Democrats, however, hoped to use it as a weapon.

CBS's political drama *Madam Secretary* did the same thing. "I've talked to White House Counsel and the attorney general, and though there is a 'fog of law' surrounding Section 4 of the 25th Amendment, because it's never been invoked, they assured me that if the heads of the executive departments plus the vice president vote by simple majority, the president will be removed from office, and Vice President Hurst will become the acting president....If ever there were a time to set aside politics

---

[103] Newsbusters "'Homeland' Invokes 25th Amendment on 'Unconstitutional' President" by Lindsay Kornick (April 16th 2018)

and do what's best for the country, this is it," says the White House Chief of Staff.[104]

After the Cabinet voted in favor of removing the President by enacting the 25th Amendment, he addressed the nation to announce that he would be stepping down and thanked them for putting their country first! "I thank the brave cabinet secretaries who voted to invoke the 25th Amendment. They are all true American heroes and patriots. They put their country ahead of their personal relationship with me. That's what separates us from dictatorships and oligarchies. Without people of such courage, our democracy would be lost, and they will forever have my gratitude. And because of them, I have never felt more proud to be an American."[105]

Kiefer Sutherland's *Designated Survivor* series on ABC also aired a 25th Amendment fantasy, where his vice president plotted to invoke the power hoping to have him removed as President after notes about his therapy sessions were leaked to the public, causing concerns about his mental stability as he tried to cope with the death of his wife.[106]

Michael J. Fox guest-starred as the prosecutor for the Cabinet, which ultimately failed in removing Sutherland, but succeeded in making an entire episode about the 25th Amendment, which was the whole point in the first place.

---

[104] Newsbusters "'American Heroes' Invoke 25th Amendment, Remove 'Unfit' President in Liberal Fantasy Show" by Lindsay Kornick (January 15th 2018)

[105] Ibid.

[106] RealClear Politics "ABC's 'Designated Survivor' Uses 25th Amendment To Remove President" by Ian Schwartz (April 16th 2018)

Even The CW's superhero series *Supergirl*, a derivative of the *Superman* franchise that focuses on Superman's cousin, also aired an episode where Kara (aka Supergirl, who, like Clark Kent works as a reporter) published an exposé on the President conspiring with arch villain Lex Luther, resulting in the cabinet invoking the 25th Amendment to have him removed. As the characters are watching a news broadcast about the situation, one turns to Kara, congratulating her, saying, "Talk about the power of the press."[107]

She replies, "These have been some dark days. And I'll admit, there were some times where I thought we would never get out of it, but we didn't give up, and we kept chipping away, until we brought the truth to light. Can you believe the Fourth Estate saved the day?"[108] The "Fourth Estate" refers to the news media, which functions as an unofficial fourth branch of government that is supposed to help keep political power in check.

Are There Any Conservative Celebrities?

Sometimes people may wonder "why are there so few conservative celebrities?" The answer is that there may not be as few as it appears because they keep quiet about their politics knowing that if they were vocal about their beliefs it would virtually end their career. Being a conservative in Hollywood has always been difficult but in the Age of Trump, it has never been more dangerous.

There are a few rare exceptions like conservative comedians Dennis Miller, Larry the Cable Guy, and Jeff

---

[107] IMDB "Super Girl" (Episode: The Quest for Peace) 2019

[108] Ibid.

Foxworthy, but they are allowed to exist because they have a niche market, and only as long as they don't come out too hard against the Left. They won't do jokes about gays, transgenders, Black crime, or other topics they know will cause them to be canceled. They have to stay in their lane.

There are some Republican actors like Jon Voight, and Dean Cain who are public about their beliefs but open conservatives in Hollywood are mostly lower-level actors who make a good living, but aren't A-listers. Those who want to be megastars know what needs to be done, and what must not be done—or said publicly.

James Woods says that after he was asked at a Hollywood Foreign Press Association junket (the organization that runs the Golden Globe awards) if he would support Hillary Clinton for president, he was blacklisted from Hollywood for saying no.[109]

After President Trump became elected Woods began tweeting support for him, and his tweets became increasingly political. He was later dropped by his talent agent who gave him no other reason than, "I don't want to represent you anymore."[110]   Woods is now basically retired but still enjoys tweeting his disgust for liberals on a regular basis.

Kanye West says it took him a year to "have the confidence" to publicly support Trump and wear a MAGA hat. He would later say that wearing the hat "represented overcoming fear and doing what you felt no matter what

---

[109] USA Today "James Woods: I was 'blacklisted' like Brendan Fraser but for my conservative politics" by Maria Puente (February 23rd 2018)

[110] CBS News "James Woods dropped by 'liberal' agent on Fourth of July" by Andrea Park (July 5th 2018)

anyone said."[111]   When Kanye was the musical guest on *Saturday Night Live* for the season premiere in 2018 he wore his MAGA hat on stage for his performance, and afterwards he started ranting about how the staff and producers were not happy about it.

"They said, 'don't go out there with that hat on.' They bullied me backstage. They bullied *me!* And then they say I'm in a sunken place." He then went on to say that ninety percent of news is liberal, "So it's easy to make it seem like it's so one-sided."[112]   He got a lot of backlash and was even called a White supremacist, but he is a big enough star to weather the storm and eccentric enough for many to dismiss his political views as him just "being Kanye."

But there is no tolerance for ordinary actors or actresses just starting their career. *Mean Girls* was a movie and is now a play on Broadway, and one of the stars (Laura Leigh Turner) made headlines because someone snooping around her Twitter account noticed that she was following various popular conservatives, including President Trump and Sean Hannity.[113]   She then un-followed Trump hoping to avoid any more negative attention.

Something similar happened to a contestant on *The Bachelorette* in the 2018 season when it was discovered that the frontrunner had "liked" various Instagram posts

---

[111] NME "Kanye West says speaking out about Trump support 'represented overcoming fear'" by Rhian Daly (August 10th 2018)

[112] New York Times "Kanye West Ends 'S.N.L.' With Speech About Trump and Bullying" by Joe Coscarelli (September 30th 2018)

[113] The Daily Dot "'Mean Girls' Broadway actress called out for following right-wing Twitter accounts" by Esther Bell (February 11th 2020)

that made fun of feminists and illegal aliens. After making headlines for his "egregious behavior" he deleted his account so more wouldn't be uncovered and issued a lengthy and pathetic apology.[114]

Because of the increasing persecution of conservative celebrities, actor Gary Sinise founded a "secret society" of sorts called the Friends of Abe in 2004 to function as a support group and networking organization for conservatives in the entertainment industry. "Abe" refers to Abraham Lincoln, and at one time the group supposedly had around 2000 members, including Kevin Sorbo, Jon Voight, Scott Baio, and Kelsey Grammer. They used to meet once a month and would host guest speakers like conservative pundits as well as Republican politicians.

When the organization filed for a 501(c)(3) tax exempt status in 2011, the Obama-controlled IRS demanded a list of their members in order to process their application which is not a requirement for a group to be granted a non-profit status.[115] It was during this same time that the IRS was later found to have discriminated against over 400 different conservative groups, especially if they had "Tea Party" in their name.[116] After getting some negative press for trying to find out the names of everyone associated with Friends of Abe, the IRS reluctantly approved them as a 501(c)(3).

---

[114] Variety "'Bachelorette' Frontrunner Apologizes for Controversial Instagram Likes" by Ellis Clopton (May 31st 2018)

[115] Variety "Hollywood Conservative Group Grapples With IRS Scrutiny As It Seeks Tax-Exempt Status" by Ted Johnson (January 22nd 2014)

[116] Reuters "Justice Department settles with conservative groups over IRS scrutiny" by Brendan O'Brien (October 26th 2017)

It is said that they disbanded in 2017 over divisions about President Trump, but there are rumors that a new "Friends of Abe" may have formed, possibly under a different name.[117] Being a conservative in Hollywood has always been difficult, but in our modern age with political correctness run amok and Thought Police ready to destroy anyone's career for having the "wrong" opinion, it has caused most conservatives in the entertainment industry to stay hiding in the closet.

It's not just Donald Trump that Hollywood is waging war on—it's what he represents. He's a nationalist, not a globalist. He puts America First, and unlike most other recent presidents won't surrender our sovereignty to the United Nations. But Hollywood isn't just trying to destroy him and his supporters. They're waging war on the entire country, our culture, our history, and our families.

---

[117] The Guardian "Club for Hollywood Republicans locked in dispute – caused in part by Trump" by Rory Carroll (June 13th 2017)

Author's Note: Please take a moment to rate and review this book on Amazon.com, or wherever you purchased it from if you're reading the e-book, to let others know what you think. This also helps to offset the trolls who keep giving my books fake one-star reviews when they haven't even read them.

Almost all of the one-star reviews on Amazon for my last three books, "The Liberal Media Industrial Complex," "The True Story of Fake News," and "Liberalism: Find a Cure" are from NON-verified purchases which is a clear indication they are fraudulent, hence me adding this note.

It's just more proof that liberals are losers and can't play fair, so if you could help me combat them as soon as possible since you actually bought this book, that would be great!

Thank you!

War on America

Since the Leftists are trying to overthrow the United States of America and replace our Republic with a socialist dictatorship they are heavily promoting illegal immigration, demonizing the police, and are relentlessly attacking American culture, customs, symbols, and holidays. This is all obvious today, but back in the late 1940s and early 50s there were widespread concerns about communists and communist sympathizers working in Hollywood who may use their positions to do just that.

Numerous individuals were blacklisted and basically banned from working in the industry to prevent them from spreading anti-American sentiments. In 1947, ten writers and directors refused to testify about their suspected communist ties or sympathies before the House Un-American Activities Committee, likely because they didn't want to incriminate themselves.

The communist purge back then was widely criticized as an overreaction and a witch hunt (often referred to as McCarthyism), but it's obvious—the seeds of Marxism have taken root in Hollywood and now, as Tim Allen said, being a conservative in that town today is like being a Jew in 1930s Germany.[118]

Orson Bean, who was a popular gameshow host in the 1960s, later noted, "Sitcoms and movies today hate old-fashioned values. There's more anti-American

---

[118] The Hollywood Reporter "Tim Allen Compares Being Conservative in Hollywood to 1930s Germany" by Arlene Washington (March 19th 2017)

propaganda today than the Soviets could have ever worked into our culture through their covert party members who were writing screenplays."[119]

A former KGB Agent named Yuri Bezmenov who defected to Canada in the 1970s would later give a series of interviews and lectures in the United States detailing how the Soviet Union was working to undermine the United States as part of their long term goal to end our reign as the world's premier superpower. He described the process as "ideological subversion" which was comprised of four different parts: Demoralization, Destabilization, Crisis, and Normalization.[120]

He said the Marxists knew it would take an entire generation to accomplish, but were patiently and persistently working towards the goal. "What [ideological subversion] basically means is: to change the perception of reality of every American to such an extent that despite [an] abundance of information, no one is able to come to sensible conclusions in the interest of defending themselves, their families, their community, and their country," he explained.[121]

Basically, the communists planned to cause cultural chaos by encouraging Americans to embrace socially toxic ideas they knew would ultimately lead to self-destruction down the road.

---

[119] Newsweek "The Hollywood Blacklist Then And Now: The Late Actor Orson Bean On Anti-American 'Propaganda'" by Paul Bond (February 29th 2020)

[120] Epoch Times "How Soviet Russia Conducted 'Ideological Subversion' in Western Nations" by Michael Wing (January 29th 2020)

[121] BigThink "34 years ago, a KGB defector chillingly predicted modern America" by Paul Ratner (July 18th 2018)

It's obvious that each phase of the Ideological Subversion plan has been successful. Hollywood has warped the minds of tens of millions of people causing irreversible damage, brainwashing them into believing that America is an evil country built entirely on the backs of slaves while the greedy 1% control all the wealth, so why bother trying to earn an honest living.

They've destabilized the nuclear family causing a sociological crisis like the world has never seen, with the majority of children now being raised by single parents; they've normalized the most unhealthy sexual behaviors and lifestyles anyone could imagine; and recently we've been faced with numerous crises from the coronavirus pandemic to the ongoing racial conflicts from Black Lives Matter. All of which have thrown America into a tailspin.

The ongoing attacks on American culture are stunningly similar to the "Cultural Revolution" in China which was launched by communist dictator (and mass murderer) Mao Zedong in the 1960s to purge any remaining elements of capitalism from the country along with anything else that may be an obstacle to his power. The Communist Party claimed that although the capitalists had been overthrown they were "still trying to use the old ideas, culture, customs, and habits of the exploiting classes to corrupt the masses, capture their minds, and stage a comeback."[122]

To solidify his power Mao Zedong had his Red Guards (a network of student groups) violently target what were called the "Four Olds"—meaning old customs, old culture, old habits, and old ideas; in order to

---

122 The Communist Party's "Decision Concerning the Great Proletarian Cultural Revolution" also known as the Sixteen Points (August 8th 1966)

"transform education, literature and art, and all other parts of the superstructure that do not correspond to the socialist economic base, so as to facilitate the consolidation and development of the socialist system."[123]

This is exactly what the social justice warriors of today are doing in the United States by targeting gender norms, the nuclear family, American holidays, our history, capitalism, and free speech.

Socialism's Emergence in America

Bernie Sanders popularized socialism perhaps more than anyone else in a generation, and now an increasing number of wealthy celebrities have taken up the cause. Mark Ruffalo was one of the first to endorse Sanders' presidential campaign. The *Avengers* star is worth over $30 million dollars and earned $6 million playing the Hulk in just one of the many *Avengers* films but he thinks "It's time for an economic revolution," and claims, "Capitalism today is failing us, killing us, and robbing from our children's future."[124]

John Cusack also endorsed Bernie Sanders and at one of his rallies said we need to end "predatory capitalism," which basically means forgive all debt and offer everyone free stuff paid for by those of us who work hard and save our money.[125] It's *our fault* that others frivolously spend

---

[123] Ibid.

[124] Fox News "Actor Mark Ruffalo attacks capitalism for 'failing us' in tweet, but boasts 7-figure net worth" by Melissa Robert (December 3rd 2019)

[125] Fox News "John Cusack at Bernie Sanders rally: World has 10-12-year window to stop climate change, 'predatory capitalism'" by Bradford Betz (January 19th 2020)

their money on things they don't need instead of saving it or investing it, and now they feel they deserve ours. Jim Carrey, Britney Spears, and others are also encouraging Americans to "say yes to socialism."[126]

The Democratic candidates for president in 2020 were in a competition to see who could offer voters more free stuff: Free health care, free college, forgiving all student loans, reparations for Black people and gays, and more. Recently we've started seeing blatant anti-capitalism and pro-socialism themes in major movies and television shows which is exactly what Joseph McCarthy was worried communist sympathizers would do.

Such messages seem to have been glossed over in 2019's *Joker* by most viewers who were captivated by Joaquin Phoenix's disturbing performance, but they were actually at the core of the movement the Joker would come to lead. "Kill The Rich—A New Movement?" is the headline on a tabloid the Joker had in his apartment as civil unrest erupted in Gotham. "Fuck the rich! Fuck Thomas Wayne! That's what this whole fucking thing is about! Fuck the whole system!" screams one protester.

A reporter asks Mr. Wayne (Batman's father) about the "groundswell of anti-rich sentiments," adding, "It's almost as if our city's less fortunate residents are taking the side of the killer."

"What kind of coward would do something that cold-blooded?" he responds, speaking of Arthur Fleck killing three men who assaulted him on the subway, sparking his transformation into Joker. "Someone who hides behind a mask. Someone who's envious of those more fortunate than themselves."

---

126 Washington Post "Jim Carrey tells Democrats: 'We have to say yes to socialism'" by Amy B. Wang (September 10th 2018)

At the very end when the Joker is a guest on a popular late-night talk show, he begins the interview saying, "It's been a rough few weeks Murray...ever since I killed those three Wall Street guys."

"Okay, I'm waiting for the punchline," Murray (Robert De Niro) responds.

"There is no punchline. It's not a joke."

He goes on to rant about how awful society is and how nobody is civil anymore. "Do you think men like (billionaire) Thomas Wayne ever think what it's like to be someone like me? To be somebody but themselves? They don't!"

He continues ranting and gloats about the riots on the streets and the police officers who have been harmed and then shoots Murray in the face live on the air. The Joker is hailed as a hero by the mobs gathering in the streets for fighting back against the system. Throughout the riots some people are seen holding signs that say "Resist"—the same signs anti-Trump "Resistance" activists often use at their protests.

The hacking thriller *Mr. Robot* has been praised for its anti-capitalism themes. The main character "Elliot" wants to cause "the single biggest incident of wealth redistribution in history," by deleting all financial records of credit card debt and mortgages.[127] *The Atlantic* said, "for the most part the show plays like an Occupy Wall Street fever dream."[128] Another critic called it, "the anti-capitalist TV show we've been waiting for," and praised it

---

[127] Los Angeles Times "TV Preview: Wealth disparity, hackers and cyber threats in 'Mr. Robot'" by Alan Everly (May 29th 2015)

[128] The Atlantic "Whose Side Is *Mr. Robot* On, Anyway?" by Spencer Kornhaber (August 6th 2015)

because it, "makes socialism a vibrant force again in popular culture."[129]

Justin Timberlake stars in the 2011 film *In Time* about a future world where people are genetically programmed to stop aging at 25, and then die a year later if they can't afford to buy any more "time." Their remaining lifespan counts down on a timer implanted in their arm which shows how much longer they have to live. The rich people are able to afford more "time" and can live for hundreds of years, but the poor people can't, and have to borrow "time" at high rates of interest. So Justin Timberlake decides to steal a whole bunch of "time" and distribute it to the poor people in order to "crash the system."[130]

The Netflix series *The Society* is about a small town where all the adults mysteriously disappear, leaving a group of high schoolers stuck in what appears to be a parallel universe to fend for themselves while they struggle to build a new "society" in order to survive on their own.

After some of the kids decide to raid the local hardware store for supplies, fighting with each other as they scramble to take what they can, it results in a town meeting where the natural leader (the new "mayor," who was student body president in their previous world) tells everyone they're going to take inventory on all the food and other resources in the town and begin eating meals communally in the school cafeteria to ration it.

129 InTheseTimes "Mr. Robot Is the Anti-Capitalist TV Show We've Been Waiting For" by Brian Cook (August 4th 2015)

130 Reuters "Dopey socialist parable 'In Time' a slick, fun ride" by Alonso Duralde (October 27th 2011)

A group of the jocks are later shown laying around reflecting on what they had done to the hardware store and discussing the emerging government. One of them begins, "I've been thinking—what if we didn't, like, take stuff? Like food or whatever. Wouldn't be the worst thing in the world, right? Sharing. It could be like socialism. There's no "I" in team, right?"

Another says it "kind of worked" in China because "everything's made in China."

"Well. Socialism it is," they conclude.[131]

But sharing food and work responsibilities angers some of the rich kids from the town (the "haves") who don't want to give up their property to others (the "have nots") or work at what they see as jobs that are beneath them, so a power struggle ensues and the "haves" organize a coup, seizing political power of the town proving how "ruthless" rich people are and the lengths they'll go to maintain their lifestyle at the "expense" of others.

In season two of Amazon Prime's *Jack Ryan* series, the cause for Venezuela's economic and humanitarian crisis isn't said to be from socialism failing the country, but because the president is a "nationalist." The president's opponent however, is "running against him on a social justice platform and on the strength of, in my humble opinion, just not being an asshole," explains Jack Ryan.[132]

The Foundation for Economic Freedom denounced the series, pointing out that, "By making the villain of *Jack Ryan* a nationalist, the writers take a not-so-subtle

---

[131] The New Yorker "'The Society,' Reviewed: A Teen Dystopia, but with, Like, Socialism" by Doreen St. Felix (May 22nd 2019)

[132] Jack Ryan Season 2 Episode One on Amazon Prime

jab at US President Donald Trump, whose 'America First' slogan has been described as nationalism 'that betrays America's values.'"[133]

The growing pro-socialist messages woven into the plots of TV series and movies caused the Orange County Register to ask, "Why does Hollywood smear capitalism, promote socialism?"[134] The answer is clear—the Marxists embedded in Hollywood are using their positions in the industry just as the Red Scare of the 1940s and 50s had feared.

In February 2020 a "Netflix for the Left" was launched called *Means TV* by a group of socialist film makers who helped produce campaign ads for Alexandria Ocasio-Cortez's 2018 election to Congress.[135] It's an "anti-capitalist" subscription service that streams documentaries, news shows, and even cartoons and comedies in order to "create the cultural foundation and need to build socialism in the U.S."[136] It is an admittedly Marxist service that aims to incite people to rise up and "seize the means of production."[137]

---

[133] Foundation for Economic Freedom "'Jack Ryan' Gets 4 Pinocchios on Venezuela" by Jon Miltmore (January 15th 2020)

[134] Orange County Register "Why does Hollywood smear capitalism, promote socialism?" by John Stossel (December 4th 2019)

[135] USA Today "'Radicalized' couple behind viral AOC ad launches pro-socialism, Netflix-like service" by JC Reindl via Detroit Free Press (April 13th 2019)

[136] Deadline Detroit "'Netflix For The Left': Socialist Streaming Service Launches In Detroit" (February 25th 2020)

[137] HuffPost "The Couple Behind The Viral AOC Ad Plans A Streaming Channel For Socialists" by Christopher Wilson (May 17th 2019)

Black Lives Matter Riots of 2020

After a man named George Floyd, who was high on fentanyl and methamphetamine,[138] died while in police custody in Minneapolis, it kicked off nationwide riots and looting that went on for over a week.[139] They started locally in Minneapolis, Minnesota, where the Black community looted and burned businesses and even took over the local police station and burnt that down too.[140]

The riots and looting quickly spread to other cities across the country largely due to the mainstream media fanning the flames of racial tensions by reporting half-truths and gaslighting, giving gullible people the impression that African Americans are being systematically hunted by police and around every corner Black people minding their own business are confronted by "White supremacists."

Celebrities were more than happy to pour gasoline on the fire, and many of them announced that they were donating money to bail out the rioters. Justin Timberlake, Chrissy Teigen, Steve Carell, Seth Rogan and many more declared that they were on the side of the mob and were helping to fund them. Others, including John Legend, Lizzo, Natalie Portman, Common, and more all signed a

---

[138] Newsweek "George Floyd Was on Fentanyl, Medical Examiner Says, As Experts Dispute Cause of Death" by Daniel Villarreal (June 2nd 2020)

[139] Fox News "Rioting, looting linked to George Floyd protests leaves trail of destruction across American cities" by Greg Norman (June 1st 2020)

[140] Fox News "Minneapolis Third Precinct police station set on fire after rioters break in" by Dom Calicchio (May 28th 2020)

petition supporting the new anti-police agenda calling for police departments to be defunded and shut down.[141]

Just days later the Los Angeles mayor announced that he was cutting $100 to $150 million dollars from the LAPD budget and diverting the money to communities of color.[142] New York City mayor Bill de Blasio followed suit saying he too was cutting the NYPD budget by one *billion* dollars to defund the police.[143]

This just after iconic stores like Macy's on Fifth Avenue had been looted because police were too busy dealing with rioters in other parts of the city. "We don't want no more police," one protest leader told Minneapolis mayor Jacob Frey before the mob ran him out of an event for not supporting the cause.[144]

Defunding and disbanding police departments as part the Black Lives Matter "revolution" certainly wasn't enough to satisfy the angry mob, so soon they began calling for all TV shows and movies about cops to be canceled. *The Washington Post* led the charge with the headline "Shut down all police movies and TV shows— Now," and just a few days later the popular "Cops" reality show was pulled from TV because it "glorified police."[145]

---

[141] Rolling Stone "John Legend, Common, the Weeknd, Lizzo Sign Open Letter to Defund the Police" by Jon Blistein (June 2nd 2020)

[142] NPR "Amid Protests Against Police Violence LA Mayor Eric Garcetti Announces Cuts To LAPD" by Vanessa Romo (June 3rd 2020)

[143] CBS News "De Blasio seeks to cut $1 billion from NYPD budget" (June 29th 2020)

[144] New York Times "For Mayor Jacob Frey of Minneapolis, a Stinging Rebuke" by Michael Levenson (June 7th 2020)

[145] New York Times "'Cops,' Long-Running Reality Show That Glorified Police, Is Canceled" by Nicole Sperling (June 9th 2020)

It had been on air for 33 seasons, beginning in 1989. Another popular cop reality show, *Live PD*, was also canceled.[146] These unscripted series show the dangers police officers face firsthand, but since they humanize them, the Marxists wanted the shows banned. And all this happened within two weeks of Black Lives Matter resurging.

They even targeted *Paw Patrol*, a cartoon for kids about dogs who work a variety of jobs like a dalmatian firefighter, a bulldog construction worker, and a German shepherd police officer.[147] The Left doesn't want children to have any positive depiction of police so they can more easily indoctrinate them into their nihilist cult and the "ACAB" (All Cops Are Bastards) ideology. It's a miracle Will Smith and Martin Lawrence didn't apologize for starring in the action comedy *Bad Boys* since it makes cops seem funny and cool.

Apple Music even disabled the search feature for a day, called Blackout Tuesday, to help raise "awareness" for Black Lives Matter—as if we all hadn't been hearing enough about them on the news and social media. Instead of letting people find the music they wanted to listen to, Apple replaced the Browse feature with a special curated playlist containing Black power music, including NWA's infamous "Fuck the Police."[148]

They continued marching in the streets for months claiming the United States is inherently racist against

[146] Entertainment Weekly "Live PD host slams cancellation: 'There's an overreaction going on'" by James Hibberd (June 11th 2020)

[147] New York Times "The Protests Come for 'Paw Patrol'" by Amanda Hess (June 10th 2020)

[148] Rolling Stone "What Music's Tech Companies Are Doing on Blackout Tuesday" by Ethan Millman (June 2nd 2020)

Black people and that they are being oppressed by "systemic racism" that keeps them from succeeding in life. This, while every major social media platform coddles them and even gives Black people special privileges and perks.[149] The terms of service forbidding "hate speech," harassment, and inciting violence are rarely enforced when such violations are made by non-White users.

During the 2020 Riots countless major corporations including Facebook, Twitter, Google, Amazon, Disney, McDonalds, Starbucks, Bank of America and many others released statements declaring their support for the Black Lives Matter movement and donated hundreds of thousands, or even millions of dollars each to Black communities and causes.[150]

Cable networks, including the Discovery Channel and the Disney Channel were airing Black Lives Matter PSAs,[151] and several video games including Call of Duty and FIFA 20 (soccer) added a "Black Lives Matter" message every-time the games were booted.[152]

Black Lives Matter is not about "ending racism" or "helping" Black people—it's a front for a neo-Marxist

[149] TubeFilter "YouTube Hosts Inaugural #YouTubeBlack Event To Support Creators Of Color" by Geoff Weiss (April 11th 2016)

[150] CNET "These are the major brands donating to the Black Lives Matter movement" by Mercey Livingston (June 16th 2020)

[151] Fox 23 "Disney releases video showing support for Black Lives Matter movement" by Katlyn Brieskorn (June 14th 2020)

[152] CNN "'Call of Duty' games now display a Black Lives Matter message" by Steve Dent (June 5th 2020)

movement attempting to overthrow the United States government and uproot our Constitutional Republic.[153]

One of their original online manifestos (which has since been toned down a bit) read, "Black people will never achieve liberation under the current racialized capitalist system...The White supremacist, imperialistic, patriarchal systems needs not reform but radical transformation...We must remake the current U.S. political system in order to create a real democracy where Black people and all marginalized people can effectively exercise full political power."[154]

One of the original "founders" of the movement, Patrisse Cullors, openly admits she's a Marxist and her "intellectual influences" are Karl Marx, Vladimir Lenin, and Mao Zedong.[155] Other Black Lives Matter leaders like Yusra Khogali have written that White people are "subhuman" and are "genetic defects."[156]

They are also calling for a universal basic income [UBI], universal healthcare, reparations for slavery, the release of "all political prisoners" meaning Black people incarcerated for committing any crime, and want "a radical and sustainable redistribution of wealth."[157]

---

[153] The Telegraph "Make no mistake – BLM is a radical neo-Marxist political movement" by Alexandra Phillips (June 12th 2020)

[154] Breitbart "Black Lives Matter Anti-Cop Protests Part of Agenda Seeking Socialist Revolution" by Joshua Klein (June 12th 2020)

[155] Time "Black Lives Matter Co-Founder Patrisse Cullors on Her Memoir, Her Life and What's Next for the Movement" by Aric Jenkins (February 26th 2018)

[156] The Blaze "Toronto Black Lives Matter co-founder says white people are 'genetic defects'" by Tre Goins-Phillips (February 13th 2017)

[157] Breitbart "Black Lives Matter Anti-Cop Protests Part of Agenda Seeking Socialist Revolution" by Joshua Klein (June 12th 2020)

Such extremist ideas had been festering on the fringes of the Black power movement since the 1960s but now they have the unwavering support of virtually every celebrity and the entire Hollywood machine has been recalibrated to promote their cause.

Christianity Under Attack

In order to destroy America, the conspirators are determined to eradicate faith in God and dismantle organized Christianity. Attacking Jesus and Christianity is a sacrament in Hollywood because the far-Left hates Jesus and everything He stands for. It's not an overstatement to say that many in key positions of power in the entertainment industry (and politics) are Satanists who will someday openly embrace Lucifer as the rebel angel kicked out of Heaven for defying God.

"I'm glad the Jews killed Christ," ranted comedian Sarah Silverman in one of her comedy specials. "Good. I'd fucking do it again!" she declares, as her audience agrees in laughter.[158] While accepting an Emmy Award one year Kathy Griffin said, "A lot of people come up here and they thank Jesus for this award. I want you to know that no one had less to do with this award than Jesus. He didn't help me a bit…so all I can say is suck it Jesus! This award is my god now!"[159]

I'm not saying people shouldn't be able to make fun of Christians, but no mainstream celebrity would dare

---

158 Sarah Silverman in her 2005 show "Jesus is Magic." Clips of the segment are currently available on YouTube and elsewhere online if you search for "Sarah Silverman Says I Would Kill Christ Again"

159 Reuters "Kathy Griffin's Jesus remark cut from Emmy show" (September 11th 2007)

make such insults or jokes about Muhammad because Muslims (and Jews) are vigorously protected against any criticism or mockery and only wonderful things can be said about them. Even a slightly edgy joke ignites a barrage of attacks with cries of "Islamophobia" or "anti-Semitism" and gears start moving in the well-funded and massive smear machines like the ADL and the SPLC which quickly move to destroy the person's career before they can utter another word.

Hating Christians is almost as necessary as believing in climate change if you're going to be a mainstream Hollywood celebrity. There are very few open Christians in Hollywood, most of them are has-beens like Kevin Sorbo and Kirk Cameron who have been basically blacklisted since being open about their faith.

Kevin Sorbo was banned from Comicon because he's a conservative and "pals with Sean Hannity."[160] He and other Christian actors are stuck doing low budget films that get little attention. They're allowed to exist (for now) as long as they never point out the Bible's teachings on homosexuality. Only watered down and generic Christian messages are allowed to be said.

After *Guardians of the Galaxy* star Chris Pratt appeared on *The Late Show* with Stephen Colbert and happened to discuss his "spirituality," many online began attacking him for being a Christian and attending a church. Actress Ellen Page (a lesbian) from the *X-Men* and *Inception* tweeted, "If you are a famous actor and you belong to an organization that hates a certain group of people, don't be surprised if someone simply wonders

---

[160] Daily Caller "Daily Caller: Comic Convention Bans Christian Conservative Actor Kevin Sorbo For Friendship With Hannity" by Ian Miles Cheong January 14th 2018)

why it's not addressed. Being anti LGBTQ is wrong, there aren't two sides. The damage it causes is severe. Full stop."[161]

Singer Ellie Goulding threatened to back out of her scheduled performance at the 2019 Thanksgiving NFL halftime show if the Salvation Army didn't pledge to donate money to LGBT causes. She got the idea after her Instagram comments were flooded with complaints from her fans because the Salvation Army was sponsoring the game to announce their annual Red Kettle Campaign (bell ringers) fundraiser for the homeless.[162] Since the Salvation Army is a Christian charity, Goulding's fans freaked out, accusing them of being "homophobic" and "transphobic."

They quickly bowed to the pressure and "disavowed" any anti-LGBT beliefs, which basically means they're disavowing the Bible because even the New Testament denounces homosexuality in Romans 1:26-27 and 1st Corinthians 6:9-10. Many critics claim that only the Old Testament does, but the Book of Romans makes it clear that just because Jesus came to offer salvation doesn't mean God's law regarding homosexuality changed.

The Salvation Army also removed a "position statement" from their website that had made it clear "Scripture forbids sexual intimacy between members of the same sex," and replaced it with one saying "We embrace people regardless of race, gender, ethnicity,

---

[161] NBC News "Ellen Page doubles down on criticism of celebs who attend anti-gay churches" via Variety (February 11th 2019)

[162] Dallas News "Ellie Goulding threatens to cancel her Cowboys Thanksgiving halftime show over Salvation Army concerns" by Dan Dinger (November 12th 2019)

sexual orientation, or gender identity."[163] One of the world's largest Christian charities whose very name "The Salvation Army" refers to the salvation of Christ, cowardly bowed down to the Leftist activists out of fear they would be branded "homophobic."

Christians are easy targets since they're much more passive than Jews and Muslims when attacked, and Hollywood loves to stereotype them as a bunch of superstitious bigots who don't know how to have fun. In the rare case that there is a movie favorable to Christianity that gets widespread distribution, that too is attacked.

Passion of the Christ was deemed "anti-Semitic" because it depicts the story of Jesus' arrest, sham trial, and crucifixion.[164] It was the most popular film about the events to be made and wasn't a straight to DVD release like most others. With Mel Gibson behind it, the film became a huge success, which caused a tremendous backlash.

The ADL [Anti-Defamation League] denounced the film, saying it "continues its unambiguous portrayal of Jews as being responsible for the death of Jesus. There is no question in this film about who is responsible. At every single opportunity, Mr. Gibson's film reinforces the notion that the Jewish authorities and the Jewish mob are the ones ultimately responsible for the Crucifixion."[165] That's because that's what happened!

---

[163] USA Today "Ellie Goulding threatens to quit Thanksgiving NFL game; Salvation Army says she's a go" by Charles Trepany (November 13th 2019)

[164] The Telegraph "Mel Gibson's film on Christ condemned as anti-Semitic" June 29th 2003)

[165] ADL.org "ADL and Mel Gibson's 'The Passion of the Christ'" (January 2nd 2013)

Technically, the Romans did it, but at the behest of the Jewish leadership in Jerusalem at the time. The Bible makes it very clear what led to Jesus being crucified. Pontius Pilate is quoted in Matthew 27:24 saying, "I am innocent of this man's blood," and "It is your responsibility!" meaning the Jewish Pharisees. They were the ones who conspired to have Jesus arrested and killed for "blasphemy" and being a "false" messiah. Pontius Pilate even offered to release Jesus, but the crowd demanded he release Barabbas instead, another man who was being detained for insurrection against Rome, and for murder.[166]

A critic for the *New York Daily News* called *The Passion of the Christ*, "the most virulently anti-Semitic movie made since the German propaganda films of the Second World War."[167] Many others angrily denounced the film when it came out in 2004. Some in the media even blamed it for a supposed "upsurge" in anti-Semitic hate crimes.[168]

When the History Channel miniseries *The Bible* was released in 2013, the same cries of "anti-Semitism" rang out.[169] *The New York Times* opinion editor Bari Weiss

---

[166] Luke 23:19

[167] The New York Daily News "The Passion of the Christ" by Jami Bernard (February 24th 2004)

[168] The Guardian "Mel's Passion blamed for rise in anti-semitic attacks" (March 16th 2005)

[169] The Guardian "History Channel's The Bible series is worse than reality TV" by Alan Nyuhas (March 25th 2013)

went so far as to say that it's a "conspiracy theory" that Jews killed Jesus.[170]

Even though most Christmas movies aren't overtly Christian and instead focus of the importance of families reuniting and spending time together, that doesn't mean they're not going to come under attack. As the war on western culture continues, the Marxists have set their sights on Christmas too.

Online liberal cesspool Salon.com ran a headline reading "Hallmark movies are fascist propaganda," and complained they promote "heteronormative whiteness" because there aren't enough LGBT characters or people of color in them.[171]

"Hallmark movies, with their emphasis on returning home and the pleasures of the small, domestic life, also send a not-at-all subtle signal of disdain for cosmopolitanism and curiosity about the larger world," Salon said, "which is exactly the sort of attitude that helps breed the kind of defensive White nationalism that we see growing in strength in the Donald Trump era."[172]

The article went on to say that because the Hallmark Channel airs so many Christmas movies, it is promoting, "a set of patriarchal and authoritarian values that are more about White evangelicals defining themselves as an ethnic group, and not about a genuine feeling of spirituality... The very fact that they're presented as harmless fluff makes it all the more insidious, the way they work to

---

[170] Real Time with Bill Maher "Bari Weiss: How to Fight Anti-Semitism" Segment posted on the show's official YouTube channel (September 13th 2019)

[171] Salon.com "Hallmark movies are fascist propaganda" by Amanda Marcotte (December 25th 2019)

[172] Ibid.

68

enforce very narrow, White, heteronormative, sexist, provincial ideas of what constitutes 'normal.'"[173]

The article wasn't satire. Salon.com has a deep-seated hatred of Christianity, conservatives and families, and is another cog in the Cultural Marxist machine working to destroy the United States.

Comedian Whitney Cummings was reported to the Human Resources department of a major Hollywood studio after she wished the crew of a TV show she was working on "Merry Christmas" when they wrapped up for the year. She made the revelation while speaking with Conan O'Brian the following December. "Last year, I was working on a TV show, [and] got in trouble with Human Resources for saying 'Merry Christmas' to an intern," she began.[174]

Conan asked her if she was being serious and she said it was a true story, elaborating, "I was leaving, like on the 18th or whatever…and I was like, 'Bye guys, Merry Christmas.'" When she returned from vacation after New Year's she was called to HR and scolded. She joked, "I don't even care how your Christmas was. It was just a formality. It's what you say when you leave."[175]

Conan O'Brien then replied, "In these times we're in, that could trigger someone or offend them if it's not their holiday."[176] She didn't say which network it was, but she's been involved with some major shows like NBC's *Whitney* (where she played the main character), as well as

---

[173] Ibid.

[174] Breitbart "Whitney Cummings Says She Was Reported to HR for Saying 'Merry Christmas'" by David NG (December 20th 2019)

[175] Ibid.

[176] Ibid.

the CBS sitcom *2 Broke Girls,* which she created and was a writer for.

While today it may seem impossible that Christmas movies may become a thing of the past, nobody could have ever guessed that reruns of the classic *Dukes of Hazzard* would get banned after the Confederate flag was deemed a "hate symbol" in 2015, or that Aunt Jemima pancake syrup, Eskimo Pie ice cream bars, and Uncle Ben's Rice would be deemed "racially insensitive" and pulled from production a few years later.[177]

Once someone reminds liberals that the word *Christmas* is derived from *Christ's Mass* and that it is actually a commemoration of the birth of Jesus, they may finally go over the edge and deem Christmas just as offensive as Columbus Day or the Fourth of July. And with the Muslim and Sikh populations increasing in the United States, the American standard of Christmas music playing in shopping malls and retail stores all month long every December may one day come to an end because it's not "inclusive" and leaves non-Christians feeling "ostracized."

Glorifying Satanism

Since the Hollywood elite hate God and everything that is normal and good, it would only make sense that they have embraced Satan as their symbolic (or literal) master. The Church of Satan is an organization started by Anton LaVey in the 1960s which gained popularity among a few celebrities at the time like Sammy Davis Jr.

---

[177] Wall Street Journal "Aunt Jemima and Uncle Ben's, Rooted in Racist Imagery, to Change" by Annie Gasparro and Micah Maidenberg (June 17th 2020)

and Jayne Mansfield. The "church" was really just Anton LaVey's house, but he was a showman, so in the late 1960s and early 70s he was able to get some media attention for openly embracing satanism and engaging in various theatrical rituals and stunts (like serving an amputated leg for dinner that one of the members stole from a hospital he worked at).[178] While the group's 15 minutes of fame soon faded away, satanism in Hollywood didn't.

Rock stars and heavy metal bands in the 1980s and 90s continued to promote satanism through their music. Marilyn Manson, the self-described "anti-Christ superstar," would often tear out pages from the Bible on stage as part of his shows. Of course he would never do that to a Quran because radical Muslims would put out a fatwa calling for him to be executed, not to mention he would be denounced as "Islamophobic," but attacking Christians gets one hailed as a hero in Hollywood.

In the early 2010s we began to see an explosion of pop stars promoting a new brand of satanism, in the form of the Illuminati. The original Illuminati was a secret society founded in Bavaria, Germany in the late 1700s by a law professor at the University of Ingolstadt named Adam Weishaupt. While the Founding Fathers in America openly declared their views and goals to gain independence from the King of England, the Illuminati sought secrecy and subversion to escape the grasp of the Monarch in Germany.

After many of the members were discovered, rounded up and arrested, it was said the secret society was no more, but rumors have persisted for over two hundred

---

[178] *The Secret Life of a Satanist: The Authorized Biography of Anton LaVey* by Blanche Barton page 78 (Feral House 1992)

years that they survived and continued on. The group's original plans—many of which had been discovered by seizing their letters of correspondence—detailed how the organization was structured to avoid collapsing if any of its cells were discovered. Some trace their symbols, slogans, and activities to the Skull & Bones secret society founded in 1832, and later to the Bohemian Grove, and the Bilderberg Group.[179]

Aside from being a mafia of sorts, consisting of powerful politicians, bankers, and businessmen—many people believe that these "Illuminati" members are privy to ancient philosophical secrets about the history of mankind and the "true" nature of divine forces.

Concerns and conspiracy theories about the Illuminati were mostly contained on the fringes of the Internet until the early 2010s when allegations of celebrity Illuminati involvement went viral through YouTube videos and social media postings.[180] Many rappers and pop stars began incorporating Illuminati symbols into their music videos and hinting that they were somehow a part of it. None of these musicians were members of Skull & Bones or attending the Bohemian Grove, but by promoting the Illuminati and satanism as cool, they laid the foundation for the widespread acceptance of satanism—or Luciferianism as it is also called.

Those who follow this secret doctrine believe that the God who created the world (and all living things) was actually a lower level god called the Demiurge (Jehovah), who essentially enslaved mankind through our very creation, either through malevolence or ignorance of its

---

[179] See my previous book, *Inside the Illuminati* (2014)

[180] The Daily Beast "How the Illuminati Stole the Mind, Soul, and Body of Hip-Hop" by Rob Brotherton (January 2nd 2016)

own lack of abilities; and so Satan/Lucifer, the "supreme" being of the Universe from this point of view, decided to enter the Demiurge's creation to "save" mankind by convincing Adam and Eve to eat from the tree of the knowledge of good and evil, giving them consciousness.[181] This strange belief that Satan is the savior, and God (the creator) is evil, is found at the core of most occult fraternities and secret societies.[182]

Such esoteric ideas had remained mostly hidden from public view for thousands of years, but now a large number of Hollywood celebrities seemed to be embracing the idea that Satan/Lucifer is good, and giving a wink and a nod that they too know the Illuminati secret.[183]

While the Illuminati fad in pop culture has passed, the open embrace of this idea—that Satan/Lucifer is actually the "savior"—will no doubt return someday and catch on like wildfire among the high priests of pop culture. A-list celebrities will declare that Satan is "king" and countless people will blindly follow their lead as they always do.

Bible prophecy predicts that one day a counterfeit Christ (the Antichrist) will declare that *he* is "God" and the ruler of the earth, and such proclamation will be

---

[181] Manly P. Hall wrote, "The serpent is true to the principle of wisdom, for it tempts man to the knowledge of himself. Therefore the knowledge of self resulted from man's disobedience to the Demiurgus, Jehovah." — *The Secret Teachings of All Ages* page 272 (Tarcher/Penguin 2003)

[182] Aleister Crowley wrote "This serpent, Satan, is not the enemy of Man, be He who made Gods of our race, knowing Good and Evil; He bade 'Know Thyself!' and taught Initiation. He is 'the Devil' of the book of Thoth, and His emblem is Baphomet, and Androgyne who is the hieroglyph of arcane perfection." — *Magick: In Theory and Practice* page 193

[183] Rolling Stone "Katy Perry: I Want to Join the Illuminati!" (August 1st 2014)

welcomed by billions of people. And thanks to the massive cultural shifts that are taking place, the path is being paved for the widespread acceptance of the "secret doctrine" that Satan/Lucifer is really the "good" God and here to "save" mankind from the inept or malevolent creator who made a flawed world.

Abortion

Because liberals celebrate hedonism, debauchery, and tend to live in the moment without any concern for the consequences, unwanted pregnancies are a common occurrence. And instead of accepting responsibility for their actions, they usually decide to kill the baby and have its remains vacuumed out of the womb, seeing such barbarism as no different than getting a wart removed. But they're upset that such a procedure has a negative stigma for so many people, so the Hollywood propaganda machine has been working behind the scenes to change that.

It's not enough for abortion activists to hope that writers will decide on their own to include pro-abortion messages in their scripts, so Planned Parenthood took it upon themselves to create their own entertainment liaison who lobbies studios to insert such themes on their behalf.

A woman named Caren Spruch is the current director of the Arts & Entertainment Engagement department at Planned Parenthood, and the *Washington Post* calls her their "secret weapon," admitting, "She encourages screenwriters to tell stories about abortion and works as a script doctor for those who do."[184] Spruch said that

---

[184] Washington Post "Planned Parenthood's Secret Weapon" by Nora Caplan-Bricker (September 23rd 2019).

Planned Parenthood has advised studios on over 150 different movies and television shows since 2014. Their first project was a "comedy" called *Obvious Child* which is about a girl who has a one-night stand with some random guy after breaking up with her boyfriend and later finds out she's pregnant and gets an abortion on Valentine's Day.[185]

One of the many shows Planned Parenthood's entertainment liaison office helped "advise" is the Hulu series *Shrill*, which shows the lead character (Aidy Bryant) getting pregnant and deciding to have an abortion "before it becomes illegal." After killing the baby she tells her roommate she's glad she "got out of a huge fucking mess" and, "I feel very fucking powerful right now. And I just feel like I need to go out [and party]."[186]

A sociologist at the University of California, San Francisco wants more comedies about abortion to help destigmatize it. "The purpose of including an abortion plot line is simply to make jokes about abortion, recognizing that such satire is valuable for some people as both a means and an end," said Gretchen Sisson, PhD.[187]

She continued, "This should not be surprising: comedy has often been used as a subversive way of challenging predominant social structures," and she thinks abortion is "intuitive new ground for comedy to address."[188]

---

[185] Ibid.

[186] Newsbusters "Hulu Character Feels 'Really, Really Good,' 'Very F**king Powerful' After Abortion" by Rebecca Downs (March 18th 2019)

[187] Campus Reform "Sociologist calls for more abortion-based comedy" by Toni Airaksinen (January 2nd 2018)

[188] Ibid.

NBC's *Parenthood* included an episode where a character (played by Skyler Day) visited a Planned Parenthood clinic to get an abortion despite her boyfriend's wishes she keep the baby and the two "start a life" together. "If I have this baby, my life is over" she told him, and proceeded to kill the child.

Depicting characters getting an abortion was rare back in 2013 for network television, and the episode was celebrated for "bravely" tackling the topic.[189]   The *Huffington Post* praised the episode as well, noting "Amy's mind was made up and there was nothing Drew could do to stop her."[190]

Melanie Roussell Newman, who works as Planned Parenthood's senior vice president of communications and culture, admitted, "We've seen pop culture change views around LGBTQ issues, for example, and pop culture has the power to challenge abortion stigma, too."[191]   Yes, that's a real job position—they have a "communications and culture department" (as well as their Arts & Entertainment Engagement office).

One Planned Parenthood affiliate even said that there should be a cartoon where a Disney princess gets an abortion.[192] Many people believed the statement to be an Internet hoax, but it is real, and they later explained,

---

[189] Salon "'Parenthood' bravely tackles abortion" by Willa Paskin (January 9th 2013)

[190] HuffPost "'Parenthood': Dramatic Episode Tackles Teen Pregnancy And Abortion" (January 9th 2013)

[191] PlannedParenthood.org "Planned Parenthood Announces New Senior Hires" Press Release (January 11th 2019)

[192] USA Today "Planned Parenthood called for Disney princess 'who's had an abortion' in now-deleted tweet" by Josh Hafner (March 27th 2018)

"Planned Parenthood believes that pop culture—television shows, music, movies—has a critical role to play in educating the public and sparking meaningful conversations around sexual and reproductive health issues and policies, including abortion."[193]

Another organization called the Center for Reproductive Rights was recently formed to promote abortion through entertainment.[194] Chairwoman Elizabeth Banks said her goal is to make abortion stigma-free and wants girls getting one to be seen as symbolic of "liberty itself."[195]

Comedian Michelle Wolf had a short-lived show on Netflix where she once did a segment titled "Salute to Abortions" which consisted of her being joined on stage by a marching band as she shouted to the audience, "It doesn't have to be a big deal, it's actually a great deal! It's about $300 dollars. That's like six movie tickets." The segment ended with her declaring, "God bless abortions, and God bless America!"[196] She later revealed that she herself had gotten one and it made her feel "very powerful" and "like God."[197]

---

[193] WNEP 16 ABC "Planned Parenthood Keystone: 'We need a Disney princess who's had an abortion'" by WNEP Staff (March 27th 2018)

[194] Hollywood Reporter "Elizabeth Banks to Lead Center for Reproductive Rights Creative Council" by Lindsay Weinberg (October 29th 2019)

[195] Washington Times "Elizabeth Banks: Abortion can be stigma-free, seen as 'liberty itself' with the right storytellers" by Douglas Ernst (March 5th 2020)

[196] Netflix "The Break with Michelle Wolf" (June 2018)

[197] Washington Examiner "'I am God': Comedian says abortion empowered her and encourages others to get one" by Spencer Neale (December 18th 2019)

Actress Lena Dunham once admitted she *wished* she had gotten an abortion so should could "better understand" other women who have had them.[198]   When actress "Busy Philipps" was at a pro-abortion rally in March 2020 she stood at the podium and screamed (literally *screamed*) about how glad she was to have gotten one when she was a teenager since it allowed her to become a star.

"Soon I would be driving my hybrid [car] to my beautiful fucking home...and I have all of this! All of it! Because I was allowed bodily autonomy at fifteen!"[199]

"I will not be shamed into being quiet. *We* will not be shamed into being quiet. Never again! I will never stop talking about my abortion or my periods or my experiences in childbirth, my episiotomies, my yeast infections, or my ovulation that lines up with the moon!"[200]   After seeing her unhinged rant, one might think it was someone playing a character and doing a parody sketch of a pro-abortion activist, but she really meant it and screamed it at the top of her lungs. She was happy to sacrifice her baby for fame and fortune.

Bowing to China

It's interesting to note that Hollywood is increasingly bowing to China's cultural standards in order to maintain

---

[198] New York Magazine "Lena Dunham: 'I Still Haven't Had an Abortion, But I Wish I Had'" by Gabriella Paiella (December 20th 2016)

[199] Townhall "Actress Busy Philipps Screams She's Proud of Her Abortion at 15-Years-Old Because It Helped Her Career" by Julio Rosas (March 5th 2020)

[200] Ibid.

distribution channels there. The Communist government has strict rules about which films are allowed to be seen in China, and in hopes of pleasing them, various plots are changed and scenes altered before they are put into production.

When the trailer for the *Top Gun* sequel was released, some eagle-eyed fans noticed that a Taiwanese flag patch which had been sown onto Tom Cruise's jacket along with a few other country's flags where his father had flown missions, was now missing.[201] Taiwan has been in an ongoing dispute with China trying to become an independent country, but China still claims the island as their territory and in another apparent attempt to appease the Chinese government, *Top Gun* producers removed the Taiwanese flag from Cruise's jacket because it simply being there symbolized Taiwan was not part of China, but their own country.

DC Comics also censored a promotional image for a Batman comic that was posted on their Instagram and Twitter accounts after some people in China interpreted it as supporting Hong Kong in *their* struggle for independence. The picture showed Batman throwing a Molotov cocktail with the caption "the future is young."[202]

Protests by separatists had been growing in Hong Kong, and mostly involved college age people using social media to organize, and some read too much into the

---

[201] Hollywood Reporter "'Top Gun: Maverick' Trailer Sparks Controversy as Fans Notice Taiwanese Flag Missing From Tom Cruise's Jacket" by Patrick Brzeski (July 22nd 2019)

[202] Hollywood Reporter "DC Comics Faces Backlash for Deleting 'Batman' Artwork That Caused Controversy in China" by Abid Rahman (November 28th 2019)

Batman picture thinking it supported them, so DC Comics deleted it so it wouldn't cause any issues with their distribution there.

The 2015 film *Pixels* starring Adam Sandler and Kevin James about aliens in the form of popular video game characters invading planet earth was altered so China wouldn't get offended. While waging war against our planet—in one scene an Arkanoid paddle, similar to Breakout, was supposed to destroy part of the Great Wall of China since in the game players bounce a ball against bricks to break them apart, but the censors changed that scene to depict the object destroying the Taj Mahal in India instead.[203]

The zombie action movie *World War Z* was based on a book that described the virus outbreak turning people into zombies starting in China, which is ultimately nuked, leaving Lhasa, Tibet the largest remaining city in the world. But for the film, producers changed the location of the outbreak to Korea and of course China wasn't nuked because they had nothing to do with it.

Apparently the Chinese government has banned the distribution of any films featuring zombies, and the *Hollywood Reporter* noted that a sequel was in the works for *World War Z* but later canceled because Paramount wouldn't be able to distribute the film internationally there.[204] The Chinese market is huge, and if studios are pitched a film they know won't be allowed in China, they're often inclined to pass on making it altogether.

---

[203] The Big Think "The silent Chinese propaganda in Hollywood films" by Scotty Hendricks (December 10th 2018)

[204] Hollywood Reporter "Zombie Films at Cannes: What's Up With All the Undead?" by Tatiana Siegel (May 18th 2019)

"You're not going to see something that's like *Seven Years in Tibet* anymore," said Larry Shinagawa, a college professor at Hawaii's Tokai International College.[205] The 1997 film which stars Brad Pitt takes place in the 1940s and 1950s when Tibet was struggling for independence from China, but that's too offensive to the Chinese these days and similar films may hurt distribution deals for other, unrelated projects.

Richard Gere's *Red Corner* (1997) was perhaps the last major film critical of Communist China to be made. In it, Gere plays a businessman who is framed for the murder of a Chinese general's daughter while on a trip there, and soon realizes how corrupt their legal system is.

In *First Man* (2018), a biopic about Neal Armstrong and the Apollo 11 landing on the moon, the film didn't show one of the most iconic scenes in history—Neal Armstrong and Buzz Aldrin planting the American flag on the moon once they arrived. When viewers noticed this strange omission Ryan Gosling, who played Armstrong, defended its absence saying landing on the moon was a "human achievement" not an American one.[206]

Others had their suspicions the scene wasn't depicted to avoid making the film too American in hopes it could be distributed in China. It doesn't make any sense that a movie about one of America's greatest achievements wouldn't proudly show the historic scene of the American flag being victoriously planted in the ground on the moon after we won the Space Race.

---

[205] The New York Times "How China is Writing Its Own Script" by Amy Qin and Audrey Carlsen (November 18th 2018)

[206] CNN "Ryan Gosling defends 'First Man' amid American flag controversy" by Sandra Gonzalez (August 31st 2018)

Ryan Gosling and the producers couldn't admit to the public the real reason for omitting the scene, because it would shock filmgoers across the country and perhaps cause people to boycott the movie for downplaying our own greatness in attempts to make more money through distribution in China. Hollywood stays very quiet about the lengths they go to in hopes of achieving that.

Even the NBA has sold out to China. When the general manager of the Houston Rockets basketball team tweeted support for Hong Kong in the midst of growing protests there hoping to gain their independence, it sparked an enormous problem for the NBA because their games are broadcast in China since they are surprisingly very popular there. Adding to the problem was Chinese native Yao Ming (the 7-foot 6-inch star) had played for the Houston Rockets before retiring.

Stars like James Harden praised China saying "We apologize. You know, we love China."[207] LeBron James said the coach "wasn't educated" about the situation and that his tweet "harmed" people financially and could have "physically" harmed them as well.[208] Despite celebrity athletes always supporting "good causes" and denouncing racism, police shootings, and human rights abuses around the world, none of them were saying a word about how China treated their citizens or that one million Muslims have been locked up in re-education camps there.[209]

---

[207] ESPN "James Harden apologizes as controversy grows: 'We love China'" (October 6th 2019)

[208] ABC News "LeBron James says general manager who tweeted in support of Hong Kong protesters 'wasn't educated' on the issue" by Meghan Keneally (October 15th 2019)

[209] New York Times "In China's Crackdown on Muslims, Children Have Not Been Spared" by Amy Quin (December 28th 2019)

Immigration

To say that the United States is being invaded by illegal immigrants is an understatement, but we're now living in a period of time where certain facts are considered to be "hate speech" and the liberal media gaslights their audience trying to get them to deny their own lying eyes. Over 20 million illegal aliens have breached our border and are currently living in the United States,[210] most of which drain financial and social resources which they don't even pay into—but to admit the extent of the illegal alien problem is strictly forbidden. In fact, the term "illegal alien" is now considered "hate speech."[211]

In 2019 almost 400,000 anchor babies were born in the United States from illegal alien mothers. In 48 of the 50 states there were more babies born by illegal alien mothers than ones who were born by women who are U.S. citizens.[212]

Flooding the United States with immigrants from third world countries is a primary objective of the globalists because it erodes patriotism, our cultural heritage, and hastens their planned economic collapse which they look

[210] The Hill "Yale, MIT study: 22 million, not 11 million, undocumented immigrants in US" by Rafael Bernal (September 21st 2018)

[211] CBS News "New York City's anti-discrimination policy warns against terms like 'illegal alien'" by Christopher Brito (October 1st 2019)

[212] Breitbart "Nearly 400K Anchor Babies Born in 2019, Exceeding U.S. Births in 48 States" by John Binder (January 5th 2020)

to seize upon in order to launch their socialist revolution. During the early Democratic presidential debates for the 2020 election, every single Democrat candidate on stage raised their hand when asked if they support giving free healthcare to illegal aliens.[213]

There are even reports of Mexicans waiting (and hoping) for Donald Trump to lose his re-election bid in November 2020, who plan to then illegally enter the U.S. because they feel their chances of getting in and being able to stay will be almost assured.[214] The more illegals the better for Democrats, who hope to one day grant them all amnesty and make them U.S. citizens (and their new voter base), destroying any chances of Republicans winning a national election again for generations.

So aside from the Democrat Party and the mainstream "news" media calling for a nonstop influx of immigrants to bring this about, Hollywood is helping as much as they can as well. Often brief pro-illegal immigration messages will be inserted into the dialogue of a show or a character will comment how "terrible" President Trump's immigration policies are, but now we're even seeing entire television series dedicated to promoting illegal immigration and demonizing anyone who wants to secure the border.

We all know Hollywood loves to reboot old shows from decades ago, from *Hawaii Five-0* and *Murphy Brown* to *MacGyver*, hoping to cash-in on the nostalgia original fans had for the series. One of those reboots was

---

[213] CNN "Democrats want to offer health care to undocumented immigrants. Here's what that means" by Tami Luhby (September 11th 2019)

[214] Washington Times "Illegal immigrants lying in wait for Trump to lose election" by Stephen Dinan (January 17th 2020)

Party of Five, which originally aired in the 1990s and was about a family of five kids (ages one to twenty-four) who had to fend for themselves after both of their parents were killed in a car accident by a drunk driver.

But in 2020, it was rebooted to depict a Mexican family whose parents got deported because of President Trump's crackdown on illegal aliens! The five kids (who are anchor babies because they were born in the U.S.) are then left here to fend for themselves.[215] The show was canceled after just one season.[216]

In 2017, the *New York Times* expressed their frustration that there weren't enough illegal aliens in starring roles or television shows that focus on them and their struggles, so they called on studios to green-light more series about "Dreamers"—the millions of illegal aliens smuggled into the United States by their parents that President Obama gave amnesty to.[217] Producers listened, and soon plots about "innocent" illegal aliens being persecuted would become a common occurrence.

ICE Are the New Bogymen

After Roseanne Barr's character was killed off and the series renamed *The Connors* due to her infamous "offensive tweet" about Obama administration official Valerie Jarrett, her daughter "Becky" in the show got knocked up by an illegal alien who worked as a busboy at

215 NPR "In 'Party Of Five' Reboot, Deportation Separates The Family" by Michael Martin (January 11th 2020)

216 Hollywood Reporter "'Party of Five' Reboot Canceled at Freeform" by Lesley Goldberg (April 17th 2020)

217 The New York Times "Hollywood's Diversity Problem and Undocumented Immigrants" by Monica Castillo (October 20th 2017)

the same Mexican restaurant she waitressed at. He later called her one day to let her know that he got caught up in an ICE (Immigration and Custom Enforcement) raid and she breaks down in tears out of fear that now the baby is going to have to grow up without a father because he's being deported.[218]

NBC's sitcom *Superstore* featured ICE agents coming to the fictional retail giant "Cloud 9" (the "superstore" at the center of the show) to arrest an illegal immigrant who works there in the season finale. Her fellow employees tried to help her escape the agents.[219]

Netflix's female prison drama *Orange is the New Black* also featured ICE agents as the bad guys who arrested a major character just when she was about to be released from prison for an unrelated crime, leaving her boyfriend waiting outside with a bouquet of flowers devastated that he wasn't getting reunited with her.[220]

In an episode of the CW's *Two Sentences Horror Story,* a Latino nanny fends off would-be robbers trying to break into the family's home that she works for, but when the heroic nanny makes the news, ICE agents discovered she was undocumented and soon paid her a visit, thus the horrifying twist at the end.[221]

---

[218] NewsBusters "'Roseanne' Spinoff: Illegal Immigrants 'Just Trying to Have a Better Life'" by Dawn Slusher (January 23rd 2019)

[219] Vulture "America Ferrera Says Superstore Season Four ICE Raid Could Shape the Show for Years" by Jordan Crucchiola (July 19th 2019)

[220] The Hollywood Reporter "'OITNB' Star Opens Up About Tackling 'Dangerous' Immigration Storyline" by Jackie Strause (August 1st 2018)

[221] Newsbusters "New CW Anthology Advises Illegal Immigrants To 'Hide'" by Lindsay Kornick (August 15th 2019)

Charisse L'Pree Corsbie-Massay, a professor at the Newhouse School of Public Communications at Syracuse University, says, "ICE has emerged as a villain in popular discourse, and now we're seeing that on screen. But these ICE agents are one-off characters with no lines and no names. They're just representations of ICE, the faceless government entity. Their only role is to play the villain to our characters."[222]

Pamela Rutledge, the director of the Media Psychology Research Center, said, "Making ICE agents as bad guys exacerbates the political fission surrounding the immigration issues…Whether you agree or disagree with current policies, it is important to understand how fiction can inform beliefs on current issues where most people have little actual experience."[223]

During the Trump administration we've seen more open border messages being sprinkled into shows than ever before. In Showtime's *Shameless* one character (Frank Gallagher) played by William H. Macy, announces he's having a keg party at his house and is charging people 10 bucks at the door to get in, and adds that unlike this "piece of shit country," his "border" turns away no one.[224]

Pop singer Kesha released a song and music video dedicated to DACA illegal aliens (Dreamers) called "Hymn" where she sings, "Even the stars and the moon don't shine quite like we do. Dreamers searchin' for the

---

[222] Daily Beast "ICE Agents Are Television's Newest Bogeymen, From Netflix's 'Orange is the New Black' to NBC's 'Superstore'"

[223] Ibid.

[224] Breitbart "Showtime's 'Shameless': America Is a 'Piece of Shit Country'" by Alana Mastrangelo (November 25th 2019)

truth. After all we've been through, no, we won't stand and salute [the flag]."[225]

The medical drama *Grey's Anatomy* had an episode about an illegal immigrant who reluctantly takes her daughter to the hospital to finally get healthcare she's been neglecting out of fear that she would get deported. Lobbying agency Hollywood, Health & Society convinced the writers to include that plot point to highlight the concerns illegal aliens have about getting deported if they go to a hospital.[226]

Even the rebooted *Twilight Zone* on CBS featured an episode where "welcoming illegal immigrants" was the "moral of the story" at the end. An upper middle class woman's housekeeper is detained by ICE and scheduled to be deported, and despite working for the family for over a decade, the family's friends seem fairly callous about her situation. "These people know the risks when they come here," a neighbor says.[227]

The homeowner herself, Eve, is later revealed to be an illegal immigrant as well—from another dimension, who came to ours thirty years ago to live among humans on earth after fleeing terrible living conditions on her own planet. In the end, she is also detained and hauled off screaming, now facing deportation herself, back to where she came from.

---

[225] Rolling Stone "Watch Kesha Celebrate DACA Dreamers in Moving 'Hymn' Video" by Jon Blistein (May 31st 2018)

[226] New York Observer "Hooray for Hollywood: How Charities Influence Your Favorite TV Shows" by Anne Easton (October 28th 2015)

[227] Newsbusters "'The Twilight Zone' Defends Illegal Immigration: 'We Are All Immigrants From Somewhere'" by Lindsay Kornick (May 16th 2019)

The episode concludes with narrator Jordan Peele giving the "moral" of the story, saying, "We are all immigrants from somewhere, be it another city, another country, or another dimension. As a child, Eve Martin escaped to what should have been a better world. A world where the skies are blue. But now those skies have darkened, and the land below them is a place she is no longer welcome. For Eve Martin, there's no passport to be stamped for passage out of the Twilight Zone."[228]

Other Attempts

There were reports that *Jane the Virgin* star Gina Rodriguez was hoping to produce a TV series about a college student who found out they were an undocumented immigrant, and reportedly had a pilot episode made for the CW network, but so far it hasn't been picked up.[229] Then CBS reportedly bought the rights and hoped they could get the show to air under the working title of *Rafa the Great*.[230]

Gina Rodriquez is also trying to get another show called *Have Mercy* produced, which is about a Latina doctor who immigrates to Miami but is unable to practice medicine in the United States for whatever reason (probably because the medical school she went to is considered substandard), and so she decides to open an

---

[228] Ibid.

[229] Vulture "Why You Could Be Seeing a Lot of Immigrant Stories on TV This Fall" by Maria Elena Fernandez (January 23rd 2018)

[230] Hollywood Reporter "'Jane the Virgin,' 'Vida' Writers Talk Onscreen Representation" by Jenna Marotta (October 3rd 2018)

illegal clinic run out of her apartment to help her Latino neighbors.[231]

CBS shot a pilot episode for *In the Country We Love*, based on Diane Guerreros's memoir of having her parents deported back to Columbia when she was a teenager, but it doesn't appear to have been picked up.[232] Probably because it's too similar to the *Party of Five* reboot.

Another planned series called *Casa* (Spanish for Home) was shopped around which is about a family of immigrants who have to fend for themselves after their parents are deported.[233] It's unknown if the idea was dropped because it's identical to the *Party of Five* reboot, or if the series was just rebranded as that. It's likely numerous different scripts about the same premise floated around Hollywood before one of them finally got picked up since it's such a predictable plot, and several different writers probably thought it was the next big idea.

DACA dramas are becoming "TV's new obsession" in the United States.[234] Even Apple TV, which has recently joined the television production business, produced an immigration series called *Little America* about a 12-year-old boy from India whose parents were deported, and he is left to run his father's hotel. Each episode tries to "go beyond the headlines to look at the funny, romantic, heartfelt, inspiring and unexpected lives of immigrants in

[231] Variety "Gina Rodriguez Developing Pair of Latino Series at CBS, CW" by Joe Otterson (September 6th 2017)

[232] Variety "Immigration Projects Take Center Stage at Broadcast Networks" by Joe Otterson (September 8th 2017)

[233] Washington Post "TV dramas and sitcoms are suddenly all about immigration" by Travis M. Andrews (October 13th 2017)

[234] The Guardian "'Daca dramas': How immigration become US TV's new obsession" by Lanre Bakare (September 13th 2017)

America, at a time when their stories are more relevant than ever."[235]

In 2019 Netflix released a documentary titled *After the Raid* which follows the lives of several people in a small town in Tennessee after ICE officers conducted a roundup of illegal aliens there in order to guilt trip White people into feeling bad for the "Latino families" that were "broken up."[236] Netflix is also producing a documentary series about illegal aliens with singer/actress Selena Gomez called *Living Undocumented*, which follows around eight families that are at risk of being deported.

Gomez told the *Hollywood Reporter* that, "I chose to produce this series, *Living Undocumented*, because over the past few years, the word 'immigrant' has seemingly become a negative word. My hope is that the series can shed light on what it's like to live in this country as an undocumented immigrant firsthand, from the courageous people who have chosen to share their stories."[237]

Executive producer Aaron Saidman said, "*Living Undocumented* is designed to illuminate one of the most important issues of our time. But rather than discussing this issue with only statistics and policy debates, we wanted viewers to hear directly from the immigrants

235 Deadline.com "'Little America' Immigrant Anthology Series In Works At Apple From 'The Big Sick' Writers, Lee Eisenberg & Alan Yang" by Nellie Andreeva (February 8th 2018)

236 The Daily Beast "How an ICE Immigration Raid Tore Apart a Small Midwest Town" by Nick Schager (December 20th 2019)

237 Hollywood Reporter "Selena Gomez-Produced 'Living Undocumented' Docuseries a Go at Netflix" by Rick Porter (September 17th 2019)

themselves, in their own words, with all the power and emotion that these stories reflect."[238]

It's not just TV shows. For years feature length films have been subtly promoting immigration. *District 9* put a unique spin on an alien invasion story by depicting the aliens arriving to earth, not to kill us and conquer our planet, but apparently in a desperate search of a new home. The friendly aliens were malnourished and weak from their long journey and presumably came here looking for help, only to be mistreated by humans and forced to live in a slum called "District 9" that serves as a giant internment camp surrounded by barbed wire and armed guards.

In the end, the lead "immigration" official who had previously harassed and abused the aliens is turned into one himself after being exposed to a DNA-mutating agent, and is forced to live in District 9 as one of them. The entire film was a cheesy allegory about racial segregation and xenophobia.[239]

In *Machete* (2010), Danny Trejo plays an illegal immigrant and vigilante living in Texas who is seen as a folk hero for killing a bunch of evil White people trying to stop illegal immigration. The film's catchphrase is "We didn't cross the border, the border crossed us." The White people are depicted as stupid or evil and at one point Robert DeNiro's character, who is part of a volunteer border patrol group, even murders a Mexican kid after they catch him trying to cross the border. "Welcome to America," he says, just before pulling the trigger. Danny Trejo then kills all the White "devils."

[238] Ibid.

[239] The Guardian "District 9: South Africa and apartheid come to the movies" by David Smith (August 20th 2009)

When some people denounced the film for seemingly encouraging anti-White violence, the Southern Poverty Law Center stepped in to defend it, calling it, "an argument for comprehensive immigration reform,"[240] meaning an argument for open borders since the bad guys in the film (aside from the Mexican drug cartel) were White people who didn't want illegal aliens crossing the border into the United States.

Elysium is a 2013 science fiction action film starring Matt Damon about a futuristic society where most of the inhabitants of earth live in extreme poverty and lack basic healthcare, while a small elite group live in luxury on a space station (called Elysium) that orbits the planet. Those not authorized to land on Elysium are deemed illegal immigrants and are "deported" or even have their aircraft shot down before reaching it.[241] Matt Damon's best friends' daughter has leukemia and is in need a medical treatment, so he helps smuggle her to the space station to save her, despite the elite's best efforts to stop him.

A film critic from *Variety* wrote that *Elysium* was, "one of the more openly socialist political agendas of any Hollywood movie in memory, beating the drum loudly not just for universal healthcare, but for open borders, unconditional amnesty, and the abolition of class distinctions as well."[242]

---

240 SPLCenter.org "Does Robert Rodriquez's 'Machete' Advocate 'Race War?'" by Alexander Zaitchik (September 10th 2010)

241 Philadelphia Inquirer "'Elysium' - the rich above, the slums below" by Steven Rae (August 8th 2013)

242 Variety "Film Review: 'Elysium'" by Scott Foundas (August 1st 2013)

Entertainment Weekly critic Sean Smith said, "If you are a member of the 1 percent (referring to the Occupy Wall Street movement which was occurring at the time the film was released), *Elysium* is a horror movie. For everyone else, it's one step shy of a call to arms."[243]

Mexican Drug Cartels Are Good

Action films need "bad guys," and for generations those bad guys have often been Mexican or Colombian drug cartels, but now those kinds of plots have been deemed xenophobic and racist out of concerns that they cast Latinos in a negative light. When the trailer dropped for Sylvester Stallone's latest Rambo film (*Last Blood*) it showed the iconic character fighting against a Mexican drug cartel and liberals immediately called it "xenophobic" and "anti-Mexican" propaganda.[244]

Rambo's adopted niece, who is of Mexican descent, runs away to Mexico hoping to find her birth mother, but is kidnapped by the cartel and forced into prostitution, but leave it to liberals to defend sex trafficking and get upset because an iconic American film hero hunts down and kills the traffickers! *The Daily Beast* said the film was "designed to prove the president's claim that we need to Build That Wall," and that "Rambo has gone full MAGA."[245]

---

[243] Entertainment Weekly "'Elysium': Future Shock" by Sean Smith (July 26th 2013)

[244] Worcester Telegram & Gazette "Movie review: Xenophobic 'Rambo: Last Blood' should be end of the line for character" by Katie Walsh (September 19th 2019)

[245] Daily Beast "'Rambo: Last Blood' is a Trumpian, Anti-Mexican Nightmare" by Nick Schager (September 20th 2019)

One reviewer called it "deeply xenophobic" and said that the film "should be end of line for the character."[246] Another critic called it a "hyper-violent xenophobic revenge fantasy" and said "It's all a setup for *Last Blood* to live out every assault rifle owner's worst fears and most insane fantasies about Mexico. The only way it could be more transparent is if Stallone had growled 'I. Am. The Wall!' in his best Judge Dredd voice."[247] Some idiot even called it a "radicalizing recruitment video," for right wing extremists.[248]

On Rotten Tomatoes it got only a 27% positive rating from critics, while 85% of viewers gave it a thumbs up— a disparity often seen on Rotten Tomatoes where critics now trash politically incorrect comedy specials and movies that are well-received by viewers.

In 2018, *Sicario: Day of the Soldado* was released starring Josh Brolin and Benicio del Toro who battle drug cartels in the stereotypical fashion, and it too set off a wave of crying critics, one saying "it doubles down on violent fantasies about another Mexican-American War," and "feels like a piece of state-sanctioned propaganda, a

---

[246] The Spokesman-Review "Deeply Xenophomic, lazy 'Rambo: Last Blood' should be end of line for character." by Katie Walsh via Tribune News Service (September 19th 2019)

[247] Uproxx "'Rambo: Last Blood' Is A Rollicking Good Time Of Hyper-Violent Xenophobic Revenge Fantasies" by Vince Mancini (September 18th 2019)

[248] The Playlist.net "'Rambo: Last Blood': Sylvester Stallone Leads A Manic MAGA Fever Dream & Radicalizing Recruitment Video [Review]" by Charles Barfield (September 21st 2019)

MAGA-sploitation thriller that does not see humanity in our neighbors."[249]

Jennifer Garner starred in a film called *Peppermint* (2018) in which her husband and daughter are murdered by a drug cartel, so she becomes a vigilante hunting and killing them. *The New Yorker* called the movie "racist" and "ignorant."[250] Another critic said it was "irresponsible" to make movies where the bad guys are Mexican drug cartels anymore because they "portray Latinos as animals."[251] *NBC News* said the film "is a poorly written blockbuster filled with racist stereotypes. Hollywood should know better."[252]

Until the Trump era, nobody thought that films about fighting Mexican drug cartels were problematic, but because of the hyper-vigilant Twitter outrage mobs that organize harassment campaigns hoping to stomp out any opposing ideas, the entire plot point may be all but abandoned by studios out of fear that their movies will be poorly reviewed by critics who deem them "racist."

---

[249] Indiwire "'Sicario: Day of Soldado' Doubles Down on Mexican Stereotypes and Violent MAGA Fantasies — Opinion" by Monica Castillo (June 29th 2018)

[250] The New Yorker "'PEPPERMINT,' REVIEWED: JENNIFER GARNER STARS IN AN IGNORANT, RACIST DRUG-TRADE REVENGE FILM" by Richard Brody (September 7th 2018)

[251] Latino Rebels "'Liberal' Hollywood Is Reinforcing Trump's Hate" by Alejandro Diaz (July 25th 2018)

[252] NBC News "'Sicario: Day of Soldado' is a poorly written blockbuster filled with racist stereotypes. Hollywood should know better." by Ani Bundel (July 1st 2018)

The Immigration Endgame

Pat Buchanon warned in his 2002 book *The Death of the West* that, "Uncontrolled immigration threatens to deconstruct the nation we grew up in and convert America into a conglomeration of peoples with almost nothing in common—not history, heroes, language, culture, faith, or ancestors."[253]

He goes on, "Millions have no desire to learn English or become citizens. America is not their home; Mexico is; and they wish to remain proud Mexicans. They have come here to work. Rather than assimilate, they create Little Tijuanas in U.S. cities, just as Cubans have created a Little Havana in Miami...With their own radio and TV stations, newspapers, films, and magazines, the Mexican Americans are creating an Hispanic culture separate and apart from America's larger culture. They are becoming a nation within a nation."[254]

Many Latinos actually want to create a new country in the Southwest called Aztlan that would include California, Arizona, New Mexico, Texas, and other states in the region.[255] The name refers to a mythical homeland of the Aztecs which Chicanos (Mexicans) want to restore. Mario Obledo, the president of the League of United Latin American Citizens, said, "California is going to be a

[253] *The Death of the West: How Dying Populations and Immigrant Invasions Imperil Our Country and Civilization* by Patrick J. Buchanon page 3 (2002 Thomas Dunne Books)

[254] *The Death of the West: How Dying Populations and Immigrant Invasions Imperil Our Country and Civilization* by Patrick J. Buchanon pages 125-126 (2002 Thomas Dunne Books)

[255] Los Angeles Times "Vision That Inspires Some and Scares Others: Aztlan" by David Kelly (July 7th 2006)

Mexican State. We are going to control all the institutions. If people don't like it, they should leave."[256] Never mind that if California was still part of Mexico the water wouldn't be safe to drink.

On college campuses in the Southwest various Chicano student groups exist to further the cause, including MEChA (the Chicano Student Movement of Aztlan) and La Raza (recently renamed to UnidosUS). These groups (and others) are really acting as agents of a foreign government, which means they should have to register with the Department of Justice as such, but it's doubtful any members of La Raza, MEChA, or any other pro-illegal alien activist groups have.

For the globalists plan for the New World Order to be complete, first large regions of the various continents must be merged into unions that act as the governing bodies for those countries, and then their different currencies merged into a single unit as well. The European Union (EU) and their common currency (the Euro) is the model for the rest of the world. Plans to merge the United States, Canada, and Mexico into the "North American Union" (NAU) which would use a new common currency (called the Amero), have been drafted, and the schemers are waiting for the day they can force their agenda through.[257]

Similar regional mergers, such as the Asian Union, the Middle Eastern Union, and the African Union, are also in the plan, which would each have their own common currency as well. And once they are all formed, the final

---

[256] FrontPageMag.com "Expressions of Ethnic Animosity" by James Lubinskas (November 24, 1999)

[257] "Building a North American Community" report by the Council on Foreign Relations (2005)

step would be to merge all of those regional unions into a single global governing system along with each of their respective currencies, ultimately forming a one world government and a single digital global currency.

War on White People

Despite Hollywood's insistence on wanting to end all bigotry and promote "tolerance" for everything; there is a growing anti-White sentiment where White people are regularly demonized, ostracized, and blamed for all the problems in the world. At the same time, Hollywood does everything they can to portray Blacks and Latinos as perpetual victims of "whiteness" whose lives have been ruined for generations because of "White privilege." According to Hollywood, Black people never do anything wrong, or if they do it's a result of the circumstances in their life which put them in that position because of "systematic" and "institutional racism" at the hands of White people.

John Langley, the creator of the reality show *COPS*, admitted he purposefully didn't allow many segments which involved police confrontations with Black suspects, and instead aired more where White people were being detained and arrested because he didn't want to promote the "stereotype" that Black people tend to be criminals.[258] Never mind Department of Justice statistics which show that Black people make up approximately 13% of the population in the United States, but are responsible for

---

[258] The Hollywood Reporter "TV Executives Admit in Taped Interviews That Hollywood Pushes a Liberal Agenda" by Paul Bond (June 1st 2001)

close to 50% of the total murders.[259]   Just pointing out statistics like that is considered to be racist, and the ADL considers 13/50 a "numeric hate symbol."[260]

"Diversity" is a code word meaning less White people, and in recent years Hollywood has been obsessed with what liberals believe are too many White people starring in films and TV shows.   In 2015 after the Academy Award nominees were announced, the hashtag #OscarsSoWhite went viral from people complaining that there weren't any Black people nominated for Best Actor or Best Actress that year.[261]   In their minds Black people are the *best*, and it must have been because of "racism" that none happened to be nominated for those spots that year.

From that point on their foot was in the door, and each year after that there would be more scrutiny over how many "people of color" were nominated and which actors won, and how many White people starred in TV shows and films.   Every time nominees were mentioned, media reports would flood the Internet about the "lack of diversity" and how "problematic" it was.[262]

"Why do snubs for women and people of color keep happening?" they would ask every time half of the

---

[259] U.S. Department of Justice "Homicide Trends in the United States, 1980-2008" by Alexia Cooper and Erica L. Smith (November 2011)

[260] ADL.org "Hate on Display™ Hate Symbols Database"

[261] CBS News "#OscarsSoWhite: Academy Awards slammed for lack of diversity" by John Blackstone (January 14th 2016)

[262] Fortune "These Oscar Best Picture nominees are 'problematic'— but will that matter?" by Paula Bernstein (January 16th 2020)

nominees weren't Black or Latino.[263]   Fans of Jenifer Lopez were so upset that she wasn't nominated for Best Actress for her role as a stripper in *Hustlers* they took to Twitter (as usual) to complain about it, demanding "Justice for J. Lo."[264] In the film she plays one of a group of strippers who drug and then defraud rich men who come into their club, running up their credit cards. Not exactly Oscar material, but she must have gotten "snubbed" because she's Latino!

Others were equally upset that Jamie Foxx (*Just Mercy*), Lupita Nyong'o (*Us*), Awkwafina (*The Farewell*), and Eddie Murphy (*Dolemite Is My Name*) weren't nominated for anything either one year. All because of "racism," not that they had mediocre performances or others who happened to be White made more of an impact.

When *Toy Story 4* was nominated for Best Animated Feature at the Golden Globes, some lunatics voiced their concerns that none of the toys in the franchise were Black![265] Keep in mind that Woody, Bow Peep, and Buzz Light Year are the only "human" toys. The rest are ones like Mr. Potato Head, a dog, a pig, a dinosaur, etc. The *Hollywood Reporter* complained about the "near-absence of people of color," despite two toys being voiced by the Black comedy duo Jordan Peele and Keegan-Michael Key, but that's not good enough.

---

[263] USA Today "Oscar nominations 2020: Why do snubs for women and people of color keep happening?" by Andrea Mandell (January 13th 2020)

[264] NBC Los Angeles "Fans Link J.Lo 'Hustlers' Snub to Oscars Diversity Problem" (January 13th 2020)

[265] The Hollywood Reporter "The Whiteness of 'Toy Story 4'" by Stephen Galloway (January 3rd 2020)

Their review went on to complain that not only are each of the lead toys Caucasian, but a new character (Forky) is a "very white fork."[266] The toy is homemade, created out of a plastic spork, some stick-on googly eyes, and has pipe cleaners for arms. It's a spork, it doesn't have a race, but the lunatic film reviewer saw it as another "Caucasian" toy because it's white, which most plastic utensils are.

The reviewer was also upset because, "in many ways [Toy Story 4's] worldview seems like an Eisenhower-era fantasy, a vision of America that might have come from the most die-hard reactionary: lovely if you're wealthy and White, but alarming if you're Black or brown or gay or a member of any other minority—in other words, more than half the U.S. population."[267]

There weren't enough Black people in *Joker* to please some critics either, even though Joaquin Phoenix's character starts dating a neighbor of his who is a single Black mother. *Time* magazine complained that her character had too small of a role, saying, "In Joker, Black women are visible but they are not seen," whatever the hell that means.[268]

The review went on to complain about the roles other Black people had in the film such as the Joker's social worker. She doesn't really listen to his problems and is just going through the motions, thus missing another opportunity to possibly steer him away from ultimately becoming a psychotic killer. That's casting a Black

---

[266] Ibid.

[267] Ibid.

[268] Time "In *Joker*, Black Women Are Visible But They Are Not Seen" by Beandrea July (October 11th 2019)

person in a negative light, and "racist." Another Black character, a random woman on a bus, scolds him to stop "bothering" her son when all he was doing was being nice to the kid, and that's perpetuating "racism" too by furthering the "angry Black woman" stereotype.

The 2019 film *Little Women,* which is based on a novel written in 1868 about four young girls living during the Civil War and coming of age, is also "too White." A writer for *Teen Vogue*, a Marxist publication dedicated to perverting the minds of teen girls, wrote that when old literary classics are made into films, they need to "better incorporate diversity."[269]

Another critic said that it "romanticizes White privilege" and that "casual racism is merely the start of its problems." They concluded that "*Little Women* is, indeed, rooted in the advantages of bourgeois White womanhood."[270] We can't have films anymore where the story just so happens to be about people who are White, because that's not "diverse" enough.

The Hollywood Reporter complained that Christmas movies on the Hallmark Channel don't have enough Black people in them and "struggles to give diversity a home for the holidays."[271] Their complaint begins with a snarky, "While other networks are viewing the holidays with an eye toward inclusion, Hallmark is delivering the dream of a white Christmas, just like the one's audiences

---

[269] Teen Vogue "'Little Women,' Laurie, and the Argument for Racebent Casting" by Natalie De Vera Obedos (December 23rd 2019)

[270] National Review "Greta Gerwig's *Little Women* Romanticizes White Privilege" by Armond White (December 27th 2019)

[271] Hollywood Reporter "Hallmark Channel Struggles to Give Diversity a Home for the Holidays" by Lesley Goldberg (November 27th 2019)

used to know," and then notes, "Of the network's record 24 original holiday movies this season, four of them have Black leads," but "that's down from last year, when five of its 21 original holiday movies had Black leads."[272] Others have complained about Hallmark movies being "too White" as well.[273]

In my previous book *Liberalism: Find a Cure* I detailed how many on the Left are upset that Santa Claus is White, and are now calling him a symbol of "White supremacy."[274] Some are so determined to destroy Santa's image that publishing giant Harper Collins released a book called *Santa's Husband* which depicts him as a homosexual "married" to a Black man. CNN gleefully gave the author airtime to promote the book when it came out.[275]

Director Tim Burton, the man behind *Edward Scissorhands* (1990), *Beetlejuice* (1988), and *The Nightmare Before Christmas* (1993) angered the Diversity Police because he didn't cast a "diverse group of characters" in his movie *Miss Peregrine's Home for Peculiar Children* (2016) since Samuel L. Jackson was the only Black person in it. He began trending on Twitter from so many "woke" people calling him a racist.[276]

---

[272] Ibid.

[273] IBTimes "Why Are Hallmark Movie Casts So White? We Asked The CEO" by Rachael Ellenbogen (December 21st 2017)

[274] Mediaite "Touré Says There's Already a Benevolent Black Man Who Gives Gifts to Kids: Obama" by Noah Rothman (December 16th 2013)

[275] CNS News "Harper, CNN Promote Gay 'Married' Santa Claus" by Michael W. Chapman (December 20th 2017)

[276] USA Today "Tim Burton's diversity comments blew up Twitter" by Carley Mallenbaum (September 29th 2016)

Actor Jonah Hill said that "real change" in the industry will come only when White men no longer run the studios and streaming companies.[277] While celebrities obsessively complain about too many White people being in positions of power in Hollywood and starring in too many shows (and winning too many awards); none of them would ever commit the cardinal sin of the entertainment industry by asking about Jewish influence in Hollywood.[278]

Everyone knows that would kill their career overnight no matter how earnestly or tactfully it was brought up, but complaining about too many White men having positions of power in the industry has become a rallying cry for social justice warriors.

There are numerous specials on Comedy Central and Netflix which feature Black and Latino comedians whose entire act is basically making fun of White people, which is fine—and sometimes funny, but we all know the double standard. Few White comedians will dare make jokes about Blacks or Latinos. Jokes about Asians used to be acceptable, but those too would be career suicide today. Blacks and Latinos can "joke" about how they "hate White people" or complain about "the problem with White people" and often their distain is obvious, and their "jokes" are just thinly veiled racism—but that's just fine.

Black sitcoms often include subplots about how the families are living in a hostile country and White people

277 Breitbart "Jonah Hill: 'Real Change' in Film Will Come When Women, Minorities Run Studios and Streaming Companies" by Warner Todd Huston (January 31st 2020)

278 Newsweek "CNN's Rick Sanchez Fired After Implying Jews Run the Media" by David A. Graham (October 1st 2010)

around every corner hate them.[279]   An entire episode of
ABC's sitcom *Black-ish* was about how "America hates
Black people" with a lead character telling members of
her family that repeatedly throughout the show.[280]

90's Sitcoms Now "Too White"

Since "diversity" dominates these days, many classic
shows from the past are now seen in hindsight as "racist"
because there are "too many" White people in them.
Beverly Hills 90210, *Seinfeld*, *Home Improvement*,
Everybody Loves Raymond, *Growing Pains*, *Family Ties*,
Cheers, *Frasier*, *Full House*, *Dawson's Creek*, *Friends*,
and more all "lack diversity."[281]

Even with the rash of revivals and reboots, critics are
upset that many of the shows' racial makeup remained the
same.   The *Hollywood Reporter* complained about the
"blinding whiteness of nostalgia TV."[282]   In the return of
Roseanne, however, producers ensured there was some
"diversity" by depicting her son D.J. as having married a
Black woman and has a Black daughter with her.[283]

Friends star David Schwimmer would later suggest
that his show be rebooted with an all-Black or Asian

---

[279] Newsbusters "'Blackish' Does Episode on Teaching Black Kids
'America Hates You'" by Amelia Hamilton (January 16th 2018)

[280] Ibid.

[281] Complex.com "The 50 Most Racist TV Shows of All Time" (June
3rd 2013)

[282] The Hollywood Reporter "Critic's Notebook: The Blinding
Whiteness of Nostalgia TV" by Inkoo Kang (March 28th 2018)

[283] Inquisitr "Roseanne Barr Explains Why She Wanted The Conners
To Have A Black Grandchild On The 'Roseanne' Revival" by
Victoria Miller (February 21st 2018)

group of friends. He went on to virtue signal that, "I campaigned for years to have Ross [his character] date women of color. One of the first girlfriends I had on the show was an Asian American woman, and later I dated African American women. That was a very conscious push on my part."[284]

These days White people are considered racist if they prefer dating only White people.[285] No other race faces the same pressures for personal relationships and families to become more "racially diverse"—only White people.

And despite David Schwimmer's hopes for a "Black Friends" reboot, that show has already been made—and *before* Friends. It was called *Living Single*, and *Friends* was basically an all-White reboot of that show, but there will never be enough "diversity" in sitcoms and feature films. No matter how many shows feature an all-Black cast, or star Black characters, the Left will never be satisfied.

There were plenty of Black sitcoms in the 1990s, like *The Fresh Prince of Bel-Air, Family Matters, A Different World, Martin, Roc, Hangin' with Mr. Cooper, The Hughleys, The Wayans Bros, The Cosby Show*, and many more. All with Black stars and few, if any, White actors involved, but God forbid sitcoms exist with a White-only cast! Of course Black-only shows were made long before the 90s, and continue to be made today—like *Empire, Power, Black-ish, Grown-ish*, and many others, and nobody complains that there aren't any White lead actors

284 The Guardian "David Schwimmer: 'I'm very aware of my privilege as a heterosexual white male'" by David Smith (January 27th 2020)

285 Slate "Is It Racist to Date Only People of Your Own Race? Yes." by Reihan Salam (April 22nd 2014)

or threaten to boycott those shows for not being "diverse" enough.

Not Enough Mexicans

The mayor of Los Angeles, Eric Garcetti, wants to double the number of Latinos in TV shows and movies within the next ten years, and launched a project called "LA Collab" in order to "connect Latinx talent, executives, and creators to opportunities in the entertainment industry."[286] *Latinx*, if you're wondering, is the new politically correct gender neutral term for *Latino*, since even that is problematic these days, but that's a topic for a whole other book.[287]

Los Angeles County contains 4.9 million Hispanics and now there are at least 60 million of them living in the United States (20 million of which are illegal aliens), so Hollywood is doing everything they can to cater to them. For example, Jimmy Kimmel's little sidekick Guillermo —who speaks broken English—is paid $500,000 dollars a year to stand off to the side of the stage and laugh at his jokes and chime in once in a while with his catch phrase, "That's right Jimmy!" Before becoming a fixture on air for the show he worked as a security guard in the parking lot of ABC Studios making $8.00 an hour.[288]

There have also been a flood of TV shows starring Latinos in recent years, including the *Magnum PI* reboot,

---

[286] CNN "Los Angeles mayor wants to double Latino representation in Hollywood in the next 10 years" by Christina Maxouris (January 20th 2020)

[287] See my previous book, *Liberalism: Find a Cure* (2018)

[288] Parade "Guillermo's Job Before Becoming Jimmy Kimmel's Sidekick" by Walter Scott (April 12th 2014)

but there will never be enough to satisfy the social justice warriors. Every show and movie must have a "diverse" cast (meaning fewer White people). Every popular series must have a Black, Asian, and Latino equivalent.

Soon there will probably be growing calls for Arab versions of hit shows, since those of Middle Eastern descent will clamor about being "under-represented" in American entertainment. And after that it will be the Indians (or Native Americans, or Indigenous people, or whatever politically correct term they're calling themselves these days), and then probably the Eskimos. We're sliding down a slippery slope of stupidity with no end.

Obsessed with White Sins of the Past

The one kind of movie Hollywood loves to make more than crime thrillers or action-adventures are ones that highlight how "racist" White people are. "Historical dramas" about how awful White people are and how the films "reflect what's still happening today" come out every year. Some of them are Black revenge fantasies like *Django Unchained*. Actor Jamie Foxx even bragged about killing a bunch of White people in the film when he was a featured guest on *Saturday Night Live*, saying, "I get to kill all the White people, how great is that?"[289]

The film incited some Black people to vent their fantasies of killing White people themselves, flooding Twitter with their hatred in tweets like, "Django got me

---

289 Washington Examiner "Jamie Foxx: It's 'great' to 'kill all the white people'" by Kelsey Osterman (December 9th 2012)

wanting to kill White people!" and "After watching Django, all I wanna do is shoot White people."[290]

Of course, you can't tell disgruntled Blacks who hate America to "go back to Africa," because that would be "racist." Everything is "racist" to liberals. Black people's obsession with racism of the past can be seen in the obvious double standard of demanding White people not be "allowed" to say "the n-word" even while singing along to popular rap songs.

Kendrick Lamar brought a fan on stage to perform one of his songs with him in 2018, but stopped the show mid-performance because the girl (who was White) rapped along to the original lyrics which included the word "nigga" in the hook. After about 30 seconds he told the DJ to stop the music and started staring at the girl. "Am I not cool enough for you, bro?" she asks, thinking that her rapping wasn't good enough. He went on to tell her the "rules" and said she had to bleep that word. She apologized, and then they started again.[291]

When Latino actress Gina Rodriguez sang a few lines from a rap song that included "nigga" in the lyrics (as most rap songs do) and posted it on her Instagram, Blacks (and SJW Whites) freaked out so bad she became the top trend on Twitter.[292] She then apologized. The same thing happened when a star of the *Bachelorette* was singing

[290] VLADTV "'Django Unchained' Viewers Tweet Desire To 'Kill White People'" by John S (January 9th 2013)

[291] BBC "Kendrick Lamar stops white fan using N-word on stage at concert" (May 22nd 2018)

[292] CNN "Actress Gina Rodriguez comes under fire over her use of the n-word" by Faith Karimi (October 19th 2019)

along to a rap song on Instagram Live.[293] Most Black people get more upset when a White person says the word than they do when gang bangers end up killing an innocent kid in their neighborhood with a stray bullet.

As Black radio host Jessie Lee Peterson points out, "They're not [actually] offended! They pretend to be in order to scare White folks and shake 'em down for stuff."[294] Imagine if White people demanded that Black people weren't allowed to use certain words! Democrats in Congress would hold hearings and pass a resolution denouncing such outrageous word policing and it would be a national scandal, but the word "nigga" mustn't be uttered out loud by White people, because it's *their* word.

On the Lookout for Racism

Many Black people (and White SJWs) are so hyper-sensitive and obsessed with racism that they hallucinate and often see it where none exists. For example, Roseanne Barr was fired from her hit TV show within just a few hours after making a joke about Valerie Jarrett, a former advisor to Barack Obama, when she tweeted that Valerie looked like a character from the *Planet of the Apes* movies; and if you saw a side by side photo of her and that character, you would know why Rosanne said that. But it turns out that Valerie Jarett is half Black, although you would never guess from looking at her. Rosanne later

---

[293] NBC News "'Bachelorette' star Hannah Brown apologizes for using the N-word" by Janelle Griffith (May 19th 2020)

[294] https://twitter.com/jlptalk/status/1262490953094295552

explained, "I thought the bitch was White!" which most people did.[295]

Her show was number one on ABC, but the network immediately fired her and then continued the show, calling it *The Conners* after killing off her character with an opioid overdose from pain pills she was taking for knee pain.[296] Of course Rosanne is not a racist, and in the 1990s the original series promoted a lot of liberal propaganda, but once someone starts trending on Twitter after getting the attention of the perpetually offended online activists, most companies feel they need to appease the mob by firing the person even if they didn't do anything wrong.

Hollywood's dogma is so rigid that if anyone dares doubt that all Trump supporters are racist *they* will be denounced for "supporting White supremacy," as a star of *Queer Eye for the Straight Guy* realized when he simply said that "not all Republicans are racist."[297] Jonathan Van Ness trended on Twitter from so many people attacking him for simply stating what should be obvious, but defending conservatives in any way is seen as a major transgression.

Sometimes when popular novels are made into movies, the studios feel the need to add some racism to "remind" the audience how terrible White people are.

---

[295] Vanity Fair "Roseanne Barr Screams About Valerie Jarrett: 'I Thought the Bitch Was White!'" by Laura Bradley (July 20th 2018)

[296] The Washington Post "Roseanne's character overdosed on opioids and left 'The Conners' behind. It's better this way." by Hank Stuever (October 16th 2018)

[297] The Wrap "'Queer Eye' Star Jonathan Van Ness Under Fire After Saying 'Not All Republicans Are Racist'" by Jon Levine (August 16th 2018)

When Tom Clancy's bestselling book *The Sum of All Fears* was turned into a film starring Morgan Freeman and Ben Affleck, the plot was changed from Palestinian terrorists trying to dupe the United States and Russia into a nuclear war because of the United States' support for Israel, to a story about White supremacists trying to trick the two super powers into a nuclear war so they could build a Whites only Europe.[298]

The movie was so different from the book that when Tom Clancy introduced himself on the DVD commentary he said he was the person who "wrote the book they ignored."[299]

Actors Denounce "White Privilege"

If White celebrities don't regularly denounce their own "White privilege" and falsely claim that their success is due to the color of their skin, then they may become a suspected White supremacist themselves, and aren't seen as an ally of the Black community. Chelsea Handler even hosted a Netflix show called "Hello, Privilege, It's Me, Chelsea" which examined "White privilege" and followed her around as she traveled across the country endlessly apologizing for being White and talking with other people about how terrible White people have made America.[300]

Jon Stewart even issued an apology for having too many White people on the staff of *The Daily Show* when

---

[298] Carolina Journal "'The Sum of All Fears' Falls Victim to Political Correctness" by Hans Marc Hurd (August 6th 2002)

[299] IGN "The Sum of All Fears: The Jack Ryan prequel hits DVD. Our full review" by Jeremy Conrad (December 13th 2018)

[300] Mashable "Chelsea Handler talks about facing up to her own white privilege" by Rachel Thompson (September 10th 2019)

he was the host.[301] He hadn't even been the host for five years and nobody was concerned about it, but he too was "sorry" and began doing various interviews to give his two cents about how America needs more "diversity." He also called for Black people to be paid reparations.[302]

When Netflix released a trailer for a forthcoming series about the crimes of serial killer Ted Bundy (played by Zac Efron), people were shocked how it glamorized him and made Bundy seem like a rock star instead of a monster.[303] Pushing back against the criticism, Zac Efron said the film highlights Ted Bundy's "White privilege" and he believed the only reason Bundy got away with his crimes for so long was because he was a "clean-cut White dude."[304]

After the Black Lives Matter riots in the summer of 2020 the media became even more obsessed with demonizing White people, and there was an endless flood of celebrities apologizing for their "White privilege" and even producing PSAs about how sorry they are and how they "take responsibility."[305]

---

[301] Rolling Stone "Jon Stewart Talks Lack of Staff Diversity During his 'Daily Show' Tenure" by Jon Blistein (June 24th 2020)

[302] Esquire "Jon Stewart: America Can Only Have Equality When Black People Are Given What's Been Taken From Them" by Justin Kirkland (June 25th 2020)

[303] Insider "Zac Efron's portrayal of serial killer Ted Bundy is being accused of romanticizing the brutal murderer" by Jacob Shamsian (January 28th 2019)

[304] Fox News "Zac Efron says white privilege allowed Ted Bundy to kill people for so long before being captured" by Jessica Napoli and Tyler McCarthy (May 3rd 2019)

[305] Los Angeles Times "White celebrities partner with NAACP to 'take responsibility' for racism" by Christi Carras (June 11th 2020)

Poor Jimmy Fallon looked like he was being held at gunpoint when he interviewed the author of "White Fragility," a book about how White people have ruined America for Black people. He had her on *The Tonight Show* to lecture the audience about White people's "inevitable and often unaware racist assumptions and behaviors," and called White people "a-holes" because we make life "miserable" for Black people.[306]

He went along with the agenda so well that he sat there agreeing with everything she said, even when she said that *he* was a racist but didn't even know it. "When I'm talking about the racism that I have, the racism that *you* have, it's the result of living in a society in which racism is the foundation. We all absorb it," she said. "There's no way we could exempt ourselves from it."[307]

There's no way White people *can't* be racist she says! The title of the segment posted on the *Tonight Show* YouTube channel is "Dr. Robin DiAngelo Wants White People to Stop Saying They're Not Racist," because she thinks we all are![308]

Watchmen

When the *Watchmen* comic book was turned into a television series on HBO, of all the villains that the superheroes could have been fighting, the producers

---

[306] The Tonight Show Starring Jimmy Fallon "Dr. Robin DiAngelo Wants White People to Stop Saying They're Not Racist" segment posted on the show's official YouTube channel (June 17th 2020)

[307] Ibid.

[308] Mashable "'White Fragility' author Robin DiAngelo explains why white people shouldn't say they're 'not racist'" by Sam Haysom (June 18th 2020)

decided to have them tackle the "problems brought about by White supremacist forces."[309] The series creator said, "In a traditional superhero movie, the bad guys are fighting the aliens and when they beat the aliens, the aliens go back to their planet and everybody wins. There's no defeating White supremacy. It's not going anywhere, but it felt like it was a pretty formidable foe."[310]

The HBO series kicked off depicting the Tulsa Race Riot of 1921, where mobs of Blacks and Whites fought and killed each other after a Black man was arrested for assaulting a White woman and a group of armed Black men came to the jail out of concern that the man had been lynched, which wasn't true. The series started with this to set the stage that "not much" has changed in the United Sates, and Black people are still supposedly being lynched on a regular basis.

The show revolves around a modern day fictional White supremacist group in Tulsa, Oklahoma called the Seventh Kavalry, who "wage war" against the local police because the city has decided to pay reparations to Black people. In order to protect themselves from the White supremacists, police hide their identities by wearing masks and costumes.

The original *Watchmen* comic book series and the 2009 movie depicted the superheroes fighting crime at the height of the Cold War between the United States and the Soviet Union. Obviously many fans were disappointed in the HBO series turning the vigilantes into social justice

---

[309] IndieWire "'Watchmen': Damon Lindelof Shares How The New HBO Adaptation Deals with White Supremacy" by Steve Greene (July 24th 2019)

[310] Ibid.

warriors and force-feeding more identity politics to the audience, but critics were eager to defend the show. Vox said, "Some Watchmen fans are mad that HBO's version is political. But Watchmen has always been political."[311] Others blamed "right-wing trolls" who gave it negative reviews online.[312]

CBS's Supernatural Drama "Evil"

CBS has a drama which is a cheap knockoff of the *X-Files* called *Evil* where a "skeptical" forensic psychologist (who's Black) works with a Catholic priest to investigate supposed supernatural events. And in one episode the skeptic investigates a case of a girl who was pronounced legally dead, but later "came back to life" once her body was moved to the morgue. After concluding his investigation he figured out that the "resurrected" girl did not experience a miracle, but was the victim of racism because she's Black!

Once he cracked the case, he heads to the office of a senior official at the hospital with two stacks of medical records, saying, "Turned out to be hyperinflation [of the lungs], and undiagnosed COPD...But it wasn't the paramedics fault."

That's when he drops the files on the man's desk. "What are those?" he asks.

---

311 Vox "Some Watchmen fans are mad that HBO's version is political. But Watchmen has always been political" by Alex Abad-Santos (October 24th 2019)

312 Esquire "The Right-Wing Troll Backlash Against HBO's *Watchmen* Is Hilariously Stupid" by Matt Miller (October 24th 2019)

"The emergency life-saving efforts of this hospital over the last year. A hundred and seventy-six in all," he replies, looking smug.

"Okay."

"These are your Caucasian patients" he says, placing his hand on one of the stacks. "Did you know that on average during a code your doctors perform fifty-eight minutes of chest compressions and rescue breathing on Caucasian patients?

"No. I didn't."

"And these are your African American patients. Your doctors on average perform chest compressions and rescue breathing *twenty-three minutes* on them. Patients like Naomi Clark" (the Black girl who supposedly died and came back to life).

"It is the stated position of this hospital that it does not distinguish on the basis of race," the hospital executive responds.

"Naomi Clark came back to life in the morgue because your E.R. staff called her time of death thirty minutes earlier than if she were White. That's why this wasn't a miracle. It was implicit racism," he concludes.

"I think you should get out of here," the executive responds. Talk about running out of ideas! Who could come up with such a ridiculous plot? And that was the big climax of the episode!

BlacKkKlansman

BlacKkKlansman (2018) directed by Spike Lee was based on a true story about a Black detective in Colorado who investigates the Ku Klux Klan in the 1970s. His partner, who is White, goes undercover and infiltrates the

KKK while the Black detective is the brains behind the operation.

There's a scene where David Duke (played by Topher Grace from *That '70s Show*) is making a toast to a group of people and talks about how great it is to be a White man in America and part of the "real America" and then says "I want to thank you so much for never putting your country second. America first!" he declares as he holds up a glass of champagne. "America first!" he repeats, to cheers from the crowd.[313]

That phrase, as you know, was popularized by President Trump, and that scene was included in the film as another attempt to tie David Duke to Donald Trump, even though Trump has denounced David Duke numerous times over the last few decades.[314]

During an interview about the film, Topher Grace said, "This is the first script when I read it that's really of the Trump Administration."[315] Of course, it's not. It's about a Black detective and his partner investigating a local chapter of the KKK for allegedly conspiring to bomb a civil rights rally, but Spike Lee decided to use the 50-year-old story to try and tie the events to President Trump.

[313] The Hollywood Reporter "Watch Topher Grace Embody KKK Leader David Duke in 'BlacKkKlansman'" by Evan Real (August 1st 2018)

[314] The American Spectator "Trump Denounced a 'White Supremacist Loser' — 19 Years Ago" by Jeffrey Lord (March 19th 2019)

[315] Interview with BlackTreeTV's YouTube Channel "Topher Grace says finding the human side of David Duke was a challenge in BlacKkKlansman" (August 16th 2018)

"Cracka"

In a series called *CRACKA,* a neo-Nazi is sent to a parallel universe that takes place in the 1800s where Whites are the slaves and Black people are in control of America. "Cracka," being an insult that angry Blacks love to call White people, a ghettoized derivative of "cracker." In the trailer, before the Nazi is transported back in time to the alternate reality, he and his friends attack a random Black man and his car is shown to have a "Trump 2020" bumper sticker on it.

The series slogan is "You stole our freedom, now we steal yours." It isn't meant to put Whites in the shoes of Blacks to make them reflect on the injustices of the past, instead *CRACKA* is a Black revenge fantasy. Posts on the series official Facebook page are filled with anti-White rhetoric like "You're in our world now!"[316] The trailer was released on Juneteenth (June 19th) the date that commemorates the freeing of the slaves, and before the comments were turned off many viewers were expressing their excitement about watching White people "get what they deserve."

Trayvon Martin's mom endorsed the series saying, "I applaud the bravery and vision for the creation of *CRACKA.*"[317]

---

[316] https://www.facebook.com/crackatv/photos/
a.119499679798117/119499656464786

[317] CrackaWorld.com - the film's official website (July 2020)

Magical Negroes and White Saviors

Since most liberals see racism everywhere, they're not even happy when films depict a Black person possessing a unique quality that is used to help others who happen to be White. That is what they call employing the "magical negro" trope. Spike Lee went off on *The Legend of Bagger Vance* because Will Smith's character comes to help Matt Damon win a golf tournament that takes place in Georgia in the 1930s. "Blacks are getting lynched left and right, and [Bagger Vance is] more concerned about improving Matt Damon's golf swing!... I gotta sit down; I get mad just thinking about it. They're still doing the same old thing ... recycling the noble savage and the happy slave," he said.[318]

Whoopi Goldberg's character in *Ghost* has been criticized as a "magical negro" (by Black people) because she helps the spirt of Patrick Swayze communicate with his widow after he dies.[319] Michael Clarke Duncan's character in *The Green Mile* also upset some Black people because he has the power to heal sickness and disease and ends up using his ability on several White people who worked at a prison he was being held in, despite being on death row for a crime he didn't commit.[320] It seems some Black people hate Whites so bad that they can't stand to see a Black person do anything nice to them. No good

---

[318] Yale Bulletin & Calendar "Director Spike Lee slams 'same old' black stereotypes in today's films" Volume 29, Number 21 (March 2nd 2001)

[319] Salon.com "The offensive movie cliche that won't die" by Matt Zoller Zeitz (September 14th 2010)

[320] NPR "'Magical Negro' Carries The Weight Of History" by Mary Louise Kelly (February 11th 2019)

deed goes unpunished, as the saying goes, and when well-meaning Hollywood studios produce films of White people helping minorities, that too is criticized as being a racist trope called the "White savior narrative."

In *Finding Forester*, Sean Connery's character is a reclusive but well-known writer who crosses paths with a Black teen who plays basketball in the courts across the street from his apartment. Connery learns the kid has a gift for writing that he helps encourage, and later the boy is accused of plagiarism because his teacher doesn't think he has the ability to write as good as he does, but Connery vouches for him in a surprise appearance at the school preventing him from failing the class.

In *The Blind Side* (2009) Sandra Bullock is considered a White savior for taking in a Black homeless kid named Big Mike who becomes a football star thanks to her help. One critic said the *Blind Side*, "peddles the most insidious kind of racism, one in which whiteys are virtuous saviors, coming to the rescue of Blacks who become superfluous in narratives that are supposed to be about them."[321]

Others attacked the film because they felt it depicted Sandra Bullock saving Big Mike from inner-city Black people who were all "poor and violent."[322] Apparently they would have been happier if she just left him to waste away in the ghetto. White people are often damned if they do, and damned if they don't.

Other popular films liberals got upset about because they feature "White saviors" are *Dangerous Minds*

---

[321] Dallas Observer "The Blind Side: What Would Black People Do Without Nice White Folks?" by Melissa Anderson (November 19th 2009)

[322] Ranker "Quietly Racist Things You Probably Missed In 'The Blind Side'" by Evan Lambert (July 13th 2020)

(because a White teacher helps educate Black and Latino students in a poverty stricken part of the city), and even *Gran Torino* because Clint Eastwood helps his Asian neighbors fight against a Black gang in Detroit.[323]

Cool Runnings, a film about a Jamaican bobsled team, was attacked because the Jamaicans wouldn't have made it to the Olympics without the "White savior" (John Candy) their trainer.[324] Even *Avatar* has been accused of this since a White character using a remote control avatar of an alien body helps the alien race save their planet from human invaders looking to take their natural resources.[325]

In the 1980s *Diff'rent Strokes* was a popular sitcom about a rich White man living in Manhattan who adopts two Black orphans from Harlem. At the time the series covered a lot of serious issues like racism, drug use, and even child molestation. But today some see it as another example of a "White savior" plot.

One online magazine even included *Diff'rent Strokes* on its "50 Most Racist TV Shows" list, writing sarcastically, "Save us, Mr. White Man! Come rescue us from Harlem and let us come live with you in yo' giant Park Avenue mansion where our po' deceased mama onced worked her fingers to the bone cleaning up after yo'

323 RacismReview.com "'Gran Torino,' White Masculinity & Racism" (January 17th 2009)

324 Slate.com "*Cool Runnings* Was Not Good, and It Is Definitely Not a 'Cult Classic'" by Justin Peters (February 16th 2014)

325 Gizmodo "When Will White People Stop Making Movies Like 'Avatar'?" by Annalee Newitz (December 18th 2009)

wrinkled White ass! We's cute, Mista Drummond, we ain't gwine start no trouble."[326]

MTV's Anti-White Agenda

In 2015, MTV aired a documentary titled "White People" that was hosted by a homosexual illegal alien named Jose Antonio Vargas who traveled around America shaming White people about their "privilege" and lecturing them for not being concerned enough about minorities.[327]

The following year MTV News released a video with "New Year's resolutions for White guys" because we're all such terrible people we need to be educated by Blacks and Latinos on how we can be better. "Try to recognize that America was never 'great' for anyone who wasn't a White guy," begins one presenter.[328]

"Nobody who has Black friends says that they have Black friends, and just because you have Black friends doesn't mean you're not racist. You can be racist with Black friends," says another.

"Look, guys, we know nobody's perfect, but honestly, you can do a little better in 2017."

They surprisingly deleted the video due to the backlash but their obsession with "White privilege" continues. MTV produced a YouTube show called

---

[326] Complex "The 50 Most Racist TV Shows of All Time" (June 3rd 2013)

[327] Vulture "MTV's New Documentary Wants to Make White People Very Uncomfortable" by Dee Lockett (July 8th 2015)

[328] RealClearPolitics "'MTV News' Deletes YouTube Video Telling 'White Guys' What They Could Do Better In 2017 After Backlash" by Tim Hains (December 20th 2016)

"Decoded" where the host uncovered White people's hidden "racism" that she sees around every corner, including decoding "micro-aggressions" and "the problem with White beauty standards."

The usual complaints about Halloween costumes being "cultural appropriation" (and thus offensive) have also been covered. Each week for several years beginning in 2015 the show would release a new episode where the host found more problems to blame on White people or ways White people are supposedly being racist.

White Replacement in Media

Recently another obsession we've seen in Hollywood is remaking popular movies or sequels and replacing the main character (if they happen to be White) with a Black actor in the name of "diversity." It's actually considered to be a "White supremacist conspiracy theory" to talk about White populations being "replaced" through mass immigration, but that is exactly what Hollywood has been doing to various characters in order to stamp out "whiteness."[329]

Generation Xers remember the musical *Annie* being about the curly redhead orphan, but when it was remade in 2014, Annie was Black with an afro. When the live-action remake of *The Little Mermaid* was announced, it was also revealed that the red-headed mermaid Ariel would be played by a Black actress instead.[330]

---

[329] The College Fix "Stanford University course to study 'abolishing whiteness'" by Matthew Stein (August 11th 2017)

[330] The Hill "Disney network defends casting black actress in 'Little Mermaid' after backlash" by Rachel Frazin (July 9th 2019)

When a reboot of *Buffy the Vampire Slayer* was announced the show cast an African-American actress as Buffy, who was originally played by Sarah Michelle Gueller in the 1990s series.[331] Two years later the show still hadn't made it to air, which likely means the pilot was so horrible it didn't get picked up. But due to the low standards of what is considered "entertainment" today, that may change if they rework the script or decide to just dump it on Netflix or Hulu. Activists also began pushing for James Bond to be played by a Black man, and it was later announced that a Black *woman* would play Agent 007, taking over Bond's famous codename.[332]

In 2010 when *The Karate Kid* reboot was released it starred Jaden Smith, Will Smith's son, who is of course Black. In 2018, *Spider-Man: Into the Spider-Verse* depicted the kid who becomes Spider Man as biracial— being half Black, half Latino.[333] There are growing calls to depict Superman as Black in future films as well.[334]

In the 2015 remake of *Fantastic Four,* Johnny Storm (the human torch character) who is White in the first two films (as well as in the comics) was played by Michael B. Jordan, a Black man.[335] This, despite being depicted as

---

[331] CNN "'Buffy the Vampire Slayer' reboot to feature African-American lead" by Chloe Melas (July 23rd 2018)

[332] The Guardian "Bond's number is up: black female actor 'is the new 007'" by Steph Harmon (July 15th 2019)

[333] NBC News "In Marvel's 'Spider-Verse,' Spider-Man's mom is alive and Puerto Rican" by Arturo Conde (December 13th 2018)

[334] Forbes "Science Says Superman Should Be Black" by JV Chamary (March 31st 2016)

[335] The Guardian "Fantastic Four film-makers respond to criticism of decision to cast black actor" by Ben Child (June 4th 2015)

the brother of a fellow "Fantastic Four" member, Sue Storm, who is White.

Samuel L. Jackson plays Nick Fury in *The Avengers* series even though the character is White in the comics. In the late 1990s a made for TV movie titled *Nick Fury: Agent of S.H.I.E.L.D.* aired on FOX where the character was true to the comic depiction (played by David Hasselhoff), but when Marvel launched their *Avengers* film series they chose Samuel L. Jackson for more "diversity." Another comic book superhero called Domino was turned Black when she made an appearance in *Deadpool 2*.

After the original actress who played Batwoman in The CW television series didn't renew her contract, she was replaced by a Black girl.[336] ABC announced plans to reboot *The Wonder Years*, a hit coming-of-age comedy-drama about a typical kid growing up in suburban America in the late 1960s, only this time...you guessed it —the family is Black.[337]

For Black History Month (February) in 2020, Barnes & Noble planned to release special editions of various literary classics like *The Wizard of Oz*, *Romeo and Juliet*, and *Alice in Wonderland* with new covers depicting the lead characters as African Americans. They called it the Diverse Editions program, but canceled their plan after critics complained that it was "literary blackface" and said

---

[336] NBC News "'Batwoman' casts Black, bisexual actress Javicia Leslie to play superhero" by Tim Fitzsimons (July 9th 2020)

[337] Variety "'Wonder Years' Reboot With Black Family in the Works at ABC, Lee Daniels to Produce" by Joe Otterson (July 8th 2020)

they should have just promoted actual books written by people of color instead of doing something so dumb.[338]

When *Harry Potter* was turned into a play, a Black actress was chosen to play the character Hermione Granger, who is described as White in the books, and was played by Emma Watson in the films.   Writer J.K. Rowling later denied that she wrote the character as White, but in the books she is specifically described as such.[339]

Other films are being remade with modern day "Black" versions, like *Steel Magnolias*, originally released in 1989 about a group of women and how they cope with the death of one of their friends, and then remade in 2012 starring all Black women. The romantic comedy *About Last Night* (1986), about couples entering into committed relationships for the first time in their lives, was remade in 2014 starring an all-Black cast. And there have been others, including *Cinderella, Death at a Funeral*, and more.[340]

Remaking a "Black" version of a film is quite different than changing a well-established character like Orphan Annie or the Little Mermaid, but when race-swapping happens to Black characters, it's denounced as "whitewashing."

---

[338] NPR "Author L.L. McKinney: Barnes & Noble 'Diverse Editions' Are 'Literary Blackface'" by Audie Cornish (February 6th 2020)

[339] *Harry Potter and the Prisoner of Azkaban* by J.K Rowling

[340] BuzzFeed "10 Classic Remakes That Gave Minority Actors The Spotlight" by Doriean Stevenson (March 28th 2014)

How About Entertainment For Whites?

Once Whites are a minority in the United States (estimated to occur in 2045), will it then be okay to have a White Entertainment Channel like Black people have BET [Black Entertainment Television]?   Will White people be able to have a Miss White USA pageant since Blacks, Latinos, and Asians have their own beauty pageants for their race?   Once Whites become a minority in America can we have White students clubs on college campuses just like the Black, Asian and Latino student organizations?   Will it be okay for a White person to say that they are proud to be White?   No, it won't.

The special interest groups for Blacks and Latinos will get unhinged and scream that "White supremacy" is trying to resurrect itself and loads of "White allies" will join in on the chorus denouncing their fellow White people to show solidarity with people of color.   "White people had their turn," they'll say, and don't deserve to be proud of their race or culture because they enslaved Black people 400 years ago.

"We ended White supremacy and must ensure it never returns," they'll say.   White people must forever bow down to the new Latino/Black/Asian majority and live the rest of their lives in servitude to the new ruling class to atone for the sins of our White ancestors, they will demand.

Of course Black people ignore the fact that virtually all countries in the ancient world had slaves. Maybe we should point out that the Egyptians (Africans) enslaved the Jews. And that Black Muslim tribes in Africa actually sold other Africans to the European slave traders who brought them to North America.[341]   Africa is also the world's leader in modern-day slavery, where millions of people remain trapped in forced labor.[342]

When the question is raised about a White counterpart to BET or White-only shows and movies, the knee jerk reaction is to always claim that the majority of mainstream entertainment is produced for White people. But with forced diversity being injected into almost every single television show, movie, and even commercials which all do their best to have an equal number of White, Black, Asian, and Latino characters, the claim that White people have entertainment that is a reflection of our own family, community, and culture is rapidly becoming null and void.

Since most "White" homogeneous entertainment has been "diversified" and turned into a heterogenous multicultural mishmash, this just adds to the justification that such shows should be created and maintained. But just pointing out these issues is enough to get one tarred and feathered as a "neo-Nazi," then deplatformed from social media, and "White nationalist" added to the first sentence of their Wikipedia page.[343]

---

341 Wall Street Journal "When the Slave Traders Were African: Those whose ancestors sold slaves to Europeans now struggle to come to terms with a painful legacy" by Adaobi Tricia Nwaubani (September 20, 2019)

342 Reuters "West African slavery lives on, 400 years after transatlantic trade began" by Angela Ukomadu (August 7th 2019)

343 See my previous book *The Liberal Media Industrial Complex* (2019)

Film and Television Liaison Offices

Most people think that propaganda films were just something produced by Nazi Germany or perhaps are still made by communist regimes in North Korea or China, but the truth is the United States is the world's biggest producer of such material. For example, during World War II our government commissioned a series of documentary films called *Why We Fight* which were designed to encourage Americans to support the war. Animated segments of the films were produced by Walt Disney Studios.[344]

Disney actually produced various cartoons throughout World War II featuring Donald Duck for this same purpose. One such film titled *The Spirit of '43* encouraged Americans to file and pay their income taxes in order to help fund the war effort. "Taxes...To Defeat the Axis" was the film's tagline which was commissioned by the U.S. Treasury Secretary at the time.[345] The title, "*Spirt of '43*" was a play off the old patriotic sentiment

---

[344] PBS "The War" series directed and produced by Ken Burns and Lynn Novick in the "At Home" episode

[345] Time "The U.S. Government Used Disney Cartoons to Convince Americans That Paying Taxes Is a Privilege" by Oliva B. Waxman (April 16th 2018)

from the American Revolutionary war which was captured by the slogan "The Spirit of '76."

Another Disney war propaganda film from the era was *Der Fuehrer's Face* (originally titled *Donald Duck in Nutzi Land*), which encouraged Americans to buy war bonds to help fund World War II. In the film Donald Duck has a nightmare where he is forced to work at a munitions factory in Nazi Germany, but then wakes up in "home sweet home" and has a renewed love for America.[346] Donald Duck also starred in a short anti-Japanese propaganda film during World War II, where he parachuted into a Pacific island jungle to "wipe out" a Japanese airfield.[347]

While it's simple to make the case that these films were for a good cause, the point is that propaganda is more pervasive than people realize, and the avenues used to reach the masses aiming to persuade them are so vast that even popular cartoon characters are employed.

Most people think war propaganda films disguised as innocent entertainment is just something from the World War II era, but the practice continued—and so did the sophistication. During the height of the Cold War in the 1980s the film *Red Dawn* (starring Patrick Swayze and Charlie Sheen) depicted the Soviet Union invading the United States only to be confronted by a group of high school kids who form a militia called "the Wolverines" (named after their school's mascot) and help fight off the communists, saving their town.

It was remade in 2012 with North Korea being the invaders this time, who just so happened to be in the

---

[346] Der Fuehrer's Face (1942) produced by Walt Disney

[347] Commando Duck (1944) produced by Walt Disney

crosshairs of the Department of Defense which considered them part of the "axis of evil." Hollywood didn't just think this would be a neat plotline, the film (and many others) was actually produced with the help of the Department of Defense. An open secret in Hollywood, but something rarely ever mentioned because it would spoil the "fun," is that the U.S. government works hand in hand with writers and directors to craft blockbuster propaganda films that reinforce American foreign policy objectives.[348]

During the War on Terror in the early to mid 2000s, millions of Americans were subjected to pro-torture propaganda through Kiefer Sutherland's popular series *24* which began airing just two months after the September 11th attacks in 2001. Torturing suspected terrorists or people detained who were believed to have information about Al Qaeda was a hot topic of debate at the time, and Kiefer Sutherland was on national television with a new episode each week to show Americans that torturing the "bad guys" was "necessary" to save the world.[349]

Over a decade later the popular entertainment industry publication *Variety* would admit that "Liberal Hollywood carried water for torture."[350] The article pointed out, "Not only has torture become more frequent since the Sept. 11 terror attacks, but the acceptance of those depictions in

---

[348] Operation Hollywood: How the Pentagon Shapes and Censors the Movies by David Robb (2004 Prometheus Books)

[349] Variety "The '24' Effect: How 'Liberal Hollywood' Carried Water For Torture" by Brian Lowry (December 14th 2014)

[350] Ibid.

entertainment has been cited as a point of reference—and even an endorsement of the tactics."[351]

Zero Dark Thirty, the 2013 dramatization depicting the hunt for Osama Bin Laden, falsely depicted torture as the reason information was obtained that led to the location of his compound after years of the terror leader eluding U.S. forces. Torturing detainees had nothing to do with discovering his hideout, but the film essentially rewrote history in the minds of millions who saw it and believe it tells the real story of how it unfolded.[352]

When he was Secretary of Defense, Leon Panetta gave classified details about the raid to the producers to help them make the film.[353] *Zero Dark Thirty* later received several Oscar nominations.

Most movie lovers have no idea that many big budget blockbuster films are produced with the direct help and oversight of the United States government. How else do you think the Hollywood studios get access to aircraft carriers, F-16 jets, tanks, and other sophisticated military equipment? They can't just rent those kinds of things from a prop house. They get them from the government.

The stars will never talk about this when doing the talk show circuit promoting their films. It's kind of a trade secret really, but in the industry it's widely known that various departments of the government have what are called entertainment liaison offices which work with producers and screenwriters to get them the equipment

[351] Ibid.

[352] Washington Post "'Zero Dark Thirty' waterboarding depictions not accurate, senators say" by Ed O'Keefe and Ann Hornaday (December 19th 2012)

[353] The Atlantic "Secret Report: Panetta Gave bin Laden Raid Details to 'Zero Dark Thirty' Makers" by Philip Bump (June 5th 2013)

they want. Of course there is a price for this. It's not monetary though—it comes in the form of script approval.

The U.S. Army isn't going to lend a bunch of tanks to a producer for a film showing the dark side of war, or one that questions the WMD hoax that was used to justify invading Iraq in 2003, for example. Movies must always celebrate war and glorify it, and never doubt the reasons for starting one. Such deals have been made for films like *Zero Dark Thirty, Red Dawn, Top Gun, American Sniper*, and hundreds of others. Some have called this form of entertainment "government-subsidized propaganda."[354]

Freedom of Information requests revealed that the Department of Defense has been involved in over 800 films and television shows between 1911 and 2017, many of them since 2001 because of the War on Terror that started shortly after the 9/11 attacks.[355] It's not just the Army, Navy, Marines, and Air Force, however. The CIA has their own Entertainment Liaison Office and has also been involved in the production of dozens of different films and television shows since at least 1947.[356]

These entertainment liaison offices also include agreements that get active duty military personnel to be extras in movies when a scene calls for a large number of uniformed troops. That way the director gets their shot of hundreds of soldiers on the battlefield, but also saves the money they would have had to pay all the extras to be

---

[354] Washington Post "25 years later, how 'Top Gun' made America love war" by David Sirota (August 26th 2011)

[355] The Independent "Washington DC's role behind the scenes in Hollywood goes deeper than you think" by Matthew Alford (September 3rd 2017)

[356] Ibid.

there. Mark Wahlberg plays a Navy SEAL deployed in Afghanistan in *Lone Survivor*, which is based on a true story derived from Marcus Luttrell's biography about his experiences there in 2005, and thanks to the Department of Defense Entertainment Liaison Office the film was shot in New Mexico on Kirtland Air Force Base.[357] That way the studio didn't have to recreate an entire military base, they were able to use a real one.

Fortune magazine calls this "Hollywood's Military Complex" and explained, "Even in an age of special effects, it's exponentially cheaper to film on actual military ships with real military advisers. Despite action sequences and an A-list lead, *Captain Phillips* cost about $55 million to make (compared with a visual effects fest like *Gravity*, which cost about $100 million). The fulcrum of Hollywood's unlikely partnership is Phil Strub, a former film school student and Navy videographer, now the entertainment liaison at the Department of Defense."[358]

Fortune goes on to say, "Scripts of movies helmed by Michael Bay, Ridley Scott, and Steven Spielberg are regularly sent to an ascetic office at the Pentagon in hopes of procuring military cooperation. If he [Phil Strub] signs off, the filmmakers stand to access the most awesome arsenal in the world, and in turn, the image and message of the American armed forces get projected before a global audience."[359]

---

[357] Universal Studios "Lone Survivor Production Notes"

[358] Fortune Magazine "Hollywood's military complex" by Soo Youn (December 19, 2013)

[359] Ibid.

An official who works in the Department of Defense's Entertainment Liaison Office confirmed they maintain control over the scripts, saying, "We make sure the Department and facilities and people are portrayed in the most accurate and positive light possible."[360] That's a nice way of saying, if anything in the film paints the government or war in a bad light, you're not getting your equipment.

Before an agreement is made to allow the use of government equipment (and locations), the Entertainment Liaison Office carefully reviews a script and then raises any possible concerns with the producer; and if they're willing to change certain dialog or plot points then the government will give them basically anything they need as long as the movie will serve as an infomercial for the military.

They can be quite picky even about the smallest detail. For example, in the original script of *Hulk*, the laboratory which caused Dr. Banner's condition was a government lab, but documents obtained by a Freedom of Information Request show that the Department of Defense requested it be just a "lab" and not associated with the government at all.[361]

The Army Times admitted that "filmmakers can ask the Pentagon for assistance on their projects, from consultation on uniforms and military procedures to use

[360] Wired Magazine "CIA Pitches Scripts to Hollywood" by Mark Riffee (September 9th 2011)

[361] The Independent "Washington DC's role behind the scenes in Hollywood goes deeper than you think" by Matthew Alford (September 3rd 2017).

of real military aircraft and equipment."[362]   Or as Phil Strub, who was the head of Department of Defense's Entertainment Liaison Office for almost thirty years put it, "The relationship between Hollywood and the Pentagon has been described as a mutual exploitation. We're after military portrayal, and they're after our equipment."[363]

Sure these films are entertaining and dramatic, but they'll only tell half the story about why a conflict actually started, and what the costs will be. They also serve a secondary purpose by encouraging people to join the military because war is painted as exciting and glorious and always for a just cause, never because of misinformation or lies (as in the case of the War in Iraq).

"We want these movies to help us in terms of recruitment and retention," admitted the Department of Defense.[364]   The original *Top Gun* starring Tom Cruise was said to have spiked enrollment in the Air Force to record levels. They even called it the "Top Gun Effect" and in some cities Air Force recruiters literally set up tables outside movie theaters.[365]

Katy Perry's music video "Part of Me" was actually shot at Camp Pendleton, a massive Marine base in San Diego, California, thanks to help from the Entertainment

[362] Army Times "The Pentagon's Hollywood Liaison" by Hope Hodge (July 1 2013)

[363] Business Insider "One Man In The Department Of Defense Controls All Of Hollywood's Access To The Military" by Aly Weisman (March 5th 2014)

[364] Wired Magazine "CIA Pitches Scripts to Hollywood" by Mark Riffee (September 9th 2011)

[365] Los Angeles Times "'Top Gun' Boosting Service Sign-ups" by Mark Evje (July 5, 1986)

Liaison Office.[366] In the video she finds out her boyfriend is cheating on her and doesn't know what to do with her life, so she ends up joining the Marines.

The entire rest of the music video is literally a recruitment commercial, showing her dressed in uniform completing basic training, shooting an M-16, and riding in an Amphibious Assault Vehicle. The video also includes actual Marines as extras, marching alongside her and storming a beach with helicopters flying overhead—all provided by Camp Pendleton.

Even the creators of the popular "Call of Duty" video game series consult with the Department of Defense's Entertainment Liaison Office in order to get access to advisors in hopes of creating more realistic video games.[367]

While the government enthusiastically helps produce movies, TV shows, and music videos that will reinforce their preferred narratives, big budget anti-war films or those which depict some of the horrors of war like *Platoon* (1986), *Apocalypse Now* (1979), and *Full Metal Jacket* (1987) have to go without any of this assistance. Sometimes the studios have to actually rent military vehicles and equipment from foreign governments and film outside of the United States to get their projects made.

When *Platoon* came out, Oliver Stone, who wrote and directed the film, said, "I hope people go to see what the war was really like. That's the statement. And once you

---

366 San Diego Union Tribune "Marines say Katy Perry video is good publicity" by Jeanette Steele (March 22nd 2012)

367 Newsweek "'Call of Duty' Creators Collaborated with Pentagon Adviser in Upcoming Videogame" by Madeline Grant (August 28th 2014)

see it, you have to think about it for yourself. Think about what you think about war. Think about what it really is, as opposed to the fantasy comic book stuff of Top Gun."[368] He also said that the main character (played by Charlie Sheen) was actually based on his own experience of being in Vietnam, and how at first he wanted to do his "patriotic duty" for his country, but after seeing the horrors of the war first hand and later learning about the lies that got us there, he began to resent the U.S. government for what they had done.

During the Iraq and Afghanistan wars in the early 2000s, George. W. Bush issued a ban on any photos and video of the coffins being unloaded from airplanes after soldiers' remains were brought back to the United States.[369] It was widely known that support for the Vietnam War dramatically dropped when people began seeing footage of the tens of thousands of coffins returning, not to mention pictures of wounded soldiers, and so the Bush Administration did everything they could trying to prevent a similar situation by censoring the details of the casualties in Iraq and Afghanistan.

It wasn't just George W. Bush and the neocons' policies that caused needless death and destruction because of our involvement in the Middle East, however. Barack Obama became known as the "Drone King" for using the newly popular remote-control aircraft which ended up killing a stunning number of innocent civilians

---

[368] Oliver Stone in CNN's "The Movies" documentary series - Episode 1: The Eighties

[369] CBS News "Pentagon Defends Photo Ban" (April 23rd 2004)

while the American mainstream media provided him cover by barely, if ever, mentioning it.[370]

First Lady Michelle Obama played her part to help promote the Military Industrial Complex during the Obama administration. She actually appeared at the Oscars in 2013 via satellite to announce the winner of Best Picture which was given to *Argo*, a movie about the CIA covertly working with Hollywood movie producers so their agents could pose as film makers working on a science fiction movie in order to infiltrate Iran so they could rescue American hostages being held there.[371]

That same year *Homeland* won Golden Globe awards for the Best Actress (Claire Danes), Best Actor (Damian Lewis), and Best TV Drama for their Showtime series depicting a returning veteran secretly siding with Al Qaeda.[372] This narrative parroted a report released by the Department of Homeland Security a few years earlier that warned returning veterans should be considered possible domestic terrorists out of concerns they may join right-wing extremist organizations after supposedly having a difficult time re-integrating into their communities.[373]

The real reason for the report, which angered veterans groups when it was made public, may have been concerns that many soldiers were disgruntled with the U.S.

---

[370] Bureau of Investigative Journalism "Obama's covert drone war in numbers: ten times more strikes than Bush" by Jessica Purkiss and Jack Serle (January 7th 2017)

[371] USA Today "Michelle Obama presents Oscar to 'Argo'" (February 25th 2013)

[372] Hollywood Reporter "Golden Globes 2013: Complete List of Winners" (January 13th 2013)

[373] CBS News "DHS' Domestic Terror Warning Angers GOP" (April 16th 2009)

government after learning that the reason for starting the War in Iraq (the "weapons of mass destruction" Saddam Hussein supposedly had), turned out to be a lie.

In March 2012 a 30-minute documentary titled *Kony 2012* was posted to YouTube and immediately went viral. The film promoted a campaign to capture or kill the African warlord Joseph Kony, leader of the Lord's Resistance Army. *Kony 2012* was the first YouTube video ever to get one million "likes" and was called the most viral video ever at the time.[374]

Celebrities from Justin Bieber to Kim Kardashian helped spread it through their social media accounts and a few weeks later the U.S. Senate passed a resolution condemning Joseph Kony and agreed to send troops from the African Union to help find him.[375]

The film's surprising popularity was no accident. It was produced by a charity called "Invisible Children" which used a high-power public relations firm called Sunshine Sachs Associates to promote it. That PR firm was co-founded by a man named Ken Sunshine who has close ties with Barack Obama.

Many people became suspicious of *Kony 2012* immediately since the video seemed to come out of nowhere and went viral so quickly. In hindsight it appears it was a carefully crafted propaganda campaign to promote the United States getting involved in another conflict halfway around the world.[376]

---

[374] Time "Top 10 Everything of 2012" - Top 10 Viral Videos

[375] ABC News "Senate Resolution Condemns Uganda's Joseph Kony" by Sunien Miller (March 21st 2012)

[376] Reason "Kony 2012's Old-Fashioned War Propaganda" by Tate Watkins (March 14th 2012)

The Military Industrial Complex had been eager to become more invested in the fight against Joseph Kony and the Lord's Resistance Army, but since they weren't a threat to the United States and had no direct connections to us, drumming up support to go after him would have been impossible. But thanks to the viral *Kony 2012* video, everyone was talking about him, and despite living in a country few Americans could even find on a map (Uganda), he became public enemy number one.

The CIA In Hollywood

In the 1990s the CIA appointed a man named Chase Brandon as a their liaison to Hollywood, and he began helping the agency produce dozens of films and television shows for major studios and television networks, including documentaries on the History Channel.[377] Chase Brandon retired in 2007 and was replaced by a man named Paul Barry who continues with the task.[378] Former CIA officer Bob Baer said, "All these people that run studios—they go to Washington, they hang around with senators, they hang around with CIA directors, and everybody's on board."[379]

Just a few weeks after the 9/11 attacks CBS launched a new series about the CIA called *The Agency*, which was shot on location at the actual CIA headquarters, and

377 The Guardian "The caring, sharing CIA: Central Intelligence gets a makeover" by John Patterson (October 4, 2001)

378 PR Week "Barry named CIA Entertainment Liaison" (June 5, 2007)

379 The Guardian "An Offer They Couldn't Refuse" by Matthew Alford and Robbie Graham (November 13th 2008)

largely focused on the hunt for Osama Bin Laden and how the CIA was tirelessly working to keep America safe.

The director of *The Recruit* (2003) a spy thriller starring Al Pacino and Colin Farrell, was invited to visit the CIA's headquarters in Langley, Virginia so he could "understand how the space worked and looked."[380] He wasn't just brought there for a tour, the CIA's Entertainment Liaison Office was involved in the production of the film to make sure it didn't cast the CIA as a whole in a negative light, only Al Pacino's character who is a corrupt agent and is eventually discovered.

Over a decade later, *The Atlantic* would publish a story titled, "How the CIA Hoodwinked Hollywood" which explained, "The agency has established a very active spin machine in the heart of the entertainment capital, which works strenuously to make sure the cloak-and-dagger world is presented in heroic terms. Since the mid-1990s, but especially after 9/11, American screenwriters, directors, and producers have traded positive portrayal of the spy profession in film or television projects for special access and favors at CIA headquarters."[381]

Robert DeNiro played a retired CIA officer in *Meet the Parents* who famously hooks Ben Stiller up to a lie detector as part of his over-protective antics to determine if Stiller can be trusted to marry his daughter. Apparently the original script included a brief scene showing "torture manuals" on DeNiro's book shelf once Stiller stumbled across his secret office in the basement and learned of his future father in law's true identity, but the CIA told the

---

[380] Cinema Review Magazine "The Recruit: About the Production"

[381] The Atlantic "How the CIA Hoodwinked Hollywood" by Nicholas Schou (July 14th 2016)

studio not to include them on the shelf since they would cast the Agency in a negative light.[382]

Not all films about the CIA show them in a positive light, however. Those movies have to be made without the help of any government agency. Matt Damon stars in *The Bourne Identity* (2002) which is loosely based on the CIA's very real mind control experiments called MK-ULTRA.[383] Needless to say the CIA would rather sweep that under the rug and didn't provide any assistance in its production.

Syriana (2005) starring George Clooney focuses on the CIA's involvement in the Middle East where they engage in numerous shady activities behind the scenes in order to maintain control of major fields in the region— another film they prefer would have never been made.

Spy Game (2001), starring Robert Redford and Brad Pitt shows the CIA turning their back on one of their operatives in order to avoid jeopardizing a trade deal that is about to be signed between the United States and China. The Agency wouldn't have anything to do with that film because it showed senior management in an "insensitive light"[384] when in reality it showed the complexities of international relations and the difficult and sometimes coldblooded decisions that are made behind the scenes to maintain American superiority in the world.

---

382 The Independent "Washington DC's role behind the scenes in Hollywood goes deeper than you think" by Matthew Alford (September 3rd 2017)

383 Time Magazine "CIA Mind-Control Experiments" by Nate Rawlings (August 6th 2010)

384 The Guardian "The caring, sharing CIA: Central Intelligence gets a makeover" by John Patterson (October 4, 2001)

In his book *Operation Hollywood: How the Pentagon Shapes and Censors Movies*, David Robb concludes, "No society is free that allows its military to control the arts. In America, it is not only unconscionable, it is also unconstitutional."[385] He's certainly not alone in thinking that. Many legal experts believe that entertainment liaison offices actually violate the First Amendment because they only help producers whose films portray the U.S. government, the military, and various other agencies, in a favorable light.

This kind of selective help is equivalent to the government refusing to allow certain groups from reserving local town hall venues because of what those groups or their leaders believe.

Constitutional Law professor Irwin Chemerinsky, who teaches at the University of Southern California argues, "The government cannot favor some speech due to its viewpoint and disfavor others because of its viewpoint. The court has said that when the government is giving financial benefits, it can't decide who to give to, or not give to, based on the viewpoint expressed."[386]

He and others say this one-sided favoritism is no different that if the government gave one particular religious group material support or financial favors while denying those same benefits to others.[387]

---

[385] Robb, David - *Operation Hollywood: How the Pentagon Shapes and Censors Movies* page 365 (2004 Prometheus Books)

[386] Robb, David - *Operation Hollywood: How the Pentagon Shapes and Censors the Movies* page 47-48 (2004 Prometheus Books)

[387] Chemerinsky also points to the 1995 U.S. Supreme Court case Rosenberger v. the University of Virginia.

Some Actors Are Real CIA Assets

Aside from the CIA aiding in the production of various films and television shows, their involvement in the entertainment industry goes much further and sounds like something right out of a movie. A former CIA officer named John Rizzo wrote a memoir called *Company Man: Thirty Years of Crisis and Controversy in the CIA*, where he admitted the agency regularly works with production companies that allow CIA operatives to work undercover as members of film crews when a film is being shot on location in a foreign country.[388]

"Among businesses in general, the CIA has long had a special relationship with the entertainment industry, devoting considerable attention to fostering relationships with Hollywood movers and shakers—studio executives, producers, directors, and big-name actors," Rizzo explains.[389]

He also said that some celebrities have been enlisted as CIA assets through the agency's National Resources Division, which recruits foreign students studying in America, business people here on work visas, and even foreign diplomats the Agency wants to become spies for the United States when they return to their home countries.

Once initiated, the celebrities are used to relay information to the CIA about foreign leaders they meet since they'll often speak more candidly with a celebrity

---

[388] Los Angeles Times "Hollywood figures spied for CIA, book asserts" by Ken Dilanian (January 10th 2014)

[389] John Rizzo - *Company Man: Thirty Years of Crisis and Controversy in the CIA* page 63 (2014 Scribner)

than with diplomats or reporters due to being star struck and letting their guard down.[390]

"These are people who have made a lot of money basically making stuff up. A lot of them, at least the smarter and more self-aware ones, realize that what they do makes them ridiculously rich but is also ephemeral and meaningless in the larger scheme of things," Rizzo says. "So they're receptive to helping the CIA in any way they can, probably in equal parts because they are sincerely patriotic and because it gives them a taste of real-life intrigue and excitement."[391]

In his book he also says that a major film star once approached the CIA himself, wanting to work with them, "just out of his patriotic duty," after the actor learned that another major studio had a relationship with the agency. Rizzo says the actor asked his handler for $50,000 of cocaine for his services, which the agency allegedly refused.[392]

When Ben Affleck was promoting his film *Argo* (2012), which is based on the true story of the CIA working undercover with a film studio to infiltrate Iran to rescue American hostages under the guise of shooting a movie there, he was asked by a reporter if he thought there were any actors working as CIA operatives in Hollywood today. "I think there are probably quite a few. Yes, I think probably Hollywood is full of CIA agents and we just don't know it, and I wouldn't be surprised at all to

---

[390] Ibid.

[391] John Rizzo - *Company Man: Thirty Years of Crisis and Controversy in the CIA* page 64 (2014 Scribner)

[392] Ibid.

discover that this was extremely common," he responded.[393]

Knowing what happened with the Iranian hostage rescue and working on other films that are overseen by the CIA's Entertainment Liaison Office, Ben Affleck would certainly be in a position to know. He also starred in *The Sum of All Fears* (2002) where he played a CIA analyst, another film that was produced with the help of Chase Brandon, the agency's entertainment liaison at the time.[394]

Affleck's (now ex) wife Jennifer Garner also played a CIA agent in ABC's action thriller *Alias,* which the Central Intelligence Agency consulted on, so he is obviously very familiar with how close the agency works with Hollywood.

The FBI and Hollywood

The FBI has their hand in Hollywood too. On their website they admit, "If you are a writer, author, or producer who wants to feature the FBI, we may be able to work with you to create an accurate portrayal of the Bureau. We've been doing it since the 1930s."[395] They call this office the Investigative Publicity and Public Affairs Unit (IPPAU), and they work with "domestic and international screenwriters, producers, authors, and other industry personnel associated with TV programs,

---

[393] YouTube - Interview with The Guardian "Ben Affleck on Argo: Probably Hollywood is full of CIA Agents" (November 8the 2012)

[394] Los Angeles Times "The CIA Spins Itself" by Patrick Goldstein (September 29th 2001)

[395] https://www.fbi.gov/about/faqs/how-can-screenwriters-authors-and-producers-seeking-authenticity-work-with-the-fbi-

documentaries, made-for-TV movies, books, and motion pictures."[396]

J. Edgar Hoover, the infamously corrupt founding father of the FBI (and its director for almost 50 years), used his position to bully Hollywood studios into dropping certain actors from projects and got scripts changed that would have shown the agency in a negative light.

John Wayne was chosen to be the narrator for a television series called "The FBI" for the ABC network in the 1960s, but because of his connections to the right-wing John Birch Society, Hoover "vetoed" John Wayne's involvement and had ABC remove him from the project "in order to prevent any possible criticism of the Bureau by using someone with known John Birch Society connections."[397]

J. Edgar Hoover also used his position to target anti-Vietnam war musicians like Jimmy Hendrix, Janis Joplin, and especially John Lennon, who he was concerned threatened President Nixon's chances of getting reelected, so Hoover tried to have him deported back to England because he was once arrested for possession of marijuana.[398]

---

[396] Ibid.

[397] *John Wayne: American* by Randy Roberts page 569 (1995 Free Press)

[398] CBS News "The U.S. vs. John Lennon" by Jon Wiener (September 15th 2006)

Operation Mockingbird

In the news industry, intelligence agencies enjoy similar influence and have deeply embedded operatives and developed covert relationships for decades. In the 1970s a Congressional hearing uncovered a secret program called Operation Mockingbird which involved the CIA infiltrating television news networks, newspapers, and magazines, and paying off reporters and editors to do the agency's bidding.[399]

At the time there were widespread concerns that the CIA was involved in numerous corrupt and illegal activities, including spying on American citizens and assassinating foreign leaders, so Congress investigated the agency and happened to learn of their secret dealings with the media.

At one point during the hearing William Colby, the head of the CIA then, was asked if the agency had operatives working for any television networks. He refused to answer the question and said that it's something he would rather "get into" in an "executive session," meaning behind closed doors with just a small number of senators authorized to have access to classified information.[400]

The former president of CBS, Sig Mickelson, was later asked if he thought despite Operation Mockingbird being uncovered, was the CIA still engaged in the same type of operations. "Yeah, I would think probably, for a reporter it would probably continue today, but because of all the revelations of the period of the 1970s, it seems to

---

[399] Final Report of the Select Committee to Study Government Operations With Respect to Intelligence Activities. April 1976.

[400] Church Committee Hearings (1975) testimony by William Colby

me a reporter has to be a lot more circumspect when doing it now or he runs the risk of at least being looked at with considerable disfavor by the public. I think you've got to be much more careful about it."[401]

Anyone who followed the "Russiagate" scandal and the conspiracy to bring down the Trump administration by claiming he's a secret Russian agent, knows in their gut that various intelligence agencies (the "Deep State") continue to work closely with the mainstream media in order to push their agenda.

I cover Operation Mockingbird in detail in my previous book, *The True Story of Fake News*, which I encourage you to order from Amazon or download the e-book from any of the major e-book stores if you're interested in learning more about the subject. Decades have gone by since the name "Operation Mockingbird" has been mentioned on national television, and when you learn just how deep the CIA burrowed their way into the various news networks, it's chilling, especially in light of their ruthless and relentless war on President Trump.

---

[401] Sig Mickleson in a clip widely available on YouTube about the CIA and the news

Climate Change

Many of Hollywood's concerns about the environment, specifically global warming (or "climate change" as they have rebranded it) aren't really about keeping our air clean, preserving delicate ecosystems, or developing green energy, but instead is just a smokescreen to hide their true intentions.

Obviously we should take care of the environment, not litter, recycle, and be good stewards of the earth, but the fanatical doomsday warnings about global warming are designed to mobilize people to accept exorbitant carbon taxes and embrace the implementation of enormous new socialist programs.[402]

Alexandria Ocasio-Cortez's senior aide and puppet master admitted, "The interesting thing about the Green New Deal is it wasn't originally a climate thing at all... Do you guys think of it as a climate thing? Because we really think of it as a how-do-you-change-the-entire-economy thing."[403]   Ocasio-Cortez said the plan was aiming for "a new national social, industrial and economic mobilization on a scale not seen since World War II and the New Deal," in order to "provide

---

[402] CNBC "A carbon tax is 'single most powerful' way to combat climate change, IMF says" by Emma Newburger (October 10th 2019)

[403] Washington Post "AOC's Chief of Change" by David Montgomery (July 10th 2019)

unprecedented levels of prosperity and economic security for all people of the United States."[404]

Celebrities have always been "tree huggers" and concerned about the environment—which is a good cause, but their hysterical rhetoric about what humans are doing to the planet is getting increasingly radical to the point that they are literally claiming the human race will soon go extinct if we don't listen to them, and any day now when we peer outside the windows of our homes it will be as if we're looking at a scene from a disaster movie.

Because of all the "end of the world" fear mongering about climate change, some children are getting what is called "eco-anxiety" which child psychologists describe as "a form of anxiety about where the world is heading when it comes to climate change."[405] This is what caused Greta Thunberg, the teenage climate change activist from Sweden, to begin skipping school thinking she was helping save the world.

Once she caught the eye of the climate change lobby, they adopted her as their spokesperson and threw the weight of their massive propaganda machine behind her to propel her to international stardom as a child prodigy who is trying to save the planet. *Time* magazine even put her on the cover for their 2019 Person of the Year issue.[406]

Recently there have been increasing calls for geoengineering, something that was said to be conspiracy

---

[404] Politico "'Green New Deal' lands in the Capitol" by Zack Colman and Anthony Adragna (February 7, 2019)

[405] Daily Mail "The devastating rise of 'eco-anxiety': Psychologist says school kids are being damaged by the climate change debate" by Zoe Zaczek (September 25th 2019)

[406] Time magazine "Greta Thunberg: TIME's Person of the Year 2019" by Edward Felsenthal (December 11th 2019)

theory just a few years ago.[407] Some scientists want to spray little particles of glitter into the atmosphere to block out some of the sun's rays hoping that will keep the earth slightly cooler to offset the supposed "global warming" that's happening. Meanwhile geoengineering advocates ignore the law of unintended consequences, and nobody knows what kind of environmental disasters doing such a thing would cause.

Like everything liberals do, their claims of "living green" are rife with hypocrisy. Just one trip on their private jet spews more pollution into the air than several months' worth of daily commutes on the freeway in a car.[408] Just one of Al Gore's homes uses more than 20 times the amount of energy as an average home, costing an estimated $30,000 a year in utilities for the gas and electricity.[409]

Arnold Schwarzenegger said fossil fuel executives should be sued for "first degree murder" because their industry is "killing" the planet.[410] Arnold apparently forgot that he was the first civilian to buy a Hummer in 1992 when the extra-large gas guzzling military vehicle became commercially available. It famously got about 10 miles a gallon.[411]

---

[407] CNBC "This Bill Gates-funded chemical cloud could help stop global warming" by Katie Schoolov (September 7th 2019)

[408] The Independent "How Bad are Private Jets for the Environment?" by Helen Coffey (August 20th 2019)

[409] ABC News "This Bill Gates-funded chemical cloud could help stop global warming" by Jake Taper (February 27th 2007)

[410] Politico "Schwarzenegger to Sue Big Oil for 'First Degree Murder'" by Edward-Isaac Dovere (March 12th 2018)

[411] History.com "The Origins of the Hummer"

Recently Hollywood has been inserting messages about global warming hysteria into almost everything. During the Miss Universe 2019 pageant one of the contestants was asked, "Are leaders of today doing enough to protect future generations from climate change?" Steve Harvey, the host, then rolled his eyes as soon as he was done reading the question off the card.[412]

Hollywood, Health & Society (the organization that helped inject storylines about Obamacare into TV shows) also lobbies Hollywood studios about climate change. They specifically have been focusing on comedy shows because as Lizz Winstead, a writer for *The Daily Show* points out, "Comedians have become trusted as people who observe the world and talk about it truthfully. Because they're not beholden to anyone, they can call bullshit when they see it."[413] That may have been true before "Cancel Culture," but that's a whole other topic.

The organization's website openly states, "Hollywood, Health & Society assists with research, providing a range of information from experts for storylines on topics, from rising seas to melting glaciers, the increase of extreme weather to the spread of infectious diseases, from the Arctic to L.A."[414] But they're certainly not the only ones lobbying Hollywood to warn viewers about the issue.

---

[412] Fox News "Steve Harvey brings drama to 'Miss Universe' with eye roll before contestant claims 'the planet is dying'" by Melissa Roberto (December 9th 2019)

[413] New York Observer "Hooray for Hollywood: How Charities Influence Your Favorite TV Shows" by Anne Easton (October 28th 2015)

[414] HollywoodHealthAndSociety.org "Climate Change Resources"

In 2011 the Secretary General of the United Nations traveled to Hollywood during Oscar week in order to encourage industry insiders to make more films about climate change.[415] The U.N. famously recruits celebrities like Angelina Jolie and George Clooney as "ambassadors" to further their agendas since so many people view celebrities as experts in everything. Knowing that few people watch documentary films, the U.N. focused on getting the issues incorporated into television series and movies.

Ban Ki-moon, the Secretary General of the U.N. at the time, told attendees, "Animate these stories. Set them to music! Give them life! Together we can have a blockbuster impact on the world."[416] Another speaker at the event said, "There's a huge gap between what governments can do, given political constraints, and what they should do. That's where you come in...We need you to make it sexy and cool to bring about the energy revolution that has to happen."[417]

Executives working for the FOX television network (not to be confused with Fox News) once openly admitted the network uses their shows to promote concerns about global warming. Chairman Gary Newman admitted in a promotional video the company put out years ago to brag about their efforts that, "We want to set an example in our industry and other industries that no matter what the size of your carbon footprint is, you can make a difference...The biggest thing we have done is inserting

[415] The Los Angeles Times "U.N. leader asks Hollywood for help in fight against global climate change" by Margot Roosevelt (February 27th 2011)

[416] Ibid.

[417] Ibid.

messages about the environment into some of our content."[418]

The Simpsons, King of the Hill, Family Guy, 24, and many other FOX shows have all included warnings about climate change, sometimes very brief, but they are there. For example, in a scene from *Family Guy* when a character is looking around at a car dealership he asks "what kind of jerk would drive one of those?" when he comes across a Hummer.

Another FOX television executive, Dana Walden, said, "the most powerful way that we could communicate the commitment on behalf of our company was to change the practices within the production as well as work in a message about global warming, about environmental changes, and about empowering people to take responsibility."[419]

The most infamous global warming propaganda is Al Gore's "documentary" *An Inconvenient Truth* which helped jump start global warming hysteria. Devastated by losing the 2000 election to George W. Bush, Al Gore found meaning in his life traveling around the world giving his doomsday predictions to anyone who would listen.

But documentary films don't have the same impact that big budget action movies do. Jesse Bryant, who organizes an environmental film festival at Yale University, said, "It's great to publish academic journals on the issues but the real breakthrough is when pop

---

[418] Promotional video for News Corp (2006)

[419] Ibid.

culture stories are hinted towards this cliff that we are all heading off."[420]

The Film that Started it All?

Kevin Costner's *Waterworld* was perhaps the first major film used to promote fears of global warming. Released in 1995 the story takes place around the year 2500 when the polar ice caps have melted and the entire earth is covered with water, forcing citizens to live on boats. At the time, it was the most expensive film ever made, costing around 175 million dollars, and turned out to be an epic flop.[421]

An interesting spin on the climate change hysteria was *The Day After Tomorrow* (2004) which, unlike *Waterworld*, depicted the earth freezing from climate change. It's based on a crazy "non-fiction" book titled *The Coming Global Superstorm* written in 1999 by UFO buff Art Bell and another guy named Whitley Strieber.

Dennis Quaid plays a climatologist who realizes that the melting of the polar ice caps has disrupted the ocean currents and caused an enormous polar vortex which drops the earth's temperature below freezing. Soon dozens of feet of snow fall everywhere from the disruptive weather patterns, trapping everyone inside.

There's even a scene where the vice president, who looks like Dick Cheney, was chastised for not listening to scientists earlier about the looming disaster global

---

[420] Ibid.

[421] Time "Top 10 Disappointing Blockbusters" (August 24th 2009)

warming would cause.[422] The film was widely mocked as ridiculous and had the opposite effect that was intended. Instead of raising awareness for the "dangers" of climate change, *The Day After Tomorrow* became a prime example of how absurd those fears were.

Vanity Fair is upset that there aren't more films about climate change, saying, "Fifteen years after *The Day After Tomorrow,* movies about climate change remain rare, and never as serious as the problem itself."[423] The article recommended that the next *Fast & Furious* film depict the gang driving electric vehicles instead of ones with "gas-guzzling" combustion engines to "set an example." At the bottom of the article it has a note that reads, "This story is part of Covering Climate Now, a global collaboration of more than 220 news outlets to strengthen coverage of the climate story."[424]

Perhaps the writer got the idea of *Fast & Furious* using electric vehicles from Pixar's animated film *Cars 2,* which casts Big Oil as the bad guy, conspiring to prevent an alternative (more environmentally friendly) fuel from catching on.[425]

A 2012 film called *Beasts of the Southern Wild* depicts planet earth on the verge of a climate catastrophe that ends up ultimately flooding a bayou village and causing dangerous prehistoric beasts which were frozen in the

---

[422] Pittsburgh Post-Gazette "'The Day After Tomorrow' falls far short of its goal" by Tony Norman (May 27th 2004)

[423] Vanity Fair "When Will Hollywood Actually Tackle Climate Change?" By Richard Lawson (September 19th 2019)

[424] Ibid.

[425] The Wall Street Journal "In 'Cars 2,' John Lasseter Says Big Oil is the 'Uber Bad Guy'" by Ethan Smith (June 20th 2011)

polar ice caps to become free and roam the earth again when they melt.

Snowpiercer (2013) starring Chris Evans is about a future where climate change made the earth freeze over due to a failed attempt by scientists trying to use geoengineering to stop it, so the humans who remain have to live on a train that constantly travels around the world non-stop. Why do they have to live on a train, and not in a building with a furnace to keep them warm, you ask?

Because that would defeat the point of the movie about the train being an allegory for "classism" and the hierarchy of society separating the rich from the poor. The upper class members live in the cars closest to the engine, in luxury, while the poor masses are stuck living in the cars at the end of the train, in poverty.[426]

One science blog said the "Frozen earth in 'Snowpiercer' is a grim (and possible) future for our warming planet."[427]   Others liked that it wasn't just another "climate change dystopia film" but was what they called the first geoengineering dystopia film.[428] It seems some who are concerned about climate change also doubt that geoengineering could solve the problem and think hopes of geoengineering (like spraying glitter in the atmosphere to block some of the sun's rays) are only addressing the symptoms, and not the cause of global warming. In May 2020 the TNT television network aired

---

[426] USA Today "Stylish 'Snowpiercer' takes a cold look at class divisions" by Claudia Puig (June 26th 2014)

[427] LiveScience.com "Frozen earth in 'Snowpiercer' is a grim (and possible) future for our warming planet" by Mindy Weisberger (October 11th 2019)

[428] Earth Island Journal "In Review: Snowpiercer" by Jason Mark (July 19th 2019)

a reboot of the film as a television series which is said to take place in the year 2021.

The 2014 science fiction film *Interstellar* revolved around the human race having to find another planet to live on because of dust storms and crop failures, and while not mentioning the words "climate change," many saw the subtle message it was trying to make. Green Peace noted, "*Interstellar* has the potential to play a positive role in the climate movement. It can urge those who already see the impact of climate change to take activist action. And for others who have up to now have ignored the science, they may think again."[429]

But the message was too subtle for some critics. *The Atlantic* complained that "climate change" is never explicitly mentioned in the film, and instead of trying to solve the "mistakes" humans have made on earth that "caused" the planet's destruction, the characters instead decided to abandon earth and try to start over somewhere else.[430] They were upset that the space opera aspects of the film and the issues of time travel overshadowed concerns about why Matthew McConaughey and his crew had to leave the earth in the first place.

It's interesting to point out that both Jeff Bezos and Elon Musk have aerospace companies and want to colonize other planets out of fear that, because of climate

[429] GreenPeace.org "No, Interstellar doesn't mention climate change but it could still do the problem a lot of good" by Brian Johnson (November 12th 2014)

[430] The Atlantic "Interstellar: Good Space Film, Bad Climate-Change Parable" by Noah Gittell (November 15th 2014)

change and "limited resources," earth may become uninhabitable in the future.[431]

In *Downsizing* (2017) Matt Damon and Kristen Wiig play a couple who plan to undergo a new scientific shrinking procedure similar to *Honey I Shrunk the Kids*, but this time on purpose, along with thousands of other people in order to all live in miniature communities so they will use a much smaller amount of earth's natural resources. By "downsizing" they also reduce the amount of pollution they create, and help slow climate change.

Another "benefit" is that by living in the miniaturized communities everything costs less since building materials and food go much further, making ordinary middle class people wealthy in their new life. But only 3% of the population opts for "downsizing," meaning it has little effect on saving the earth from overpopulation. In the end the people who didn't succumb to the procedure are said to be on the verge of all dying from global warming, but the miniature "downsized" people were all safe in an underground bunker, and they will be the ones to repopulate the earth once the climate calamity finally ends.

In *Geostorm* (2017) special weather-controlling satellites are put in space to save the planet from all the climate change we've caused, only to get sabotaged and turned into weapons of mass destruction.[432] Despite the film's over the top special effects showing major cities around the world being completely destroyed, climate

---

[431] CNBC "Jeff Bezos: Forget Mars, humans will live in these free-floating space pod colonies" by Catherine Clifford (March 8th 2019)

[432] Variety "New 'Geostorm' Trailer: Gerard Butler Attempts to Save the World From Climate Change Disaster" by Dave McNary (July 6th 2017)

change alarmists felt it was a good try regardless since it helped raise awareness for the "ecological tipping point" they fear we are approaching and were glad that climate change had been a common theme in several movies that year.[433]

Ethan Hawke stars in *First Reformed* (2017) where he plays a minister struggling with his faith after his son died in the War in Iraq because he encouraged him to enlist in the military as part of the "family tradition." The earth is on the verge of being uninhabitable because of climate change, and at one point a woman calls him to ask if he will counsel her boyfriend out of concern for his environmental extremist views.

The woman later finds a suicide vest her boyfriend made that he planned to use to fight back against the industrialists who ruined the planet. Hawke takes it but agrees not to call the police, hoping he can talk some sense into the man and avoid getting him in trouble. The minister then researches climate change for himself, starts to agree with the man's extremist views, and begins planning to use the suicide vest himself to kill a wealthy factory owner and others who aren't good stewards of the earth. Writer and director Paul Schrader said the film reflects his own "despair" over the "climate crisis."[434]

Equally corny was the 2018 version of *The Predator* where a key part of the plot was when the humans figured out why the creatures had returned to the earth after the incident depicted in the original film. The aliens, it turns out, were worried that climate change was going to make

[433] The Guardian "Is climate change Hollywood's new supervillain?" by Greme Virtue (October 19th 2017)

[434] Variety "Paul Schrader on How 'First Reformed' Reflects His Own Despair Over Climate Crisis" by Ted Johnson (May 19th 2018)

humans extinct soon, so the creatures came to earth to collect our DNA for their own genetic experiments before it was no longer available!

"How long before climate change renders this planet unlivable? Two generations? One?" asks a federal agent trying to kill the creatures. Then it suddenly dawns on the lead scientist, played by Olivia Munn. "That's why their visits are increasing. They're trying to snap up all of our best DNA before we're gone."[435] That's literally the reason given in the film as to why they returned to earth! Climate change was going to kill us!

HBO's *Years and Years* aired an entire episode focusing on the issue. The series follows a political family over the course of 15 years, with each episode taking place in a different time period, and one in the year 2025 depicts the north pole as having melted because of global warming.

A lead character (Edith Lyons) says, "We keep saying, 'you've got ten more years to sort out climate change, you've got ten more years to sort out flooding, you've got ten more years to sort out the rain forest.' We've been saying that for 30 years. It's too late. We've run out of time. Everyone knows it."[436]

The show goes on to warn that most people will soon starve from floods destroying crops and those who survive will have to live in small huts and only have their memories of what life was like before the climate catastrophe.

---

[435] Screen Rant "The Predator: Ultimate Predator Origins, Hybrid DNA & Abilities Explained" by Hannah Shaw-Williams (September 14th 2018)

[436] NewsBusters "Futuristic HBO Drama Lambasts Trump, Pence, 'Old Men In Power Forever'" by Rebecca Downs (July 1st 2019)

Aquaman (2018) starring Jason Momoa depicted the King of Atlantis "Orm" starting a war with humans because of the decades of pollution we have been dumping into the ocean. Despite its pro-environmental message, some critics were upset that the words "global warming" were never actually explicitly mentioned in the film.

"*Aquaman* shows, with unfortunate clarity, that the superhero film genre is ill-equipped to take on serious subjects," said one critic. "Superhero stories love to imagine the end of the world, but don't have much to offer in the face of actual global catastrophes."[437]

"Aquaman" Jason Momoa took the role very seriously however. When actor Chris Pratt posted a picture on his Instagram showing himself after a workout, he got "called out" by Momoa for drinking from a "single-use" plastic water bottle. Pratt then apologized.[438] Even if you recycle your plastic water bottle, that's not environmentally friendly enough, so now the extremists are shaming people who don't drink out of re-usable water bottles instead.

In the Marvel superhero film *Venom*, the villain who is using his personal space exploration company to search for other inhabitable planets because "overpopulation and climate change" are going to make earth "uninhabitable" in just "literally" one more generation.[439] It's by accident

---

[437] NBC News "DC Comics 'Aquaman' raises questions about environmentalism" by Noah Berlatsky (December 21st 2018)

[438] The Hill "Chris Pratt apologizes for posing with single use plastic bottle" by Justine Coleman (December 4th 2019)

[439] Yale Climate Connections "Superheroes and aliens: Climate change in the movies in 2018 - with a preview of 2019" by Michael Svoboda (March 21st 2019)

that one of their probes discovers an alien symbiotic lifeform that is brought back to earth, creating the "Venom" superhero by merging with a man's DNA.

"Thanos Did Nothing Wrong"

Fighting climate change often involves reducing the earth's population, since the more people there are living on the planet, the larger our supposed accumulative carbon footprint is, and it's under this rationale that some environmentalists sided with *Avengers* villain Thanos in his quest to kill half of all life in the Universe.

In the movies, that's his goal once he obtains all of the "Infinity Stones" which would grant him supernatural power, and some critics began arguing that instead of being a psychotic villain, Thanos "did nothing wrong." The saying "Thanos did nothing wrong" had become a popular Internet meme from nihilist fans who sided with him, but some on the Left took it seriously thinking that it would help save the earth.

Forbes magazine asked "Is Thanos right about overpopulation? His rationale seems to make sense if we consider our own planet. Since the Industrial Revolution, the world population has grown rapidly. The figure is currently over 7.6 billion and is projected to reach 10 billion in 2050... Fewer people ought to mean more food and less hunger, and might lower the risk of an epidemic when overcrowding enables the spread of disease. Human activity is driving a loss of biodiversity, with about 25% of animals and plants now threatened with extinction, so halving the population would help other species. As a consequence, you could conclude that by eliminating 50% of all humans, Thanos did the Earth a huge favor."[440]

Their review concluded, "you could indeed argue that Thanos did nothing wrong—and in the long run, the villain might have actually saved the world."[441]

Population Control

The idea of dramatically reducing the earth's population in order to "save" it is actually something that environmental extremists have been promoting for decades. Back in the late 1960s, Stanford University professor Paul R. Ehrlich published a book titled *The Population Bomb*, which warned that within the next ten years society would collapse from massive famines because there were too many people on the planet using too many resources.[442]

Despite the book being wildly inaccurate and over 50 years later the predictions laughable, many activists are still warning that we need to immediately reduce the population to save the planet.[443] Some celebrities like Miley Cyrus have even said they're not going to have children because of climate change.[444] Alexandria Ocasio-Cortez has also said she too isn't sure whether or

---

[440] Forbes "The Science Of 'Avengers: Endgame' Proves Thanos Did Nothing Wrong" by JV Chamary (May 7th 2019)

[441] Ibid.

[442] Smithsonian Magazine "The Book That Incited a Worldwide Fear of Overpopulation" by Charles C. Mann (January 2018)

[443] The Guardian "Climate crisis: 11,000 scientists warn of 'untold suffering'" by Damian Carrington (November 5th 2019)

[444] Washington Times "Miley Cyrus: 'I refuse' to have kids until climate change resolved" by Jessica Chasmar (July 12th 2019)

not she wants to have kids for the same reason.[445] Many others are blaming couples who have children for contributing to the "problem."[446]

With Transhumanism appearing to be on the horizon which promises to extend our lifespan by hundreds of years (or indefinitely),[447] proponents are becoming increasingly concerned that this will cause the earth's natural resources to become even more rapidly depleted because if people are able to quadruple their lifespan, that also means they'll end up using four times as much energy, food, and other natural resources as well.[448]

The mysterious Georgia Guidestones monument located in the small town of Elberton, Georgia, was erected in 1980 to declare the "need" for such actions. The 19-foot-tall monument consists of four slabs of granite planted into the ground with 10 "commandments" engraved on each side, written in eight different languages.[449]

The first of the ten "commandments" is to reduce the planet's population down to 500 million, an over 90% reduction from its current 7.5 billion. The "Guidestones" were commissioned and paid for by an unknown man

---

445 Newsweek "Alexandria Ocasio-Cortez Asks: Is It Still OK to Have Kids in Face of Climate Change?" by Nicole Goodkind (February 25th 2019)

446 BBC "The couples rethinking kids because of climate change" by Ted Scheinman (October 1st 2019)

447 Newsweek "Silicon Valley Is Trying to Make Humans Immortal—and Finding Some Success" by Betsy Isaacson (March 5th 2015)

448 The New Bioethics: A Multidisciplinary Journal of Biotechnology and the Body "Transhumanism: How Far Is Too Far?" by Joel Thompson pages 165-182 (July 6th 2017)

449 The Elberton Star "The Georgia Guidestones: tourist attraction or cult message?" by Gary Jones (April 21st 2012)

using the pseudonym R.C. Christian who said he represented a group that wanted the monument built to send the world a message.[450]

---

[450] The man published a little-known book in 1986 titled *Common Sense Renewed* where he admits that he represented a group. In it, he also says that leather-bound copies were sent to all members of Congress. At the time of this writing in July 2020, one is for sale on E-bay, and listed for $3,500. I own a paperback version which was later published in a small quantity.

Sports "News"

Unlike politics and religion, sports is supposed to be the one universal activity that people can enjoy or discuss without the usual controversies associated with the human condition. One would expect that sports news shows and networks would be the last place you'd hear about politics, let alone be subjected to political propaganda, but unfortunately that's not true these days.

In the past, sports and politics would occasionally intersect but usually only when a star athlete joined a political cause and their involvement was part of a human-interest story. It was usually void of much controversy because often their activities weren't divisive or controversial, but instead humanitarian in nature.

But recently many sports writers, websites, and television networks have become liberal propaganda outlets, promoting left wing causes and putting athletes on pedestals who become token symbols of the liberal agenda. The entire NBA and NFL endorse the Black Lives Matter movement and have turned Colin Kaepernick, the former San Francisco 49ers player who refused to stand during the National Anthem before games, into a hero for starting the trend.

When the 2020 NBA season began after a long delay from the COVID-19 pandemic, many of the players wore special jerseys with "social justice" messages printed on them in place of their last names on the back.[451] The

---

[451] ESPN "'Equality' tops list of NBA players' most popular social justice jersey messages (July 8th 2020)

league had worked with Nike to make the "Black Lives Matter" jerseys. This was in response to the protests (and riots) that spread across the country that summer when it became mandatory for sports leagues to condemn White people for "systemically" ruining Black people's lives. Several basketball stadiums even painted "Black Lives Matter" on the courts.[452]

The NFL also kicked off the 2020 season with the "Black National Anthem" being performed at the start of each game during week one in order to help "raise awareness" of "systemic racism" in America.[453] The "Black National Anthem" is a song titled "Lift Ev'ry Voice And Sing" that many Black people consider to be "their" national anthem, instead of the Star Spangled Banner.

Even NASCAR became political in 2020 when they banned drivers *and fans* from displaying any Confederate flags at the races just two days after the league's only (half) Black driver Bubba Wallace made the demand.[454] Then a week and a half later someone allegedly hung a "noose" in his garage at the Talladega Superspeedway in Alabama right before a big race. Bubba became a hero overnight from the media endlessly reporting that a "racist" NASCAR fan upset at him for getting the

---

[452] CBS News "NBA reportedly plans to paint 'Black Lives Matter' on courts when season resumes" by Christopher Brito (June 30th 2020)

[453] USA Today "NFL will play Black national anthem 'Lift Every Voice and Sing' before each Week 1 game" by Mike Jones (July 2nd 2020)

[454] New York Times "Bubba Wallace Wants NASCAR to Ban the Confederate Flag" by Maria Cramer (June 9th 2020)

Confederate flag banned must have snuck into his garage and hung the "noose" for revenge.

At the race the next day Bubba was given a parade as he rolled out onto the track to show how the entire league supported him for being so "brave" for what he had gone through.[455] Only, as I'm sure you know, the "noose" turned out to be the handle on the end of the rope which is used to pull open the garage doors at the track.[456] But Bubba had become a star overnight and was a NASCAR hero for standing up against the imaginary "hate crime" that 15 FBI agents wasted their time investigating.[457]

After Amazon obtained the naming rights to Seattle's NHL arena, formerly called Key Arena, they changed the name to Climate Pledge Arena to "raise awareness" for climate change, so now fans can't watch a hockey game in Seattle without the constant reminder to be on the lookout for global warming.[458] Not even the Super Bowl Halftime shows are safe from becoming avenues to deliver political messages with musical guests sometimes incorporating "social justice" propaganda into their performances.[459]

---

[455] NBC Sports "NASCAR drivers push Bubba Wallace's car in act of solidarity after noose found in his garage" via Associated Press (June 22nd 2020)

[456] Boston Globe "FBI says noose in Bubba Wallace's stall was garage door-pull rope, not a hate crime" by Jenna Fryer via Associated Press (June 23rd 2020)

[457] USA Today "FBI announces noose found in Bubba Wallace's garage had been there since 2019; no federal crime committed" by Michelle R. Martinelli (June 23rd 2020)

[458] Seattle Times "Amazon buys naming rights to KeyArena, will call it Climate Pledge Arena" by Geoff Baker (June 25th 2020)

[459] CNN "Beyonce gets political at Super Bowl, pays tribute to 'Black Lives Matter'" by Deena Zeru (February 9th 2016)

Sportswriter Bryan Curtis noted, "There was a time when filling your column with liberal ideas on race, class, gender, and labor policy got you dubbed a 'sociologist.' These days, such views are more likely to get you a job."[460]

Sports broadcaster Jason Whitlock said, "ESPN and most of the mainstream media have lurched farther left. That's a complaint from middle America and, in my opinion, objective America. ESPN's own ombudsman acknowledged ESPN's hardcore progressive slant."[461]

Speaking about Fox Sports 1, a competitor to ESPN, he said, "I think we're the alternative for sports fans who respect and like traditional sports values. I think we're the alternative for mainstream sports fans, Little League coaches, athletes, sports moms and dads. I think we're the alternative for people who want to hear authentic conversation and debate rather than words crafted for Twitter applause. I think we're the alternative for middle America, blue-collar sports fans. I think we're the alternative for people who don't think every misspoken word is a fireable offense. ESPN caters to the elite, safe-space crowd. We cater to the people who love to tailgate and knock down a six-pack."[462]

Michael Brendan Dougherty, editor of *The Slurve* baseball newsletter, wrote, "It's also true that conservative ideas tend to be slower off the block. Because they are defenders of tradition, conservatives' arguments often

---

[460] The Ringer "Sportswriting Has Become a Liberal Profession—Here's How It Happened" by Bryan Curtis (February 16th 2017)

[461] SportingNews.com "Jason Whitlock sounds off on 'liberal' sports media, whether Bill Simmons should return to ESPN" by Michael McCarthy (April 12th 2017)

[462] Ibid.

strike liberals as either an unreflective devotion to the way things are (or were), or as being too subtle to be credible."[463]

For the 2015 season the NBA teamed up with Sheryl Sandberg, a radical feminist and top executive at Facebook, to promote her "Lean In" campaign which nagged men to, "take more responsibility for housework and child care," and said they need to "do their fair share of daily chores."[464] The campaign aired commercials on TV during basketball games which used NBA players like LeBron James and Stephen Curry to lecture men to help out more around the house with laundry and other chores.[465]

In 2015 ESPN gave Caitlyn Jenner the Arthur Ashe Courage Award, choosing "her" over others—including double amputee Noah Galloway, who is an Iraq War veteran—and despite missing one arm and one leg became a competitive distance runner, CrossFit athlete, and won third place on *Dancing With the Stars*.[466]

Caitlyn Jenner was also chosen over fellow nominee Lauren Hill, a college basketball player who lost her fight

---

[463] The Week "The arrogant thinking of liberal sports writers" by Michael Brendan Dougherty (February 21st 2017)

[464] Associated Press "Facebook exec, NBA team up to get men to 'lean in' for women" by Michael Liedtke (March 5th 2015)

[465] NBA.com "NBA and WNBA Partner with LeanIn.Org to encourage men to support equality at home and at work" (March 5th 2015)

[466] National Review "Yes, ESPN Did Pick Caitlyn Jenner Ahead of Iraq War Vet and Amputee Noah Galloway for the ESPY Courage Award" by David French (June 3rd 2015)

with a brain tumor.[467]   Surprisingly, veteran sports broadcaster Bob Costas admitted choosing Caitlyn Jenner was a "crass exploitation play," saying, "In the broad world of sports, I'm pretty sure they could've found someone—and this is not anything against Caitlyn Jenner —who was much closer actively involved in sports, who would've been deserving of what that award represents."[468]   Caitlyn Jenner hadn't played competitive sports since the 1980s (when "she" was Bruce). *Sports Illustrated* also put "her" on the cover at the age of 66 wearing the gold metal "she" won at the 1976 Olympics as Bruce, forty years earlier.[469]

Not long after this, ESPN fired baseball analyst Curt Schilling because he posted a meme on his personal Facebook page criticizing new transgender bathroom laws which allow biological males to use women's bathrooms, locker rooms, and showers.[470]   The meme simply consisted of a man dressed as a woman with the caption, "Let him in to the restroom with your daughter or else you're a narrow minded, judgmental, unloving, racist bigot, who needs to die!"

ESPN's President John Skipper was asked if the "perceived political shift" in sports becoming political was a "conscious decision" by the network.   He

---

[467] New York Daily News "Twitter users call for ESPN to give Arthur Ashe Courage Award to Lauren Hill, not Caitlyn Jenner, at ESPYs" by Bernie Augustine (June 2nd 2015)

[468] The Washington Post "Bob Costas: Caitlyn Jenner's ESPYs courage award is 'crass exploitation play'" by Cindy Boren (June 10th 2015)

[469] ABC News "Caitlyn Jenner Appears on Sports Illustrated Cover 40 Years After Victory" by Ricki Harris (June 28th 2016)

[470] New York Times "Curt Schilling, ESPN Analyst, Is Fired Over Offensive Social Media Post" by Richard Sandomir (April 20th 2016)

responded, "It is accurate that the Walt Disney Company and ESPN are committed to diversity and inclusion. These are long-standing values that drive fundamental fairness while providing us with the widest possible pool of talent to create the smartest and most creative staff. We do not view this as a political stance but as a human stance. We do not think tolerance is the domain of a particular political philosophy."[471]

One conservative employee at ESPN revealed, "If you're a Republican or conservative, you feel the need to talk in whispers. There's even a fear of putting Fox News on a TV [in the office]."[472]

Speaking shortly after the 2016 Presidential election, ESPN's public editor Jim Brady said, "As it turns out, ESPN is far from immune from the political fever that has afflicted so much of the country over the past year. Internally, there's a feeling among many staffers—both liberal and conservative—that the company's perceived move leftward has had a stifling effect on discourse inside the company and has affected its public-facing products. Consumers have sensed that same leftward movement, alienating some."[473]

Sportscaster Joe Buck is uncomfortable with sports recently becoming political, saying, "Unless I'm completely wrong, and I know in this case I'm not, nobody's tuning into the 49ers-Cowboys game to hear my political opinions, whether it's about Trump, or Kaepernick or Flint, Michigan. That's not why they're

---

[471] ESPN.com "Inside and out, ESPN dealing with changing political dynamics" by Jim Brady (December 1st 2016)

[472] Ibid.

[473] Ibid.

watching a football game. It's misplaced. I hear guys doing it at times. It seems self-serving. Like they want to inject themselves into the conversation. Wait for a talk show. Go on Bill Maher's show. Bill O'Reilly. Whoever. I think people watch these games to get away from that stuff. I think you risk alienating and upsetting a lot of people when you start going down that rabbit hole."[474]

NFL Promotes "Social Justice"

Shortly into the 2017 season, NFL players and owners issued a joint statement saying they held an important meeting to, "discuss plans to utilize our platform to promote equality and effectuate positive change. We agreed that these are common issues and pledged to meet again to continue this work together."[475]   Then Roger Goodell, NFL Commissioner, sent a letter to the Senate Judiciary Committee encouraging them to pass the Sentencing Reform and Corrections Act of 2017, which would reduce the prison sentences for drug offenders.

A few months later the NFL announced the creation of their new "Inspire Change" initiative which involves giving millions of dollars in grants to "social justice" causes, including "helping schools implement more

---

[474] Sporting News "Fox's Joe Buck says announcers should stick to sports" by Michael McCarthy (April 18th 2017)

[475] NFL.com "Players, owners meet to discuss social issues in N.Y." (October 17th 2017)

comprehensive African-American history education programs."[476] The NFL also started becoming concerned that the tradition of using beautiful women as cheerleaders was "sexist," so for the 2018 season they introduced male "cheerleaders" for the first time. The Los Angeles Rams and the New Orleans Saints were the first two teams to add them, and they're not there to help the girls perform stunts by tossing them into the air and catching them. They dance with the girls and do all the same routines on the sidelines, even holding pom-poms.[477] Instead of being denounced as stupid or weird, they were hailed by the liberal media for "making history."[478]

Nike also decided to get into politics recently. In September 2018 the sportswear giant put out a new ad featuring Colin Kaepernick to celebrate the 30th anniversary of the company's "Just Do It" campaign. While it was a polarizing choice, pushing half of their potential customers away who despise Kaepernick for his anti-American and anti-police activism, Nike's revenue increased over the previous year's quarter.[479]

Under their new business model they don't care how many of their previous customers will never buy a Nike product again because with Kaepernick as their new

476 Sports Illustrated "NFL Announces 'Inspire Change' Initiative, Will Boost African-American History Education in Schools" by Jenny Vrentas (January 11th 2019)

477 USA Today "Los Angeles Rams' male cheerleaders make NFL history" by Steve Gardner (March 28th 2018)

478 Los Angeles Times "Rams' male cheerleaders make NFL history at Super Bowl" by Bill Plaschke (January 30th 2019)

479 Time "Despite Outrage, Nike Sales Increased 31% After Kaepernick Ad" by Gina Martinez (September 10th 2018)

poster boy the company's focus is now on the fanatics who will buy Nike gear even more because it reflects their social justice warrior identity.[480]

As everyone knows, Black people dominate the NBA and NFL—and other sports like long distance running; but NBC Sports president Pete Bevacqua is worried that too many White people play golf. "Golf hasn't had the best history," he says. "Golf needs more diversity. How do you get more minorities playing the game, how do you get more women playing the game? I think all of golf understands that, whether it's the LPGA, the PGA Tour, the USGA, the PGA of America, Augusta National."[481]

Imagine a sports broadcaster saying there's too many Black people in the NBA, or that it needs more "racial diversity!" They would be fired within the hour, but as I detailed in the "War on White People" chapter, the liberal media has no problem with anti-White racism, and in fact encourages it.

Jemele Hill (a proud Black woman) who was co-host of SportsCenter, called President Trump a "White supremacist" in 2017 without any repercussions from the network.[482] Such an outrageous comment from the host of ESPN's flagship show drew criticism from White House Press Secretary Sarah Huckabee Sanders and even President Trump himself. Many had become accustomed

---

[480] ABC News "Why the sneaker game is becoming more political: 'It's not just good business but a net positive for the world'" by Deena Zaru (December 22nd 2018)

[481] Hollywood Reporter "NBC Sports President: 2020 Will Be 'Uniquely Combustible' as Olympics, Conventions Collide" by Marisa Guthrie (December 16th 2019)

[482] USA Today "ESPN's Jemele Hill stands by comments calling President Trump white supremacist" by Steve Gardner (February 21st 2018)

to hearing such slander from CNN and MSNBC panelists, but coming from an ESPN host took things to a new level of depravity.

"Pride Night"

All major sports leagues now host an annual "Pride Night" where they celebrate LGBT people, decorate their stadiums with rainbows, and bring special guests to the games from the gay (and transgender) community. To make sure everything is gay enough they even have gay men's choirs sing the national anthem.[483] Today, most—if not all—NBA teams now host one each year, but it's not just the NBA.

The NFL launched their own annual "Pride Night" as well, to "heighten sensitivity to the LGBTQ community" and show their "commitment to an inclusive environment in which all employees are welcome."[484] As of 2018, every major league baseball team except one hosted an annual Pride Night.[485] The following year the one hold out (the Yankees) gave in and held their first "Legacy of Pride" night and even awarded scholarships to various LGBT students.[486]

---

[483] NBA.com "Los Angeles Lakers to Hold Second Annual Pride Night" (September 24th 2019)

[484] USA Today "NFL launches LGBT initiative, NFL Pride" by Scott Gleeson (August 18th 2017)

[485] NBC News "Yankees set to be only MLB team not to host LGBTQ Pride Night" by Kit Ramgopal (July 5th 2018)

[486] USA Today "New York Yankees, the only team without a Pride Night, announce LGBT initiative for 2019" by Scott Gleeson (September 21st 2018)

Even the NHL has an annual Pride Night, where they too decorate the stadiums in rainbow colors and players even use hockey sticks wrapped in rainbow colored tape to show support for the LGBT community.[487] You can't even go to a hockey game these days without LGBT propaganda being shoved in your face.

The Super Bowl

Since the Super Bowl is the most-watched event on television every year, the NFL and their sponsors can't pass up the opportunity to spread liberal propaganda to as many people as possible. Lately we've been seeing an increasing amount of Super Bowl commercials pushing a political agenda, from Audi using a car commercial to complain about the (non-existent) "gender pay gap" to a lumber company denouncing President Trump's plan to build a wall on the U.S. / Mexico border.[488] The NFL has also reportedly refused to air pro Second Amendment commercials.[489]

Even the Halftime show, which might be the last place one would expect to push a political agenda, isn't immune. In 2016, Beyonce was the featured artist and turned her performance into a dedication to the Black

---

[487] NHL "Washington Capitals To Host Pride Night Jan. 7" (January 7th 2020)

[488] Fortune "This Will Probably Be the Super Bowl's Most Controversial Commercial" by Tom Huddleston Jr. (February 3rd 2017)

[489] Breitbart "NFL Bans Super Bowl Gun Commercial" (December 2nd 2013)

Panthers and Black Lives Matter.[490] The following year, with tensions still high from the recent Presidential election, Lady Gaga also used the spotlight to promote a political agenda, although a lot more subtle than Beyonce the year before.

Many people missed it, but it was there, and it was undeniable if you knew what to look for.[491] Gaga gave a shoutout to the anti-Trump protesters who were (at the time) out protesting the new president's temporary travel ban from seven countries which had been identified as hotbeds of terrorism.[492]

When Jennifer Lopez and Shakira performed in a sex-charged halftime show that included stripper poles, booty shaking, and crotch-grabbing; they also depicted "kids in cages" as a way to denounce President Trump's immigration policy of detaining people who cross illegally into our country.[493] Both Jennifer Lopez and Shakira are of Latin descent, and at one point during their performance they started singing in Spanish to cater to the tens of millions of non-assimilating immigrants who are occupying areas in American cities.

After the New England Patriots visited the White House following their 2017 Super Bowl win, the *New York Times* tweeted out two side by side photos, one

---

[490] CNN "Beyonce gets political at Super Bowl, pays tribute to 'Black Lives Matter'" by Deena Zaru (February 9th 2016)

[491] Vanity Fair "Lady Gaga Made an Edgy Political Statement You Might Have Missed at the Super Bowl" by Joanna Robinson (February 5th 2017)

[492] CNN "How the Trump administration chose the 7 countries in the immigration executive order" by Kyle Blaine and Julia Horowitz (January 30th 2017)

[493] CBS News "'Kids in cages' help J-Lo make powerful statement at Super Bowl halftime show" by Christopher Brito (February 3rd 2020)

showing when the Patriots visited the White House in 2015 when Barack Obama was president, and the other from the current visit, giving the impression that far fewer players showed up because they didn't want to have anything to do with President Trump.[494]

The official Patriots Twitter account then issued a statement saying, "These photos lack context. Facts: In 2015, over 40 football staff were on the stairs. In 2017, they were seated on the South Lawn."[495] Countless other people called out the *New York Times* for their fake news, and of course President Trump took to Twitter to denounce them as well.[496]

The next day the *New York Times* sports editor Jason Stallman apologized, saying, "Bad tweet by me. Terrible tweet. I wish I could say it's complicated, but no, this one is pretty straightforward: I'm an idiot. It was my idea, it was my execution, it was my blunder. I made a decision in about four minutes that clearly warranted much more time. Once we learned more, we tried to fix everything as much as possible as swiftly as possible and as transparently as possible. Of course, at that point the damage was done. I just needed to own it."[497]

But that wasn't the only politicizing of the Patriot's White House visit. Rob Gronkowski, who played tight

---

[494] USA Today "The truth behind the New York Times' Patriots photo that went viral on social media" by Luke Kerr-Dineen (April 20th 2017)

[495] CBS Boston "Patriots Hit Back At New York Times Over White House Tweet" (April 20th 2017)

[496] Fox News "Trump Blasts NY Times for 'Big Lie' About Patriots' Visit to White House" (April 20th 2017)

[497] The Washington Times "New York Times sports editor takes sole blame for Patriots tweet that elicited Trump response" by Cindy Boren (April 20th 2017)

end, interrupted Sean Spicer's press briefing that day asking if he needed any help [arguing with the fake news] in a hilarious stunt that had Spicer and the press corps laughing, but ESPN's Max Kellerman didn't think it was funny at all.

"When the press corps is cracking up at a press secretary because of an athlete's presence there, so he's lending something to the proceedings, the athlete is, and the press corps is, you know, they're having a rollicking good time...that's a very bad thing. That's an unhealthy thing to have happened," he complained on air.[498]

Kellerman went on to say that Gronkowski's prank "normalized" Sean Spicer, who he insists worked for an "authoritarian" administration.[499]

Layoffs

Many people were growing tired of politics being intertwined with sports coverage, especially when the issues weren't even remotely related, and polls began showing it was causing some viewers to tune out.[500] In April 2017 ESPN laid off about 100 people, including several on-air personalities, and six months later laid off another 150 people.[501]

---

[498] Breitbart "ESPN's Kellerman: Gronkowski Popping Into WH Press Briefing Normalizes Sean Spicer — Patriots Should've Boycotted Trip" by Trend Baker (April 20th 2017) .

[499] Ibid.

[500] Washington Times "Hollywood stars, athletes driving away viewers with political activists poll finds" by Valerie Richardson (March 21st 2018)

[501] Los Angeles Times "ESPN laying off 150 employees in another round of cuts" by Daniel Miller (November 29th 2017)

This was after ESPN had reportedly lost an average of 15,000 subscribers a day in October alone, totaling an estimated decline of 465,000 for the month.[502]   In the fiscal year of 2018 they lost two million subscribers.[503] While some of the loss can be ascribed to cord-cutters ditching cable in favor of streaming services, a significant portion was due to fans becoming sick of the players protesting during the national anthem.[504]

In October 2019 the sports news website Deadspin sent out a memo to their editors and staff telling them to stick to sports and stop covering politics since the website had steadily drifted into regularly complaining about President Trump. The memo said in part, "Deadspin will write only about sports and that which is relevant to sports in some way."[505]   The editor-in-chief then decided to plaster the entire website with political and pop culture news in protest, and was immediately fired.   He unironically tweeted, "I've just been fired from Deadspin for not sticking to sports."[506]

Members of the staff then quit en masse to show solidarity with the editor, and to also protest the new

---

[502] Media Research Center "ESPN Lost 15,000 Subscribers a Day In October" by Nick Kangadis (October 31st 2017)

[503] Variety "ESPN Loses 2 Million Subscribers in Fiscal 2018" by Cynthia Littleton (November 21st 2018)

[504] New York Post "Anthem protests biggest reason for NFL's falling ratings: study" by Richard Morgan (February 2018)

[505] USA Today "Order from management to 'stick to sports' has Deadspin site in open revolt" via Associated Press (October 30th 2019)

[506] Fox News "Top Deadspin editor says he was fired after refusing to 'stick to sports'" by Joseph A. Wulfsohn (October 29th 2019)

"stick to sports" policy.[507] Yes, people who worked for a sports website quit when management told them to write about sports!

Sports are supposed to be an outlet for people to get away from the stress and responsibilities we face during the work week. And the last thing most sports fans want is to have politics brought up when they're trying to enjoy their favorite game, but unfortunately "stick to sports" is no longer the motto for most sports entertainment outlets.

While playing sports is a great way for kids and adults to stay physically fit and learn about working together with others, the artificial importance placed on professional sports entertainment largely serves as a type of bread and circus distraction, diverting people's attention and energy away from important problems in society.

Instead, the focus is put on concerns about whose team is going to win, and which players are injured or may get traded, and other trivial and meaningless controversies which, when you boil them down, do nothing other than serve to keep people pacified with things that lack any real importance whatsoever.

George Orwell summed this phenomenon up in his prophetic novel *Nineteen Eighty-Four* when he wrote, "films, football, beer, and above all, gambling filled up the horizon of [people's] minds. To keep them in control was not difficult."[508]

---

[507] NPR "After Days Of Resignations, The Last Of The Deadspin Staff Has Quit" by Brakkton Booker (November 1st 2019)

[508] Orwell, George - *Nineteen Eighty-Four* page 63 (1983 Plume)

Author's Note: If you haven't already, please take a moment to rate and review this book on Amazon.com, Kindle, Google Play, iBooks, or wherever you bought it from, to let other potential readers know how valuable this information is.

Almost all of the one-star reviews on Amazon for my last three books "The Liberal Media Industrial Complex," "The True Story of Fake News," and "Liberalism: Find a Cure" are from NON-verified purchases which shows the "reviewers" probably didn't even read them, and just hate me.

So if you could help me offset their fake one-star reviews by leaving a real one yourself since you actually read the book, that would help a lot!

Thank you!

Late-Night Comedy Shows

For decades the late-night talk shows were something Americans could watch at the end of the day to get a few laughs about current events, celebrity stupidity, or from other theatrics. Viewers couldn't tell Johnny Carson's politics because he was an equal opportunity offender. The same was true for Jay Leno and David Letterman who were staples of late-night TV for a generation.

Starting the evening following Donald Trump's victory over Hillary Clinton in 2016, late night TV stopped being funny. In fact, the hosts were visibly distraught when they took to the air, speaking in a somber tone as if we had just experienced a national tragedy. They tried to pull themselves together over the following days and weeks, but late-night television was never the same.

Today Jimmy Kimmel, Stephen Colbert, and Jimmy Fallon aren't merely "entertainers." They are stealth propagandists; whose political messages go down easier than those from "news" outlets because it's covered in comedy. Their agenda is no longer to make people laugh, it's to get them to cheer on the liberal agenda and mock conservatives.

New York Magazine embraced comedy's new mission and asked, "How Funny Does Comedy Need to Be?" noticing that it wasn't very funny anymore. "Like post-rock, post-comedy uses the elements of comedy (be it stand-up, sitcom, or film) but without the goal of creating the traditional comedic result—laughter—instead focusing on tone, emotional impact, storytelling, and formal experimentation. The goal of being 'funny' is optional for some or for the entirety of the piece."[509] Comedy *without* comedy? At least they're honest enough to admit the shows aren't funny anymore.

When Supreme Court Justice Anthony Kennedy announced he was retiring, opening the door for President Trump to nominate a second judge to the court, the official Comedy Central Twitter account tweeted sarcastically "Thanks, Justice Kennedy," along with a graphic that read "Supremely Fucked."[510]

Comedy Central's Jim Jefferies went so far as to deceptively edit an interview with a man named Avi Yemini who is opposed to Muslims mass emigrating to European countries, but unbeknown to Comedy Central, Yemini secretly recorded the entire interview and posted it on YouTube to show how manipulated the footage was for the segment when it aired and demonstrated how many of his statements were completely taken out of context. He then sued them for defamation.[511]

Some hosts like HBO's John Oliver are steeped in guilt because they mocked the idea of Donald Trump becoming president. When guest hosting the *Daily Show,* John Oliver responded to a news clip reporting Trump was considering running in 2016 by saying, "Do it. Do it!

[509] New York Magazine "How Funny Does Comedy Need to Be?" by Jesse David Fox (September 4th 2018)

[510] https://twitter.com/comedycentral/status/1012049409503358982

[511] ReclaimTheNet.org "Avi Yemini files lawsuit against Jim Jeffries and Viacom after deceptively edited Comedy Central video" by Didi Rankovic (February 19th 2020)

I will personally write you a campaign check now!" because he thought it would make for some great material and didn't think for a moment Trump had a chance to actually win. Now John Oliver lives in misery every day of his life.

In an interview five years after he was fired from NBC as host of the *Tonight Show*, Jay Leno was asked how much different the late-night comedy shows are in the Trump era. "Do you miss being on the show, or is it such a different time that it would be hard to do?" Al Roker asked him.

"No, it's different. I don't miss it," he replied, going on to say during his time hosting he didn't want people to know his politics, so he tried to hit both sides equally.[512] "Because, you know, the theory when we did the show was you just watch the news, we'll make fun of the news, and get your mind off the news. Well, now people just want to be on the news all the time. You just have one subject that's the same topic every night, which makes it —makes it very hard. I mean, all the comics, Jimmy and Colbert and everybody else, it's tough when that's the only topic out there."[513]

Leno noted that the comedy on late-night TV is now "one-sided" and "all very serious" and that "I'd just like to see a bit of civility come back to it, you know?"[514]

Saturday Night Live alumni Rob Schneider noted today, "Much late-night comedy is less about being funny and more about indoctrination by comedic imposition.

---

[512] Today Show "Jay Leno Talks Cholesterol, Comedy And Life After Late-Night" (March 12th 2019)

[513] Ibid.

[514] Ibid.

People aren't really laughing at it as much as cheering on the rhetoric."[515]

Jimmy Kimmel

Jimmy Kimmel is largely credited with killing the Republicans' plan to repeal Obamacare after he spent several nights ranting (and crying) about it on his show in 2017, claiming it would prevent poor people from getting healthcare. He even used his newborn son Billy as a prop since he was born with a congenital heart defect and claimed that if Obamacare was repealed then other children with similar life-threatening conditions would die.

But Kimmel wasn't coming up with his Obamacare material on his own. *The Daily Beast* admitted, "Kimmel and his team were in touch with health care officials, charities and advocacy groups," as well as Senator Chuck Schumer who, "provided technical guidance and info about the bill, as well as stats from various think tanks and experts on the effects of [it]."[516]

CNN asked, "Did Jimmy Kimmel kill the health care bill?" after Senator John McCain [who cast the deciding vote] said he wouldn't support the repeal. "Kimmel's critique [of the Republican plan] inspired intense coverage and analyses, pundits debated Kimmel's expertise on the subject while others told him to stay in

---

[515] Fox News "Alec Baldwin says Rob Schneider 'has a point' in criticism of 'SNL' Trump impersonation" by Jennifer Earl (April 30th 2018)

[516] The Daily Beast "Jimmy Kimmel Got a Hand From Chuck Schumer in His Fight Against Obamacare Repeal" by Asawin Suebsaeng, Lachian Markay, and Sam Stein (September 23rd 2017)

his lane, and the comedian found himself again at the center of the health care fight."[517]

Kimmel's propaganda efforts have extended far beyond healthcare. He has used children in skits about how "disastrous" global warming is.[518] He calls CPAC the largest gathering of "anti-vaxxers" and "very angry White people."[519] And he even called for Supreme Court Justice Brett Kavanaugh to be castrated.[520]

Kimmel says, "It just so happens that almost every talk show host is a liberal and that's because it requires a level of intelligence."[521] He has also admitted that sharing his political views "has cost me commercially" but neither he nor ABC care, because it's "for a good cause."[522]

Stephen Colbert

Stephen Colbert took over *The Late Show* from David Letterman in 2015 and ever since has turned the nightly

---

[517] CNN "Did Jimmy Kimmel kill the health care bill?" by Frank Pallotta (September 22nd 2017)

[518] Mediaite "Jimmy Kimmel Enlists Little Children to Explain 'Global Warming' and Climate Change to Trump" by Tommy christopher (January 30th 2019

[519] Newsbusters "Kimmel: CPAC Is 'Largest Gathering' of Anti-Vaxxers Led by a 'Dementia'-Stricken Trump" (March 5th 2019)

[520] Newsweek "Jimmy Kimmel Suggests Cutting Off Brett Kavanaugh's 'Pesky Penis' if He's Confirmed to Supreme Court" by Janice Williams (September 25th 2018)

[521] Town Hall "Jimmy Kimmel: 'Almost Every Talk Show Host Is Liberal' Because 'It Requires a Certain Level of Intelligence'" by Timothy Meads (February 4th 2018)

[522] Daily Caller "Jimmy Kimmel: Sharing political views 'has cost me commercially'" by Justin Caruso (March 13th 2018)

monologue into an anti-Trump editorial, but his audience enjoys it, even his pathetic Donald Trump impression which should be enough for anyone with any taste in comedy to change the channel.

He plays a big role, however, in politics. Practically all the Democrat candidates running for president in 2020 appeared on his show: Bernie Sanders, Kamala Harris, Julian Castro, Beto O'Rourke, Elizabeth Warren, Corey Booker, etc. CNN admitted that, "Aides for several of the most-talked-about contenders confirmed that they view Colbert as a crucial stop on the presidential roadshow," and one campaign official who spoke off the record said, "We strategize about Stephen a lot."[523]

New York senator Kirsten Gillibrand announced she was running for President in 2020 on his show.[524] She had coordinated with them and then Stephen shamelessly had her on to awkwardly ask if she had anything to announce, and then she revealed the "big" news. Congressman Eric Swalwell also officially announced he was running for president in 2020 on Colbert's show.[525] His campaign soon embarrassingly ended with him begging people on Twitter to donate "just one dollar" in hopes he could stay in a little bit longer.

[523] CNN "Welcome to the Stephen Colbert primary" by Brian Stelter (January 14th 2019)

[524] Vanity Fair "Kirsten Gillibrand Just Announced Her Presidential Bid on The Late Show" by Laura Bradley (January 16th 2019)

[525] Rolling Stone "California Democrat Eric Swalwell Announces 2020 Presidential Run on 'Colbert'" by Ryan Reed (April 8th 2019)

Jimmy Fallon

Poor Jimmy Fallon tried not to become a rabid anti-Trump ranter out of concerns he would ostracize half his viewers, but was reportedly pressured by NBC to stop being so soft on Trump.[526] Industry-wide Fallon was shunned and denounced after his 2016 interview with then-candidate Donald Trump because he didn't use the opportunity to tear into him, and instead had a fun interview like he does with all of his guests.

Trump even famously let Jimmy mess up his hair to prove it was real, but the liberal media was furious and claimed Fallon had "humanized" him.[527] He was shut out of the Emmys that year in what many speculated was retaliation for "helping" Trump.[528] Fallon later apologized for being too friendly and said that people "have a right to be mad."[529]

Despite trying to not have a show tainted with an obvious political agenda like Stephen Colbert and Jimmy Kimmel, Fallon soon bent to the will of his producers and started focusing more on the president and other social justice issues.

---

[526] New York Post "Fallon forced to change 'Tonight Show' amid Colbert ratings wins" by Carlos Greer (March 7th 2017)

[527] Washington Post "Jimmy Fallon says people 'have a right to be mad' at his friendly hair-tousling of Trump" by Travis M. Andrews (May 18th 2017)

[528] Decider.com "Did Donald Trump Cost Jimmy Fallon His Emmy Nomination?" by Joe Reid (July 13th 2017)

[529] Washington Post "Jimmy Fallon says people 'have a right to be mad' at his friendly hair-tousling of Trump" by Travis M. Andrews (May 18th 2017)

He even had anti-gun activist David Hogg and his sister on the show to rail against the NRA and Florida Senator Marco Rubio for not supporting radical anti-gun laws.[530] Fallon had the kids recount their experience during the Parkland school shooting, because what could be a more appropriate topic for a late night comedy show than talking about a mass shooting at a school?

Saturday Night Live

Once a staple of American comedy, *Saturday Night Live* has been on a slow and continuous decline, perhaps in part to an increasing number of options for viewers with the growth of cable TV and more recently streaming services and other online entertainment; but the show's parodies of presidential politics still bring in viewers and the sketches make headlines.

More importantly than that, *Saturday Night Live* has been responsible for significantly altering how tens of millions of people view certain politicians. One critic noted, "The series has also shown a deft ability to define politicians' personas—for better or worse.

For some, Chevy Chase's exaggerated version of President Gerald Ford or Dana Carvey's over-the-top President George H.W. Bush are more familiar than the politicians' actual legacies. And sketches spoofing the likes of Michael Dukakis and Sarah Palin have had a

---

[530] The Hollywood Reporter "Parkland Survivors David Hogg and Lauren Hogg Recall Mass Shooting and Call for Change" by Katherine Schaffstall (June 20th 2018)

much longer shelf life than the real-life versions' political careers."[531]

University of Tennessee professor and blogger Glenn Reynolds admitted, "Personally, I think that Chevy Chase cost Ford the 1976 election. Well, part of it, anyway."[532] Decades later Chase admitted, "[M]y leanings were Democratic and I wanted [Jimmy] Carter in and I wanted [Ford] out, and I figured look, we're reaching millions of people every weekend, why not do it."[533]

During the 2000 presidential campaign Darrell Hammond's character of Al Gore was devastating, accentuating his dull personality to the point that the real Al Gore reminded people of Hammond's character. SNL's portrayal of a George W. Bush vs Al Gore debate showed him repeatedly referring to his "lock box" and haunted Gore for the remainder of the campaign. Will Ferrell's impression of a bumbling George W. Bush is what really launched him to stardom.

In 2008 Tina Fey's portrayal of Sarah Palin stuck like glue and many political analysts credit SNL with permanently tarnishing her image in the minds of millions of voters.[534] While the show and its cast have always leaned Left, once they came down with Trump Derangement Syndrome their sickness began showing its symptoms in their skits.

---

[531] NBC "How 'Saturday Night Live' Has Shaped American Politics" by Adam Howard (September 30th 2016)

[532] PJ Media "'The President's Watching. Let's Make Him Cringe And Squirm.'" by Ed Driscoll (December 26th 2006)

[533] CNN "Chevy Chase: I wanted Carter to win" (November 3rd 2008)

[534] Boston Globe "How Tina Fey destroyed Sarah Palin" by Kevin Lewis (March 3rd 2012)

In 2018 they sung a special rendition of Mariah Carey's "All I want for Christmas Is You" conveying their wishes to have Robert Mueller throw President Trump in prison.[535] And their anti-Trump obsession has caused them to sink so low that they actually endorsed assassinating him.

Cast member Michael Ché began, "Maybe I just don't understand politics well, because when they said Trump was gettin' impeached, I immediately thought, 'Great! Trump's fired! Let's get drunk!' But they're like 'no, he's just being impeached, but he ain't exactly impeached yet, it's still gonna take another year or so.'"[536]

The punchline was, "You know, I'll bet somebody explained how long impeachment took to John Wilkes Booth, and he was like 'Okay, well where's he at right now?'"[537]

Jokes about assassinating a current President, or any President even after they've left office, have always been out of bounds, especially for any show on network television, but *Saturday Night Live* decided to go there.

SNL alumni Norm McDonald has trashed the show's obsessive anti-Trump agenda, such as framing his 2016 election victory as if it was the end of the world. "I was like, what the fuck are we getting through? That a man was duly elected president? What are you, crazy? ...I can get through anything. I got through my own father's

[535] Newsbusters "All 'SNL' Wants for Christmas Is for Mueller to Lock Up Trump, 'Only Other Option Is a Coup'" by Nicholas Fondacaro (December 2nd 2018)

[536] Breitbart "SNL 'Weekend Update': Impeachment Process Was Too Slow for John Wilkes Booth" by David Ng (September 30th 2019)

[537] Ibid.

death. You think I can't get through a man getting elected president of the United States?"[538]

McDonald made it clear that he is certainly no fan of President Trump, but says they're "playing into Trump's hands."[539] He said he doesn't even do political jokes because he hates politics and mostly just watches sports. Pondering how comedy shows have gotten so partisan these days he said, "I wonder when it happened. Maybe with Jon Stewart. But it happened at some point that talk show hosts had to be political pundits."[540]

The Good Old Days

In a 1984 interview with Barbara Walters, late night legend Johnny Carson was asked if there were things in the world that bothered him and caused him to want to use his platform (then host of *The Tonight Show* on NBC) to raise awareness for them. He responded, "I think one of the dangers if you are a comedian, which basically I am, is that if you start to take yourself too seriously and start to comment on social issues, your sense of humor suffers somewhere."[541]

"I've seen other people, whose names I won't mention, who do humor, and then somewhere along the line they start to want to make their views known. I try to do it humorously. Some critics over the years have said

---

[538] The Daily Beast "Norm Macdonald Sounds Off on SNL: 'I Think They're Playing Into Trump's Hands'" by Matt Wilstein (July 27th 2017)

[539] Ibid.

[540] Ibid

[541] Barbara Walters interviews Johnny Carson (1984)

that our show doesn't have great sociological value, it's not controversial, it's not deep," defending the show saying it's just to entertain people and make them laugh.[542]

He was asked a few years earlier by Mike Wallace on *60 Minutes* about why he never gets political. "Do you get sensitive about that fact that people say 'he'll never take a serious controversy?'"[543]

Carson responded, "Well, I have an answer to that. Now tell me that last time that Jack Benny, Red Skelton, any comedian, used his show to do serious issues. That's not what I'm there for. Can't they see that? Why do they think that just because you have a Tonight Show that you should deal in serious issues? That's a danger. That's a real danger. Once you start that, you start to get that self-important feeling that what you say has great import, and strangely enough, you could use that show as a forum, you could sway people, and I don't think you should as an entertainer."[544]

Hate Crime Charges for Jokes?

Although mainstream shows have lost their edge and turned into social justice cesspools, some stand-up comedians are trying to save freedom of speech by carrying on the tradition of George Carlin, Lenny Bruce, and others who stood up for the right to offend people with thin skin, but comedy is under attack by the Thought

---

[542] Ibid.

[543] Rolling Stone "Flashback: '60 Minutes' Profiles Johnny Carson in 1979" by Patrick Toyle (June 23rd 2015)

[544] Ibid.

Police who want people *arrested* for telling jokes. The London *Independent* published a piece titled, "As a comedy aficionado, I'm appalled at disgusting 'jokes' creeping back into the industry" where the columnist complained, "Comedians, crying 'free speech' isn't good enough—hate crime laws should apply to all of us."[545]

She complained about what she called "Alt-Right comedy" naming YouTubers PewDiePie and Sargon of Akkod as supposedly having "persuaded some comedians that there is money to be made from belittling social justice."[546]

The writer then whined about Ricky Gervais' Netflix special *Humanity* where he "deadnamed" Caitlyn Jenner (*liberalspeak* for calling a transgender person by their legal name or birth name), and complained about Dave Chappelle cracking some jokes about transgender people too, saying, "I would go so far as to argue that some of the jokes I have heard on the comedy circuit of late constitute actual hate speech."[547]

Chappelle's 2019 Netflix special *Sticks & Stones* upset a lot of liberals since they have no sense of humor and he kept the edge he once had for his Comedy Central sketch series in the early 2000s. *Vice News* told their moronic readers that "You can definitely skip Dave Chappelle's new Netflix special *Sticks & Stones*" because he "doubles down on misogyny and transphobia."[548] The

---

545 The Independent "As a comedy aficionado, I'm appalled at disgusting 'jokes' creeping back into the industry" by Liam Evans (February 26th 2019)

546 Ibid.

547 Ibid.

548 Vice "You Can Definitely Skip Dave Chappelle's New Netflix Special 'Sticks & Stones'" by Taylor Horsking (August 26th 2019)

critics at Rotten Tomatoes, the popular entertainment rating website, gave it an approval rating of just 35% while the average audience rating is at 99%.[549]

Matt Stone, co-creator of *South Park,* said that the reason so many critics trashed it was because they were afraid to say it was actually funny. "When I read TV reviews or cultural reviews, I think of someone in prison, writing. I think about somebody writing a hostage note. This is not what they think. This is what they have to do to keep their job in a social media world."[550]

Tim Allen has said that today he couldn't do his old act from the '90s because it would be deemed too "sexist" since much of it was about the dynamics between men and women.[551] His hit show *Last Man Standing* was canceled by ABC after he appeared on the Jimmy Kimmel show and joked about how being a conservative in Hollywood these days is like being a Jew in 1930s Germany because of the persecution they face.[552]

ABC claimed it was canceled because the show wasn't performing as well as they wanted, but it was actually the network's second most watched comedy, and the third most watched show on the entire network.[553] It

---

[549] Rotten Tomatoes "Dave Chappelle: Sticks & Stones" Critics Consensus (as of February 2020)

[550] RedState "'South Park' Co-Creator Matt Stone Knows Why Critics Trashed Dave Chappelle's New Special: to 'Keep Their Jobs'" by Alex Parker (September 13th 2019)

[551] Fox News "Tim Allen decries 'thought police,' political correctness in comedy" by Sam Dorman (November 26th 2019)

[552] The Wrap "Did Tim Allen's Nazi Germany Joke Help Kill 'Last Man Standing'?" by Tony Maglio and Ryan Gajewski (May 10th 2017)

[553] Deadline "Tim Allen Comedy 'Last Man Standing' Canceled By ABC After 6 Seasons" by Nellie Andreeva (May 10th 2017)

was later picked up by FOX where it instantly became the highest rated show on its night.[554]

Many European countries have much stricter "hate speech" laws than the United States, and it's a model the Left wants to implement here, starting by amending or repealing the First Amendment to allow criminal charges for people who say things that hurt others feelings or are "divisive" and "not inclusive."[555] Scottish comedian "Count Dankula" was famously arrested *and convicted* for hate speech after he posted a video on YouTube showing that he trained his girlfriend's dog to do a "Nazi salute" as a joke to upset her.[556]

There is no doubt that Leftists would love to have political commentators like me arrested for jokes (or even sarcastic statements) about Black people, illegal aliens, gays, and transgenders. Comedy, which was once seen as the last bastion of free speech, is increasingly coming under attack by intolerant liberals who aim to use the mechanisms of government to silence people if the social media companies won't.

---

[554] Deadline "Friday Ratings: Fox's 'Last Man Standing' Returns To The Top" by Bruce Haring (March 16th 2019)

[555] The Washington Post "America Needs Hate a Speech Law" by Richard Stengel (October 29th 2019)

[556] BBC "Man guilty of hate crime for filming pug's 'Nazi salutes'" (March 20th 2018)

Award Shows

Award shows aren't just for awards. They themselves are elaborate propaganda campaigns whose winners are often chosen, not because of their extraordinary talent, but because certain songs, movies, and TV shows promote agendas the social engineers want to encourage. Movies that fail miserably at the box office are still awarded if the Hollywood elite want to highlight their "powerful" message.

In recent years the award shows have veered further left than most people could imagine, and it's impossible to make it through one now without getting browbeat by nauseating messages about "diversity," anti-White bigotry, and gender bending. For example, the 2018 Emmys began with Kate McKinnon (a lesbian) and Kenan Thompson (a Black man) saying, "Tonight is the celebration of the hard work and the talent of everyone in this room," begins Kate. "That's right," continues Kenan. "We're also celebrating the fact that this year's Emmy Awards has the most diverse group of nominees in Emmy history."

It seemed like they may have been setting up a joke for a second, but they were really being serious. A few more celebrities then came out on stage and literally began to sing a song celebrating the "diversity" of the nominees.

Halfway through their little musical number Ricky Martin entered the stage, saying, "You haven't solved it. This song is way too White!" and then the music changed to salsa music and they all started dancing again. At that point *Saturday Night Live's* Andy Sandberg joined the group and sings, "What about me? Is there any room in this song for a straight White guy like me?"

"You can't be a part of this," he is told.

"Sounds good, have fun you guys," he replies, and then walks off stage. White people should be shunned was the message. Get rid of them.

If you took a drink every time someone said "diversity" during the show you would have died of alcohol poisoning. When Jimmy Kimmel took to the stage to present he began, "We are delighted this year to have such a diverse collection of talented supporting actress nominees."[557]

Another presenter, Emilia Clarke (best known for starring in HBO's *Game of Thrones*), also had to make note of the wonderful "diversity," saying, "Tonight, we are happy to announce that the comedy writing category, once dominated by White male nerds now boasts more female and diverse nerds than ever before."[558]

But there were still too many White people winning awards despite the "diverse" group of nominees that night, so in protest when James Corden was presenting he told the audience at home to get #EmmysSoWhite trending on Twitter, which they did.[559]

---

[557] Jimmy Kimmel and Tracy Morgan present Outstanding Supporting Actress in a Comedy Series at 2018 Emmys

[558] Orange Country Register "Emmys 2018: Here's how diversity in Hollywood was handled on the awards show" by Angela Ratzlaff (September 17th 2018)

[559] Boston Herald "Focus on Hollywood's diversity at Emmy Awards" by Mark Perigard (September 18th 2018)

And we can't have an award show these days without it including a celebration of drag queens, so RuPaul was given the Emmy for his cross-dressing competition, *RuPaul's Drag Race*.[560]

The Golden Globes are basically the Oscars and Emmys combined, meaning both movies and television shows are given awards. The event is put on by the Hollywood Foreign Press Association which is an organization consisting of foreign media outlets and reporters who cover American entertainment outside the United States.

It's the typical superficial award show with celebrities who think they can save the world by giving a shout out to various causes, but once Donald Trump became president it was obligatory for at least one of the winners to denounce him while accepting their award. Meryl Streep was the first at the 2017 Golden Globes, held just two months after the 2016 election, where she gave an overly dramatic speech about how he's ruining the country for immigrants.[561]

The following year feminism was the theme of the night with host Seth Meyers beginning the show by saying, "People in this room worked really hard to get here, but it's clearer now than ever before that the women had to work even harder. So thank you for all the amazing work that you've all done, and you continue to

---

560 Hollywood Reporter "Emmys: 'RuPaul's Drag Race' Wins Best Reality Competition Program" by Allison Crist (September 17th 2018)

561 Washington Post "Meryl Streep called out Donald Trump at the Golden Globes. He responded by calling her 'over-rated.'" by Elahe Izadi and Amy B Wang (January 9th 2017)

do. I look forward to you leading us into whatever comes next. So thank you so much for letting me say that."[562]

His cucking didn't stop there. After his monologue he expressed concerns that the first presenters were going to be two White men. "Now to present our first awards, please don't be two White dudes, please don't be two White dudes. Oh, thank God! It's Gal Gadot and Dwayne Johnson everybody."[563]

The very first award of the night went to a man named Ramy Youssef who won Best Actor in a Comedy Series. As soon as he took the stage he said, "Look, I know you guys haven't seen my show," and then the entire audience laughed. "Everyone's like 'is this an editor?'" he continued.[564] He was only half joking because nobody there, and hardly anyone watching at home, knew who he was.

His show *Ramy* streamed on Hulu and was a comedy about a Muslim family from Egypt who had just moved to New Jersey. He was given the Golden Globe as a form of affirmative action to demonstrate how "woke" Hollywood is by celebrating a Muslim comedy, not because it was the funniest show, but simply for the sake of "diversity," and he knew it.

When Jessica Chastain announced the winner for Best Actress that year, she began sarcastically, "I'm so happy to announce that the winner of this category will also

---

[562] Yahoo "Golden Globes 2018: The 5 most memorable lines from Seth Meyers's monologue" by Ethan Alter (January 7th 2018)

[563] New York Times "Seth Meyers's Golden Globes Opening Monologue: Transcript" by Giovanni Russonello (January 7th 2018)

[564] Entertainment Tonight "Ramy Youssef Jokes 'I Know You Guys Haven't Seen My Show' After First Golden Globe Win" by Myeisha Essex (January 5th 2020)

receive the 23 percent of her salary that went missing in the wage gap." Chris Hemsworth, who stood there alongside her virtue signaling, added, "It's true. That's correct."[565]

When presenting the nominees for Best Actor, Geena Davis also made a sarcastic comment about the supposed wage gap, saying, "These five nominees have agreed to give half of their salary back, so that the women could make more than them."[566] But the White male bashing didn't end there. When Natalie Portman announced the winner for Best Director, she went off script, saying "And here are the *all-male* nominees," clearly upset that no women were nominated that year because of "sexism."[567]

At the end of the night Oprah Winfrey was given the Cecil B. de Mille Award for her "contributions" to the entertainment industry, where she gave a tearful acceptance speech causing liberals to become ecstatic and filled with hope that she would run for president in 2020 against Donald Trump.

NBC's official Twitter account even tweeted a picture of her and said, "Nothing but respect for OUR future

[565] Esquire "The Best, Worst, and Most Empowering Moments of the 2018 Golden Globes" by Jake Kring-Schreifels (January 8th 2018)

[566] Hollywood Reporter "Golden Globes: 'Thelma & Louise' Stars Susan Sarandon, Geena Davis Reunite Onstage" by Meena Jang (January 7th 2018)

[567] USA Today "Natalie Portman savages the Golden Globes' 'all-male nominees' for best director" by Maeve McDermott (January 7th 2018)

president."[568]   *The New Yorker* ran the headline, "Oprah Leads a Decisive Feminist Takeover."[569]

At the 2020 Golden Globes, Ellen DeGeneres was given an "Award for Excellence" for all she has done to advance the LGBT agenda.[570] The dinner which takes place before the show was an all vegan meal that year to help "raise awareness about climate change."[571] When Joaquin Phoenix won the Best Actor award for his performance in *Joker,* he began his acceptance speech thanking the Hollywood Foreign Press for "recognizing and acknowledging the link between animal agriculture and climate change." Adding, "It's a very bold move making tonight plant-based and it really sends a powerful message," referencing the vegan dinner.[572]

While Sacha Baron Cohen was presenting he took the opportunity to rip into Mark Zuckerberg for not cracking down on free speech enough on Facebook, sarcastically describing him as a "naive misguided child who spreads

[568] Entertainment Weekly "NBC apologizes for tweet calling Oprah 'our future president'" by David Canfield (January 8th 2018)

[569] The New Yorker "The 2018 Golden Globes: Oprah Leads a Decisive Feminist Takeover" by Michael Schulman (January 8th 2018)

[570] Los Angeles Times "Ellen DeGeneres accepts Carol Burnett Award at Golden Globes" by Greg Braxton (January 5th 2020)

[571] NBC News "Golden Globes will serve plant-based meal at awards ceremony to raise environmental awareness" via Associated Press (January 3rd 2020)

[572] Variety "Joaquin Phoenix Made the Golden Globes Go Vegan" by Meg Zukin and Ramin Setoodeh (January 5th 2020)

Nazi propaganda."[573] Just two months earlier Cohen gave a speech to the Jewish ADL where he aggressively called for the major social media companies to increase censorship, claiming that they're still allowing people to post "hate speech."[574]

Then during her acceptance speech for Best Actress in a Limited Series, Michelle Williams (who was visibly pregnant), admitted she once killed her other baby in an abortion and was glad that she did because if she had the kid it would have prevented her from becoming a successful actress.[575] The audience cheered her "bravery" for admitting what she had done.

The Biggest Night in Hollywood

The "biggest night in Hollywood" is the Academy Awards where the Oscars are handed out, and for many years celebrities have spewed political nonsense—often about saving the environment or some issue in a third world country, but in the Trump-era, everything is about Trump.

At the 2017 Oscars, held just one month after President Trump's inauguration, host Jimmy Kimmel called him a racist and insinuated that the entire world

---

573 Business Insider "Sacha Baron Cohen satirically described Facebook CEO Mark Zuckerberg as a 'naive, misguided child who spreads Nazi propaganda'" by Isobel Asher Hamilton (January 6th 2020)

574 Washington Post "'Your product is defective': Sacha Baron Cohen slams Facebook for allowing hate speech" by Katie Shepherd (November 22nd 2019)

575 Hollywood Reporter "Michelle Williams Delivers Empowering Acceptance Speech on Women's Rights at Golden Globes" by Katherine Schaffstall (January 5th 2020)

now hates America. "I want to say thank you to President Trump," he said sarcastically. "I mean, remember last year when it seemed like the Oscars were racist?" referring to the "Oscars so White" controversy.[576]

In 2018 *Call Me by Your Name* was nominated for "Best Picture" which is based on the true story of a 24-year-old man seducing a 17-year-old boy. Hollywood calls that a great "love story."[577]

As the Oscars kicked off that year host Jimmy Kimmel gave a shoutout to the actor who played the boy, Timothee Chalamet, saying he is "the star of a small but powerful story, *Call Me By Your Name,* which did not make a lot of money, in fact, of the nine best picture nominees, only two of them made more than 100 million dollars. But that's not the point. We don't make films like *Call Me By Your Name* for money. We make them to upset Mike Pence."[578] (Vice President Mike Pence is a devoted Christian who doesn't support same sex "marriage.")

Then came more White guilt as Black films, Black actors, and Black writers were touted as being the best. At one point Jimmy Kimmel mentioned that the new Black power film *Black Panther* wouldn't be included in that year's awards because it just came out, and then expressed his disappointment that there aren't more Black superheroes.

---

[576] New York Times "Jimmy Kimmel's Oscars Opening Monologue" by Giovanni Russonello (February 26th 2017)

[577] Tampa Bay Times "Coming-of-age love story 'Call Me By Your Name' is a rare treasure" by Steve Persall (January 11th 2018)

[578] The Hill "Kimmel: We make films like 'Call Me By Your Name' to upset Mike Pence" by Morgan Gstalter (March 4th 2018)

"It's weird that so many superheroes are White because that's what they were in the comics, right? People say, 'Well Superman is White. He's always been White. You know what else Superman has been? Not real!'"[579] Apparently it's racist now that Superman is always White in the movies, because he's White in the comics!

Then two Black women (Tiffany Haddish and Maya Rudolph) came out to present and Maya began, "We are so happy to be here, but a little nervous too, because a few years ago people were saying that the Oscars were so White, and since then some real progress has been made."[580]

Tiffany Haddish, who has a voice scratchier than Axl Rose then chimed in, agreeing. "Mmhmm. When we came out together we know some of you were thinking, 'are the Oscars too Black now?'"

Maya Rudolph replies, "Don't worry. There's so many more White people to come tonight."

"Mhhhmmm. So many! We just came from backstage and there are tons of them back there! And not just movie stars. There are White people walking about with headsets. White people with clipboards. I'm personally not a fan of White people with clip boards because I'm always wondering 'what are they writing down about me?'"[581] The message was clear. There were still too many White people around, despite the recent strides in "diversity."

---

[579] Jimmy Kimmel at 2018 Oscars

[580] Slate "Tiffany Haddish and Maya Rudolph Reassure America That The Oscars Are Still Pretty White" by Rachel Withers (March 4th 2018)

[581] Ibid.

Best documentary that year went to *Icarus*, a movie about the Russian doping scandal at the Olympics to fan the flames of the hysteria at the time about Russia supposedly helping Donald Trump win the 2016 election. Then there was more pro-immigration propaganda.

Lupita Nyong'o (who is from Kenya) and Kumail Nanjiani (who is from Pakistan) presented an award, but not before saying they're not just actors, they're also immigrants, "and like everyone in this room and everyone watching at home, we are dreamers. We grew up dreaming of one day working in the movies. Dreams are the foundation of Hollywood, and dreams are the foundation of America...To all the Dreamers out there, we stand with you," they said, to a resounding applause, referring to the millions of illegal immigrants Barack Obama granted amnesty to with his "Dream Act" executive order. "Now the nominees for achievement in production design."[582]

Rapper Common and singer Andra Day performed their social justice anthem "Stand Up for Something" with Common beginning, "We put up monuments for the feminists. Tell the NRA they're in God's way... Sentiments of love for the people from Africa, Haiti, and Puerto Rico."[583]

Later while Andra Day sung, Common continued injecting his two cents with statements like, "We stand up for the Dreamers. We stand up for immigrants." The

---

[582] ABC News "Lupita Nyong'o, Kumail Nanjiani at the Oscars: 'To all the Dreamers ... we stand with you'" by Emily Shapiro (March 4th 2018)

[583] Vibe "Oscars 2018: Andra Day and Common Celebrate Unsung Heroes During 'Stand Up For Something' Performance" by Christine Imarenzor (March 4th 2018)

eight-year-old Syrian refugee, Bana al-Abed, who (supposedly) began tweeting photos of civil war-torn Syria in 2016, was brought on stage during their performance.[584] Of course eight-year-olds don't tweet, but the girl was used as a propaganda tool to promote U.S. intervention in the country by making her a symbol of the civil war there, but that's a whole other story.[585]

Planned Parenthood CEO Cecile Richards was also on stage, along with a total of ten social justice activists invited up there during the performance because they all "Stand Up for Something."[586]

Mexican film maker Guillermo del Toro won the Academy Award for Best Picture that year for *The Shape of Water*, a movie about a woman who falls in love with a fish-man (and literally gets naked and has sex with it). Probably Hollywood's way of taking baby steps on the path to giving an Oscar to a film about bestiality.

Guillermo del Toro also won for Best Director and when he took to the stage he began, "I am an immigrant like, like my compadres, Alfonso and Alejandro, like Gael [García Bernaland] Salma [Hayek], and like many of you. And in the last 25 years, I've been living in a country all of our own. Part of it is here. Part of it is in Europe. Part of it is everywhere, because I think the greatest thing the

---

[584] Washington Post "Syrian refugee girl gets star treatment at the Oscars" by Christina Barron (March 5th 2018)

[585] NBC News "Aleppo Twitter Star Bana al-Abed Asks Trump to 'Save' Syria's Children" by Mark Hanrahan and Ammar Cheikh Omar (January 25th 2017)

[586] Variety "Here Are the 10 Activists Who Shared the Oscars Stage With Common and Andra Day" by Shirley Halperin (March 4th 2018)

industry does is erase the line in the sand," [meaning borders].[587]

The 2019 Oscars were just more of the same. At the beginning of the show Maya Rudolph announced, "Just a quick update for everybody in case you're confused. There is no host tonight. There won't be a popular movie category, and Mexico is not paying for the wall."[588] Kevin Hart had originally been scheduled to host, but he was canceled after snowflakes dug up some of his past jokes and tweets about not wanting his son to be gay, so like many others, he became a victim of the "cancel culture."[589]

Black Panther was nominated for "Best Picture" simply because it was the first Black superhero movie. Spike Lee won the Academy Award that year for Best Adapted Screenplay for *BlacKkKlansman*, and during his acceptance speech said that the 2020 election is "just around the corner" and told everyone to "mobilize" and "do the right thing" by voting Donald Trump out of office.[590]

Within just a few minutes of the 2020 Academy Awards show starting, Chris Rock was complaining that not enough Black people were nominated, but the show certainly made up for it that year with presenters. At one point a guy came on stage to announce, "The Academy

[587] USA Today "Mexico had great night at the Oscars. President Trump still tweeted smear" by Maria Puente (March 5th 2018)

[588] The Hill "Maya Rudolph hits Trump at Oscars: 'Mexico is not paying for the wall'" by Judy Kurtz (February 24th 2019)

[589] Washington Post "Trending: Kevin Hart is out as Oscars host" by Briana R. Ellison (December 9th 2018)

[590] Hollywood Reporter "Oscars: Read Spike Lee's Powerful Political Acceptance Speech" by Jasmyne Bell (February 24th 2019)

would like to acknowledge that tonight we have gathered on the ancestral lands of the Tongva, the Tataviam and the Chumash" [Native American tribes] to apologize for White people "stealing" their land.[591]

To kick off the show, singer/rapper Janelle Monae changed the lyrics in one line of her song to say "It's time to come alive, cuz the Oscars, it's so White," marking the sixth year in a row the "Oscars so White" complaint was made.[592] No amount of "diversity" could make them happy.

Hair Love won Best Short film for a 7-minute-long animation about a Black father learning to do his daughter's hair. Usually the winner for this category isn't included in the show, but because the film celebrated Black people and their "hair" the producers made a special exception this year.

When accepting the award the director encouraged people to support the Crown Act, which was pending legislation that would ban employers and schools from "discriminating" against people for their hairstyles, for example, if a business didn't want their employees to wear dreadlocks, or have an afro that sticks out two feet.[593]

A Netflix show called *American Factory* that Barack and Michelle Obama's production company made won

---

[591] The Hill "The Oscars acknowledged the indigenous land Hollywood sits on" by Anagha Srikanth (February 10th 2020)

[592] Newsweek "Janelle Monae's Oscars Performance Channels Mr. Rogers, Calls Out Lack of Diversity in Opening Number" by Samuel Spencer (February 10th 2020)

[593] Washington Post "Oscar-winning 'Hair Love' director calls attention to efforts to ban race-based hair discrimination" by Jenna McGregor (February 10th 2020)

the Oscar for best documentary in 2020, and when accepting the award, the director quoted straight from the Communist Manifesto, saying "workers of the world unite."[594]

When Joaquin Phoenix won the Oscar for Best Actor in *Joker* he rattled off as many social justice buzzwords as he could, saying, "Whether we're talking about gender inequality or racism or queer rights or indigenous rights or animal rights, we're talking about the fight against injustice," and then went on to complain about cow rights and people using milk in our cereal and coffee in the morning.[595]

After the Black Lives Matter riots of 2020 caused a surge of Black supremacist sentiments to spread across the country and endless virtue signaling by corporations and schools about how they were going to work much harder to "support the Black community," the Oscars announced that they were changing the criteria for films to be considered for the awards, adding a "diversity requirement."[596]

So now it doesn't matter how good a film is, if there isn't a Black person, a Latino, or a queer as part of the main plot, then it may get passed over in favor of another film with more "diversity."

---

[594] New York Post "Karl Marx gets shoutout during Barack Obama-produced film's 2020 Oscars speech" by Tamar Lapin (February 9th 2020)

[595] The Hill "Joaquin Phoenix makes impassioned plea for animal rights in Oscars speech" by Judy Kurtz (February 9th 2020)

[596] The New York Times "The Oscars Will Add a Diversity Requirement for Eligibility" by Nicole Sperling (June 12th 2020)

The Grammys

The Grammys used to be mostly just about the music, but now the event browbeats the audience about how there are too many White people in the United States and endlessly praises LGBT people for being "amazing." The Grammys have even openly celebrated Satanism.

In 2014, Katy Perry performed her song "Dark Horse" in a ceremony that depicted her as a witch and made headlines across the country from people saying the performance looked like a satanic ritual.[597] She did it as a collaboration with a group called Three Six Mafia—get it —three sixes "666"—the "Satanic Mafia." A few years earlier in 2012 Nicki Minaj had done a similar "satanic ritual" for her performance of her song "Roman Holiday."[598] (A "Roman holiday" means to get pleasure from someone else's pain or misfortune.)

The Grammys is supposed to be a celebration of music, but they can't make it through a show without expressing their love for the LGBT agenda. Katy Perry performed her lesbian-themed single "I Kissed a Girl" in 2009 shortly after she burst onto the music scene thanks to that song. A few years later Lady Gaga performed her "gay rights" anthem "Born This Way" during the show.[599] And now every year there are shout-outs to the "LGBT community" and how "awesome" they are.

---

[597] Christianity Today "Katy Perry satanic performance of 'Dark Horse' at Grammys called demonic glorification by Glenn Beck" by Serena McGill (January 29th 2014)

[598] Wall Street Journal "Nicki Minaj Defends 'Roman Holiday' Grammy Performance" by Lyneka Little (February 4th 2012)

[599] MTV "Lady Gaga Emerges from Egg to Perform 'Born this Way' at the Grammys (Jocelyn Vena (February 13th 2011)

In 2014 Macklemore & Ryan Lewis won a Grammy for Best New Artist and Best Rap Album as a reward for producing a "gay rights" anthem called "Same Love" which promoted gay "marriage."[600] When they performed at the Grammys that year thirty-three gay couples were married on stage as part of the show.[601] At the time, gay "marriage" still wasn't legal in all fifty states, and the issue was awaiting a ruling by the Supreme Court.

That same year Irish musician Hozier's debut single "Take Me To Church" was nominated for Song of the Year because it denounced Christianity, particularly the Catholic Church's views on homosexuality. The music video for the song was a gay anthem depicting two homosexuals being persecuted by an angry mob. It was made for just $500 and posted to YouTube when the band was still virtually unheard of, but music executives in Hollywood discovered the video and turned Hozier into a star that year because they wanted a new "gay rights" anthem to promote.

To kick off the 2017 Grammys, Jennifer Lopez said it was a really tough time in our nation's history since it was just a few weeks after Donald Trump was inaugurated as president. Sounding like she was about to breakdown and cry she said, "It is about the music, the words, and the voices. How they move us and inspire us and touch all of

---

[600] New York Times "Stars Align for Gay Marriage Anthem" by James McKinnley Jr. (June 30th 2013)

[601] The Hollywood Reporter "Grammys: Macklemore and Madonna Perform 'Same Love' As 33 Couples Wed Live on Air" by Debbie Emery (January 26th 2014)

our lives. At this particular point in history our voices are needed more than ever."[602]

There was no question what "point in history" she was talking about. Hollywood and the talking heads in the news media were still in shock that Hillary had lost. James Corden even performed a rap song at the start of the show which included lyrics about his fear of what Donald Trump was going to do to the country.[603]

Busta Rhymes later trashed President Trump on stage, calling him "President Agent Orange." He was joined by another group "A Tribe Called Quest" who made their entrance to the stage by breaking through a wall constructed of foam blocks. At one point Busta said that President Trump was "perpetuating evil" throughout the United States.[604]

The following year the Grammys were hosted by James Corden who began the show saying "This year, we don't just have the most diverse group of nominees in Grammys history, we also have, for the second year in a row, the least diverse host in Grammys history," referring to himself being a straight, White male, with blonde hair and blue eyes.[605]

---

[602] W Magazine "2017 Grammys: Jennifer Lopez Made a Moving Political Statement at the Award Ceremony" by Lynsey Eidell (February 12th 2017)

[603] Hollywood Reporter "Grammys: Read the Lyrics of James Corden's Opening Rap Number" by Lexy Perez (February 12th 2017)

[604] The Hollywood Reporter "Grammys: Busta Rhymes Refers to Trump as 'President Agent Orange' During A Tribe Called Quest Performance" by Ryan Parker (February 12th 2017)

[605] People Magazine "James Corden Jokes in Opening Monologue About Being the 'Least Diverse Host in Grammys History'" by Jeff Nelson (January 28th 2018)

Then rapper Kendrick Lamar got on stage and performed an anti-cop, pro-Black Lives Matter song. Halfway through his performance the lights dimmed and the camera cut to Dave Chappelle, who said, "I just wanted to remind the audience that the only thing more frightening than watching a Black man being honest in America, is *being* an honest Black man in America."[606]

Later Hillary Clinton made an appearance via a video which showed her reading the anti-Trump book *Fire and Fury* that was all the rage at the time.[607] The following year in 2019, they brought Michelle Obama on stage during the opening segment to talk about how much music means to her and how it keeps her going in tough times.[608]

Childish Gambino won the award for Song of the Year and Album of the Year for his racist, anti-White, anti-police diatribe "This is America," marking the first time that a rapper had won both awards.[609] When the nominees were announced a month or so earlier, he and other rappers complained that there weren't enough Black artists being nominated, so it looks like the Recording Academy tried to make it up to him by crowning him the night's big winner.

---

[606] Mediaite "Dave Chappelle Interrupts Kendrick Lamar's Grammy Performance With Joke About Race in America" by Rachel Dicker (January 28th 2018)

[607] Politico "Hillary Clinton reads from 'Fire and Fury' at Grammys" by Brent D. Griffiths (January 28th 2018)

[608] Vanity Fair "Michelle Obama Made a Surprise Visit to the 2019 Grammys" by Erin Vanderhoof (February 11th 2019)

[609] Billboard "Childish Gambino's 'This Is America' Becomes First Rap Song to Win Record of the Year Grammy" by Tatiana Cirisano (February 11th 2019)

At the 2020 Grammys, host Alicia Keys started the show playing a piano melody while doing a spoken word performance mentioning the various artists who were nominated and tossed in a line celebrating President Trump getting impeached.[610]

Broadway theater performer Billy Porter then took to the stage (dressed like a woman) and introduced the Jonas Brothers who performed a song, but not without first giving a wink and a nod to the "gender fluid" and "gender non-conforming" people. "Ladies, gentlemen, and those who have yet to make up their minds…" he said, before introducing the group.[611] Singer John Legend also gave a non-verbal shout-out to the gender "non-binary" people by wearing a "dress/suit."

Ellen DeGeneres introduced a performance by "country rapper" Lil Nas X, and after mentioning some of his accolades added, "And he's done it all by being true to himself. Unwavering in the face of prejudice, he told the world that he was gay, and overnight he became an inspiration and a role model for millions of young people around the world."[612]

Michelle Obama was then given a Grammy for "Best Spoken Word Album" for the audio book version of her

610 Newsweek "Alicia Keys References Trump's Impeachment, Tells President to 'Get Out' and Cardi B to Enter Politics at Grammys" by Christian Zhao (January 26th 2020)

611 MRCtv.org "Billy Porter 'Ladies and Gentleman and Those Who Have Yet To Make Up Their Minds'" by Rachel Peterson (January 27th 2020)

612 Hollywood Reporter "An Epic Performance and 2 Wins: Lil Nas X's Big Night at the Grammys" by Evan Real (January 26th 2020)

memoir *Becoming*.[613] There was also a performance by a Spanish singer who goes by the name of "Rosalia" who sung a few songs in Spanish to pander to the tens of millions of non-assimilating Mexicans and other Latinos who have invaded the United States.

The American Music Awards and the Billboard Music Awards are just more of the same. Taylor Swift even "broke her political silence" at the 2018 AMAs to encourage her fans to vote Democrat in the upcoming midterm elections.[614] For her entire career she stayed out of politics completely, but the pressure was building for her to denounce the Trump administration, so she eventually did.

MTV Awards

The most degenerate of award shows can be found on MTV. Their annual Movie Awards and VMAs (Video Music Awards) are geared for kids, which makes them even more disturbing. The only time anyone really tunes in to MTV anymore is for these award shows once a year since music videos are all released on YouTube now, and it's been a decades-long running joke that MTV (which stands for Music Television) doesn't play any music anymore because the network mostly consists of teen dramas.

---

[613] Hollywood Reporter "Grammys: Michelle Obama Wins Best Spoken Word Album for 'Becoming'" by Katie Kilkenny (January 26th 2020)

[614] ABC News "Taylor Swift breaks her political silence, endorses Democrats in passionate post on midterm elections" by Deena Zaru (October 8th 2018)

MTV's VMAs gave birth to Miley Cyrus with her 2013 performance where she introduced "twerking" to the world, a form of "dance" she popularized which simply consists of shaking one's butt in a rapid motion, although that's just the beginning of MTV's degeneracy.

They have unique awards compared to other shows, for things like the Best Villain and Best Fight, and even the Best Kiss. And in 2017, the Best Kiss award went to two men for a "gay coming-of-age" film called *Moonlight*.[615]

The following year in 2018, it was given to two men again, one of them (Keiynan Lonsdale) identifying as a "pansexual" (meaning someone who will have sex with a person of any gender, including trans people). Their movie was another teenage gay "romantic comedy" called *Love, Simon*. While accepting his "Best Kiss" award the pansexual told the audience, "You can live your dreams and wear dresses."[616]

In 2017 the MTV Movie Awards announced it was going to be a "genderless" award ceremony, meaning they weren't giving different awards for best actor or best actress because that was "sexist" and "divisive." They boasted that it was the first "gender-neutral" awards show in history.[617] To emphasize their idiotic idea, the first presenter of the evening was a real life "gender non-binary" person named Asia Kate Dillon who nobody has

---

[615] Time "*Moonlight* Stars Dedicate MTV Best Kiss Award to 'Those Who Feel Like the Misfits'" by Megan McCluskey (May 8th 2017)

[616] MTV "Love, Simon's Keiynan Lonsdale Accepts Best Kiss Award with a Magical Speech" by Crytal Bell (June 18th 2018)

[617] Variety "The MTV Movie & TV Awards: A New Gender Revolution?" by Owen Gleiberman (May 7th 2017)

ever heard of. Her "preferred pronouns" are "they" and "them," and of course she has a shaved head.

The Wikipedia entry for Asia Kate Dillon reads, "Dillon was born in Ithaca, New York. *They* were assigned female at birth, but identifies as non-binary. Dillon explained around 2015, *they* began removing gendered pronouns from *their* biography, and auditioning for the part of Mason helped *them* understand *their* gender identity. Dillon identifies as pansexual, stating *they* are attracted to multiple genders."[618]

It's confusing because using the pronoun "they" to refer to one person is usually grammatically incorrect, but even the Merriam Webster dictionary has caved in to the craziness and recently updated the "rules" for grammar to accommodate gender non-binary or non-conforming people and their "preferred pronouns."[619]

Emma Watson won the first award that night for the live-action remake of *Beauty and the Beast* and made sure to start off her acceptance speech by praising how great of an idea it was to go "genderless," saying, "Firstly, I feel I have to say something about the award itself. The first acting award in history that doesn't separate nominees based on their sex says something about how we perceive the human experience. MTV's move to create a genderless award for acting will mean something different to everyone, but to me, it indicates that acting is about the ability to put yourself in someone else's shoes. And that

[618] https://en.wikipedia.org/wiki/Asia_Kate_Dillon

[619] Time "'Social Forces Change Language.' Merriam-Webster Adds Gender-Neutral Pronouns to Dictionary" by Suyin Haynes (September 17th 2019)

doesn't need to be separated into two different categories."[620]

This was all part of the show. She was just reciting the script that MTV's producers had given her to emphasize the "historic" genderless theme of the night. Everything in Hollywood is fake, even the award shows.

When Vin Diesel was given the Generation Award, he made sure to go along with the social justice agenda and said the only reason that the *Fast & Furious* series was a success is because the younger generation is accepting of multiculturalism. "Most importantly, I got to thank a generation that was willing to accept this multicultural franchise where it didn't matter what color your skin was or what country you were from, when you're family, you're family."[621]

Multiculturalism had nothing to do with the franchises' success. It's an action movie series about *cars*, and a lot of people love car movies, and the chase scenes and action sequences are amazing, but the Hollywood elite never miss an opportunity to sing praises of their precious "diversity."

In 2018, rapper "Logic" wore a t-shirt that said "F*ck the Wall" and dozens of Mexican immigrants were brought out on stage during his performance who had shirts on that read "We Are All Human Beings."[622] The previous year a "descendent" of Robert E. Lee, the

[620] Washington Post "Emma Watson takes first major gender-neutral movie award" by Travis M. Andrews (May 8th 2017)

[621] Entertainment Weekly "Vin Diesel pays tribute to Paul Walker as *Fast & Furious* wins MTV Generation Award" by Derek Lawrence (May 7th 2017)

[622] Variety "VMAs 2018: Logic Wears 'F— the Wall' Shirt in Bold Statement on Immigration" by Rachel Yang (August 20th 2018)

Confederate Army general, was brought on stage to denounce racism. "We have made my ancestor an idol of White supremacy, racism, and hate," he began. "As a pastor, it is my moral duty to speak out against racism, America's original sin."[623] The man was the great-great-great-great (four "greats") nephew of Robert E. Lee.

He went on to tell the audience, "Today, I call on all us with privilege and power to answer God's call to confront racism and White supremacy head on. We can find inspiration in the Black Lives Matter movement, the women who marched in the Women's March in January, and especially Heather Heyer, who died fighting for her beliefs in Charlottesville."[624]

Then Heather Heyer's mother was brought on stage, whose daughter was killed during the infamous 2017 Unite the Right rally in Charlottesville, to announce the winner of the "Best Fight Against the System" award. All the nominees had music videos denouncing racism, anti-immigrant sentiments, and promoted "diversity."

While opening the show in 2019, Taylor Swift had the words "Equality Act" projected on the stage in giant letters under a rainbow.[625] The Equality Act is a proposed bill by Democrats that would amend the Civil Rights Act and mandate someone's gender identity be legally recognized no matter which one of the 58 different

[623] The Daily Beast "MTV VMAs Unite Heather Heyer's Mom and Robert E. Lee's Descendant Against Racism" by Matt Wilstein (August 28th 2017)

[624] Ibid.

[625] The Hollywood Reporter "Taylor Swift Promotes Equality Act During 2019 VMAs Performance" by Katherine Schaffstall (August 26th 2019)

"genders" they claim to be.[626]   It would also severely restrict the religious freedom of individuals and groups who don't accept the positions of LGBT extremists. The following year the Supreme Court ruled on similar legislation, declaring that business owners can't fire employees for being gay or transgender, nor refuse to hire them.[627]

---

[626] Forbes "What Is The Equality Act And What Will Happen If It Becomes A Law?" by Eric Bachman (May 30th 2019)

[627] The Hill "Workers can't be fired for being gay or transgender, Supreme Court rules" by Harper Neidig (June 15th 2020)

Feminism

The Left has a saying that "representation matters," which means the more on-screen depictions of certain kinds of characters, lifestyles, and behaviors, the more the general public warms up to accepting those kinds of things in real life. And part of paving the path to what they hope will be a woman President of the United States someday involves producing a variety of shows focusing on a female character who holds that position.

In the years preceding Hillary Clinton's long-expected attempt at a presidential bid there were almost a dozen television shows that had a woman president as the central part of the plot. Geena Davis starred in *Commander in Chief*, a short-lived series from 2005 to 2006 where she was originally the Vice President, but then had to takeover after the president died of a brain aneurysm. In FOX's thriller *24*, the show had a female president for two seasons in 2008-2010. Julia Louis-Dreyfus ascended to the presidency in her series *Veep* after the president resigned, leaving her in charge. And that was just the beginning.

State of Affairs, which aired for just one season on NBC, depicted a Black woman as the president, and CBS's political drama *Madam Secretary* revolved around a female Secretary of State (obviously modeled after Hillary Clinton), and at the end of the fifth season the character decided to run for President and won. The following season (which was its last) the series focused on the new female president but kept the name *Madam Secretary.*

But Hollywood's feminist propaganda goes far beyond hoping to normalize the idea of a woman president. Liberals are obsessed with uprooting the traditional gender roles of men as providers and protectors, and women as nurturers and caretakers. They are determined to "empower women" at any cost and embrace the disastrous effects on family dynamics and society as a whole that their radical agenda is causing.

"The future is female" is their mantra, showing they have no concern for equality, but instead have a thirst for power and want to dominate instead of cooperate. They despise traditional families and gender roles, and are on a mission to undermine the very foundational relationships of human society.

To feminists, being a stay at home mom is slavery. Women cooking for their family is "oppression" under the Patriarchy, and men are all scumbags; but having unprotected sex with an endless line of them while avoiding any committed long-term relationships is the ideal life. That's what Hollywood wants women to believe.

Their latest plan to promote "women empowerment" is hijacking popular franchises and then completely changing the major characters and turning good old-fashioned action films into social justice warrior propaganda. Not just swapping male characters for females, or adding strong female leads, but by also portraying men as inept and incompetent losers who always need to be rescued from their own stupidity.

When the *Star Wars* series was revised in 2015 with *The Force Awakens*, it diverted from the usual storyline featuring male leads (Luke Skywalker in the original trilogy and Anakin Skywalker in the prequels) to a totally new character invented by JJ. Abrams named Rey, a female loner.

A female Yoda-type of creature named Maz first starts teaching Rey about the force once she happens to discover Luke Skywalker's old lightsaber lying around. And throughout the film Rey keeps proving to everyone that a girl can do amazing things like pilot a ship, and even fix one with her ingenuity, saving the Millennium Falcon from exploding. After there was an electrical overload and Han Solo didn't know what to do, Rey saved the day. For extra diversity the new *Star Wars* teased a possible interracial romance between Rey and Finn (the Black former stormtrooper).[628]

In the next film, *Star Wars: The Last Jedi* (2017), all women are in charge of the Resistance (the good guys), giving the orders to subservient and bumbling men. The tension keeps building between Poe Dameron and Vice Admiral Holdo (his superior) with them butting heads numerous times and Poe facing repeated snarky comments from her. *The Last Jedi* was hailed as "the most triumphantly feminist Star Wars movie yet," because of this odd storyline.[629] And critics hailed it for "awakening the feminist force in little girls everywhere."[630]

---

[628] Digital Spy "How Star Wars: Episode VIII could break Hollywood's final taboo" by Al Horner (December 23rd 2015)

[629] The Guardian "A Force for good: why the Last Jedi is the most triumphantly feminist Star Wars movie yet" by Anna Smith (December 18th 2017)

[630] The Guardian "Star Wars is a game-changer, awakening the feminist force in little girls everywhere" (December 29th 2015)

At one point Poe and the other men take over the ship at gunpoint, tired of the perceived inability of the women to lead the mission. They committed mutiny only to later learn that Vice Admiral Holdo had a great plan but they just didn't know it, and now Poe had put everyone at risk. The women save everyone though, and he's sorry for ever doubting them.

Even the *Star Wars* spinoff *Rogue One* starred a woman. NBC News noted that, "Not only is *Rogue One* continuing *The Force Awakens* trend of putting a young woman in the center of the action, but it appears to provide prominent roles for African-American, Latino and Asian actors as well—a relatively new development in the Star Wars universe."[631] They loved the "diversity."

George Lucas, the creator of *Star Wars*, sold the rights to Disney in 2012 and later said he felt "betrayed" after the entertainment giant decided to "go in another direction" from his original ideas.[632] He once referred to the films as his "kids" and said that he regretfully sold them into slavery.[633]

In 2015, a new installment of *Mad Max* was released titled *Mad Max: Fury Road*, but instead of starring Mad Max it starred Charlize Therone's character "Imerator Furiosa." It was declared the "feminist picture of the year."[634] And instead of Max being a hero like the

[631] NBC News "'Rogue One: A Star Wars Story' Diversity a Selling Point" by Adam Howard (August 13th 2016)

[632] NME "George Lucas 'felt betrayed' by Disney's plans for 'Star Wars' sequel trilogy" by Sam Moore (September 24th 2019)

[633] Business Insider "George Lucas says he sold 'Star Wars' to 'white slavers'" by Jason Guerrasio (December 31st 2015)

[634] New York Post "Why 'Mad Max: Fury Road' is the feminist picture of the year" by Kyle Smith (May 14th 2015)

previous films, he was depicted as an idiot who had to be repeatedly rescued by women.

In Disney-Pixar's animated *Incredibles 2*, a "superhero mom" named Elastigirl (Mrs. Incredible) is chosen for a secret mission over her husband, who led the superhero family in the first film, because he has the tendency to cause unnecessary "collateral damage" and the superhero organization felt they needed to change the image of superheroes in the public's mind. She then leaves her husband at home to watch the kids while she takes off on her mission. When she calls to check on how things are going, the husband is depicted as being in over his head and not able to handle taking care of the kids and running the house.

The London *Guardian* called the film a "feminist triumph."[635] *Bustle*, an online women's magazine, wrote, "In a time when conversations about representation are more prevalent than ever, showing the diversification of familial roles is definitely fitting. Though not entirely out of the ordinary, seeing a father—especially one as domineering as Mr. Incredible—taking on more of a domestic role will definitely serve as a comedic relief for some, but will also, hopefully, contribute to larger conversations surrounding familial structures and their many forms."[636]

Their glowing review continued, "The responsibilities of family life should be divvied up amongst its members, and gender shouldn't play a determining factor in who takes on whichever task. In this way, *The Incredibles 2* is

---

[635] The Guardian "How Incredibles 2 goes to work for the feminist superhero" by Anna Smith (June 28th 2018)

[636] Bustle "'Incredibles 2' Has A Feminist Message That Couldn't Be More Timely" by Ashley Rey (June 6th 2018)

adding some much-needed perspective to conversations surrounding family dynamics and female empowerment. But, though extremely relevant and important to discuss today, true progressiveness will be measured once conversations about strong female leads and diverse familial structures are no longer needed."[637]

Birds of Prey is a spin-off from *Suicide Squad*, a film based on DC Comics' characters, focusing on Harley Quinn (played by Margot Robbie) who just broke up with her boyfriend the Joker and must survive as a supervillain in Gotham City with no man to protect her.

Some critics called the character's portrayal in *Suicide Squad* sexist and misogynistic, so for the spin-off producers decided to atone for their "sins" by making *Birds of Prey* a hyper-feminist film where all of the bad guys aren't just criminal masterminds, but misogynists who treat women poorly and deserve to be punished.[638]

Ewan McGregor, who plays the crime lord Black Mask, said, "What interested me with *Birds of Prey* is that it's a feminist film. It is very finely written. There is in the script a real look on misogyny, and I think we need that. We need to be more aware of how we behave with the opposite sex. We need to be taught to change. Misogynists in movies are often extreme: they rape, they beat women ... and it is legitimate to represent people like that, because they exist and they are obviously the worst. But in the *Birds of Prey* dialogues, there is always a hint of everyday misogyny, of those things you say as a man

---

[637] Ibid.

[638] Metro UK "Bird Of Prey's Ewan McGregor is proud to be part of the 'feminist film that tackled misogyny'" by Zara Woodcock (January 30th 2020)

you do not even realize, mansplaining ... and it's in the script in a very subtle way. I found that brilliant."[639]

Salon.com raved, "Harley Quinn is back to take down the patriarchy, and this revolution brings scrunchies."[640] Another critic loved that it was about "women's emancipation," because the character proved she could be a supervillain on her own without a boyfriend.[641]

Like most "woke" movies, the film bombed its opening weekend, so the producers changed the title to *Harley Quinn: Birds of Prey*, hoping to spark people's interest because the character had become a breakout star from *Suicide Squad*. The film was still a huge loss for the studio, but Hollywood can't take a hint. They'll keep making feminist propaganda pieces and have their favorite critics try to sell them to viewers no matter how much they suck and how poor they perform at the box office.

Gender Swaps

In 2016 a new *Ghostbusters* film was released, but instead of starring Bill Murray and the gang it featured four women as the Ghostbusters. At the end of the movie the girls shoot the giant evil ghost in the crotch with their proton packs to finally destroy him. Actress Leslie Jones, who was one of the Ghostbusters, quit Twitter and said she cried because she was getting "harassed" by people

[639] CinemaBlend.com "Ewan Mcgregor Calls Birds Of Prey A 'Feminist Film'" by Corey Chichizola (October 10th 2019)

[640] Salon.com "'Birds of Prey' is a fantabulous, feminist grenade" by Mary Elizabeth Williams (February 8th 2020)

[641] Digital Spy "Birds of Prety does feminism in a way Endgame never could" by Gabriella Geisinger (June 2nd 2020)

who hated the film.[642] It completely bombed at the box office and cost the studio an estimated $125 million dollars in losses.[643]

A few years later when it was announced that a new *Ghostbusters* was in the works that would continue the original series and "hand the movie back to the fans," the director Jason Reitman was called a "sexist" because that meant it wouldn't be another feminist empowerment film.[644]

In the 2019 film *Terminator: Dark Fate*, John Connor, the future leader of the "Resistance" against the machines, is killed in the first few minutes, making all of the previous films completely pointless since the primary mission was to ensure that he lives so he can grow up to lead the war against the machines. Then Sarah Connor, along with the help of another "good" time-traveling Terminator (who is an "enhanced" cyborg woman) help another girl evade a new advanced "bad" Terminator which is on a mission to kill *her* before *she* becomes a threat to the machines in the future.

"If you're at all enlightened, she'll play like gangbusters," director Tim Miller said, speaking of the "good" female cyborg. "If you're a closet misogynist, she'll scare the fuck out of you, because she's tough and strong but very feminine. We did not trade certain gender

---

[642] ABC News "'Ghostbusters' Star Leslie Jones Quits Twitter After Online Harassment" by Luchina Fisher and Brian McBride (June 20th 2016)

[643] Forbes "'Ghostbusters' Brand Crosses The (Revenue) Streams For Halloween" by Simon Thompson (July 17th 2019)

[644] Fox News "'Ghostbusters' reboot director faces sexism accusations for saying he's handing the film 'back to the fans'" by Joseph A. Wulfsohn (February 21st 2019)

traits for others; she's just very strong, and that frightens some dudes. You can see online the responses to some of the early shit that's out there, trolls on the internet. I don't give a fuck."[645] The film bombed, reportedly losing 100 million dollars,[646] and the *Hollywood Reporter* said the studio had no future plans for any other Terminator movies.[647]

Ocean's Eleven was a popular heist film that originally starred the Rat Pack in 1960 and was remade in 2001 featuring an ensemble cast led by George Clooney. The reboot, which did very well, was followed up with two sequels, (*Ocean's Twelve*, and *Ocean's Thirteen*) but then in 2018 the gender swap mania infected the franchise and *Ocean's 8* was released, re-envisioning the professional burglars as a group of all women, led by Sandra Bullock.

As I'm sure you expected, the film bombed, and the actresses blamed bad reviews on men of course, saying they were due to a "lack of diversity" among the critics.[648]

In 2019, a crime drama called *The Kitchen* was released as an all-woman gangster film starring Melissa McCarthy because someone thought it would be a good idea to make such a ridiculous movie. It wasn't even a

---

645 IndieWire "Tim Miller Says 'Terminator: Dark Fate' Will 'Scare the F*ck' Out of Misogynistic Internet Trolls" by Zack Sharf (July 10th 2019)

646 Variety "Box Office Bomb: 'Terminator: Dark Fate' Could Lose Over $100 Million" by Rebecca Rubin (November 3rd 2019)

647 Hollywood Reporter "'Terminator: Dark Fate' Puts Franchise on Ice, Faces $120M-Plus Loss" by Pamela McClintock (November 3rd 2019)

648 IndieWire "Sandra Bullock and Cate Blanchett Second Brie Larson in Championing More Diversity Among Film Critics" by Jenna Marotta (June 15th 2018)

comedy, which made it even more absurd. The title refers to Hell's Kitchen, a neighborhood on the West Side of Midtown Manhattan where the women "gangsters" live. The plot revolves around them collecting protection money from local businesses and running the neighborhood as part of the Irish mafia. It was a complete bomb and lost the studio tens of millions of dollars which should come as no surprise.[649]

Disney announced they were going to reboot the 1990s *Doogie Howser M.D.* series about a teenage genius who becomes a doctor which originally starred Neil Patrick Harris, but the remake will star a 16-year-old girl as the child doctor.[650] Disney is also producing an all-female version of *Pirates of the Caribbean* that will star Margot Robbie.[651]

Steven Spielberg said that his iconic character Indiana Jones should take "a different form" and be played by a woman named "Indiana Joan."[652] Vin Diesel even said that an all-female version of *Fast & Furious* was in the works.[653]

---

[649] Deadline "'Hobbs' Hauls $25M; 'Scary Stories' Frighten 'Dora'; 'Kitchen' Sinks Melissa McCarthy & Tiffany Haddish To Career B.O. Lows – Sunday Final" by Anthony D'Alessandro (August 11th 2019)

[650] Hollywood Reporter "'Doogie Howser' Reboot in the Works at Disney+" by Rick Porter (April 8th 2020)

[651] Entertainment Weekly "Margot Robbie set to star in new Pirates of the Caribbean movie" by Nick Romano (June 26th 2020)

[652] The Sun "INDIANA JOANS - Ready Player One director Steven Spielberg says it's time for a woman to play Indiana Jones" (by Grant Rollins (April 3rd 2018)

[653] Entertainment Weekly "Vin Diesel says a female Fast & Furious spin-off is coming, so here are some we'd love to see" by Derek Lawrence (January 24th 2019)

In 2017 when the film *Dunkirk* was released, which depicts the historic Dunkirk evacuation during World War II when Allied soldiers pulled out of the Dunkirk harbor in France, liberals were upset that the film didn't gender-swap some characters to make it more "diverse."[654] Of course that wouldn't have been historically accurate, or made any sense because women were not on the battlefield, but that didn't stop the snowflakes from complaining about the soldiers being all men.

The Institute on Gender in Media

In 2004 actress Geena Davis started a non-profit research organization to study "gender representation" in media. The "Institute" on Gender in Media is obsessed with monitoring the number of women vs men in TV shows and movies and tracking what percentage of them have speaking roles and how many of them have power.

Their website says, "we're the only organization working collaboratively within the entertainment industry to engage, educate and influence the creation of gender balanced onscreen portrayals, reducing harmful stereotypes and creating an abundance of unique and intersectional female characters in entertainment targeting children 11 and under."[655]

Another pointless project the "Institute on Gender in Media" has been working on is a computer program that checks scripts for "gender bias" language to make sure they're "inclusive." Not only does the software scan

---

[654] Washington Times "'Dunkirk' review in USA Today warns 'no lead actors of color' in WWII-inspired film" by Douglas Ernst (July 19th 2017)

[655] https://seejane.org/about-us/

scripts for words and phrases like *fireman*, *postman*, and *mankind*; but it also produces a report on the percentage of characters who are "people of color" and even LGBTQ so the writers and producers can make sure their projects are "diverse" enough.[656]

Television Commercials Turn Feminist

For many years feminists have been upset about the way cleaning products are marketed, so recently there are an increasing number of commercials for laundry detergent, vacuums, and mops depicting men using the products. Creating "gender equality" in commercials for cleaning products has even been called "the final feminist frontier."[657]

Some companies are even promoting feminism in their commercials even when their products have nothing to do with gender at all. For example, some morons in the marketing department at Anheuser-Busch thought it would be a good idea for Bud Light to promote the supposed "wage gap" in an incredibly unfunny ad featuring Amy Schumer and Seth Rogan. It begins with Schumer saying, "Bud Light party here, to discuss equal pay."

Seth Rogen goes on to complain that "Women don't get paid as much as men and that is wrong!"

The two banter back and forth about women supposedly having to pay more for cars, dry cleaning and

---

[656] Hollywood Reporter "Geena Davis Unveils Partnership With Disney to 'Spellcheck' Scripts for Gender Bias (by Patrick Brzeski (October 10th 2019)

[657] The New Republic "Cleaning: The Final Feminist Frontier" by Jessica Grose (March 18th 2013)

shampoo, but "Bud Light proudly supports equal pay. That's why Bud Light costs the same, no matter if you're a dude or a lady," explains Schumer.

Forbes magazine called the commercial "unusual" and the writer wondered, "So why did Bud Light choose to make what might be the first civil-rights-inflected beer ad...Are they targeting Hillary voters? Are they simultaneously making fun of 'equal pay' claims by subverting the meaning of the term to be about a non-problem—what men and women pay for beer? Or are they trying to thread the needle with comedy to speak to both audiences?"[658]

Their beer sales soon declined, and they pulled the ad.[659] When journalists started inquiring about the company's own business practices regarding "equal pay" they declined to reveal how many women work for the company or how their salaries compare to those of their male counterparts.[660] Bud Light even took the video off YouTube trying to distance themselves from the mess they created.

In 2018 Burger King launched an ad campaign to "raise awareness" about "gender inequality." Using a hidden camera in one of their restaurants they served what they called "Chick Fries" (which were just thin chicken strips or "chicken fries") to customers, but when women ordered them, they were served the chicken strips in a pink box and were told they had been charged a few

---

[658] Forbes "What Amy Schumer And Bud Light Have To Say About Marketplace Inequality" by Ian Ayres (August 15th 2016)

[659] New York Post "Bud Light abruptly pulls Amy Schumer, Seth Rogen ads" via Fox News (November 1st 2016)

[660] CNBC "The big problem with Bud Light's new commercial" by Sarah Whitten (June 30th 2016)

dollars more than men "for the pink box."[661]

When some of them got upset and started arguing with the cashier (who was an actor) about how they shouldn't have to pay more just because the box is pink for women, the cashier began lecturing them about how women's razors supposedly cost more than men's "just because they're pink" and asked them why they didn't complain about that too. Why not just promote their chicken fries and say they taste great and are on sale you may be wondering? That's what a normal person would do, but we're talking about people who have become infected with the liberal pathogen.

The Audi car company aired a Super Bowl commercial showing a group of kids racing in a pine box derby, while focusing on the only girl in the group. As the race begins her dad is the narrator, musing aloud wondering how he was going to teach her about sexism. "What do I tell my daughter? Do I tell her grandpa is worth more than her grandma? That her dad is worth more than her mom? Do I tell her that despite her education, her drive, her skills, her intelligence, she will automatically be valued as less than every man she meets?"[662]

She then wins the race, beating the boys, and it concludes with him saying, "Or maybe I'll be able to tell her something different," and then the words "Audi of America is committed to equal pay for equal work," and "Progress is for everyone," are shown on the screen.[663]

---

[661] ABC News "Burger King raises awareness of the pink tax with 'Chick Fries' that cost $1.40 more" (July 28th 2018)

[662] Wall Street Journal "Audi's Super Bowl Ad on Gender Pay Gap Faces Criticism" by Alexandra Bruell (February 2nd 2017)

[663] Ibid.

The "Secret" women's deodorant brand aired a Super Bowl-themed commercial showing a kicker kick the winning field goal at the end of a game and then when "he" takes off "his" helmet the crowd realizes it was a woman and goes silent, but after a moment of surprise they begin cheering even more and then the catchphrase "Let's Kick Inequality" is shown on the screen.[664]

Companies often use their big Super Bowl commercials to really promote the liberal agenda instead of their product. The "Unstereotype Alliance" campaign launched by the United Nations notes, "Advertising is a particularly powerful driver to change perceptions and impact social norms," and says they are "excited to partner with the foremost industry shapers in this Alliance to challenge and advance the ways women are represented in this field."[665]   It's impossible to escape liberal propaganda, even when viewing commercials for cars and deodorant!

Jared jewelers even released a commercial encouraging women to propose to their boyfriends with the tagline "Dare to ask him."[666] One ad shows a woman drop down on one knee holding the ring, and then as she slides the ring on his finger the camera cuts to their friends seated at a nearby dinner table all celebrating his acceptance, having witnessed her pop the question.

---

[664] Men's Health "Secret Deodorant's Super Bowl Ad Contains a Powerful Message About Gender Equality" by Philip Ellis (January 31st 2020)

[665] UnstereotypeAlliance.org "About the Unstereotype Alliance"

[666] The Federalist "In Flight of Idiocy, Diamond Ad Tells Women to Propose to Men (by David Marcus (November 19th 2018)

Fat is "Beautiful"

No fat jokes (or "fat shaming" as they're called now) are allowed anymore, because they're considered "bullying" and "hate speech" so liberals have been promoting "body positivity" which is a more politically correct term for the "fat acceptance movement" in which morbidly obese women are said to be "beautiful" by those who pity them.

Despite becoming obese later in her career, Amy Schumer was reportedly in talks to play Barbie in a live-action film based on the doll—in what some people thought was a joke, but it turned out to be true.[667] She was then pulled from the project, probably due to the ridicule she was receiving or after producers realized the movie would be a complete flop because of their idiotic idea.[668]

Lena Dunham is another token fat ugly girl in Hollywood who is always promoted as a feminist icon.[669] Dunham has posted pictures on her Instagram over the years celebrating her weight gain, once posting a before-and-after photo showing her of average weight in the past next to a current photo of her 24-pounds heavier (weighing in at 162 pounds).[670] The post got almost 500,000 likes from people who were proud of her for being happy that she was obese. A year later she posted a

---

[667] US Weekly "Amy Schumer Is Reportedly in Talks to Star in Live-Action Barbie Movie" by Stephanie Webber (December 2nd 2016)

[668] Variety "Amy Schumer Drops Out of 'Barbie' Movie" by Justin Kroll (March 23rd 2017)

[669] Time Magazine's 2013 List of Most Influential People

[670] Breitbart "Lena Dunham Celebrates Gaining 24 Pounds" by Ben Kew (July 11th 2018)

picture of her lying in bed wearing lingerie, noting that "I weigh the most I ever have," and saying she's the "happiest I've ever been."[671]

By accepting obesity as "normal" and banning criticism of obesity as "fat shaming" people are only contributing to the problem. It would be like claiming you were "bullying" people by declaring opioid use is dangerous and something that should be shunned and avoided.

Singer Lizzo, best known for being the 300 pound Black girl who likes bouncing around on stage during her performances, was hailed as "brave" and "beautiful" after she posted a semi-nude photo of herself on Instagram.[672] During the coronavirus pandemic of 2020 she posted a picture of herself wearing a face mask and matching bikini, and one tabloid reported that it was a balance of "safety with sex appeal."[673]

Hollywood's new affinity for fat women is causing some older TV shows and movies to come under scrutiny. As part of the storyline in *Friends*, Monica (Courtney Cox) was depicted as severely obese when she was younger, but then ended up losing a bunch of weight and became hot. In flashbacks, Courtney would wear a fat suit and a prosthetic chin playing her old self, but now *Entertainment Weekly* calls "Fat Monica" the "ghost that continues to haunt *Friends* 25 years later," and complains

[671] Breitbart "Lena Dunham Posts Lingerie Photo to Celebrate Weighing 'The Most I Ever Have'" by Justin Caruso (February 27th 2019)

[672] ET Online "Lizzo Poses Fully Nude in Racy Instagram Photos and Video" by Paige Gawley (December 2nd 2019)

[673] Page Six "Lizzo's bikini and matching face mask balance safety with sex appeal" by Elana Fishman (May 25th 2020)

that the show used her to get "cheap laughs in the laziest ways possible."[674]

Shallow Hal and *The Nutty Professor* have since been deemed the most "fat-phobic" movies of all time for their use of fat suits.[675] It probably won't be long now until the practice of actors wearing fat suits for comedic effect will be banned industry wide, and the those kinds of characters will be deemed just as offensive as someone wearing "blackface" which used to be a staple of comedy with people like Jimmy Kimmel, Jimmy Fallon, Howard Stern, Dan Aykroyd, Robert Downey Jr. and many others once doing skits as a Black person.

Most have recently apologized for what were actually hilarious characters after old clips circulated on Twitter with people denouncing them for being "racist."

Feminists even got upset when Pixar's *Wall-E* came out, which depicts a dystopian future where the earth is evacuated because it has turned into a trash heap from all the garbage humans were creating. The online outlet *Slate* was upset that the movie "goes out of its way to equate obesity with environmental collapse."[676] They complained, "It plays off the easy analogy between obesity and ecological catastrophe, pushing the notion that Western culture has sickened both our bodies and our planet with the same disease of affluence. According to

---

[674] Entertainment Weekly "'Fat Monica' is the ghost that continues to haunt *Friends* 25 years later" by Clarkisha Kent (September 4th 2019)

[675] The Revelist "The 8 most fat-phobic movies in Hollywood, ranked by awfulness" by Lauren Gordon (October 3rd 2016)

[676] Slate "Fat-E: The new Pixar movie goes out of its way to equate obesity with environmental collapse" by Daniel Engber (July 10th 2008)

this lazy logic, a fat body stands in for a distended culture: We gain weight and the Earth suffers."[677]

The London *Telegraph* noted that fat pride groups, "believe the film propagates anti-obesity hysteria comparable with the quest for the perfect body by the eugenics movement in Nazi Germany."[678] Yep, *Wall-E* is Nazi propaganda to these lunatics!

Since the Left is so concerned with "global warming" and people's "carbon footprint," you'd think they would start calling out fat people for using triple or quadruple the natural resources as the average person, but that would hurt people's feelings—so instead they're trying to convince trendy social justice warriors to eat bugs because the cow farts from beef-producing cattle are supposedly destroying the planet.[679]

In 2019, Victoria's Secret hired a plus-size model named Ali Tate-Cutler in order to be "more inclusive."[680] And what a surprise—later that year they canceled their annual fashion show, citing declining sales and ratings! That same year they had also celebrated hiring their first transgender model in the name of "diversity" so it's no wonder the Victoria's Secret brand had become less appealing to so many people.[681]

---

[677] Ibid.

[678] The Telegraph "WALL-E's 'fattist' satire angers fat pride groups" by Tim Shipman and Rowena Mason (July 12th 2008)

[679] CNN "The food that can feed, and maybe save, the planet: Bugs" by Sandee LaMotte (October 25th 2019)

[680] USA Today "Victoria's Secret just got its first plus-sized model: 'It felt surreal'" by Rasha Ali (October 8th 2019)

[681] The New York Times "Victoria's Secret Casts First Openly Transgender Woman as a Model" by Christine Hauser (August 5th 2019)

The move came after lunatics on Twitter kept complaining they were "discriminating" against transgender people by having only (actual) women as models.[682]

Abercrombie & Fitch also decided to be "more inclusive" by distancing themselves from their well-established brand of flawless models in their catalogs and have now embraced the "body positivity" movement by using "plus-sized" (fat) models and LGBTQ people in their ads.[683]

The *Sports Illustrated Swimsuit Edition* has also featured a "plus size" (fat) model on the cover recently, but she doesn't attribute her success to the fat acceptance movement. She believes it's because of White privilege! "I know I'm on this pedestal because of White privilege," she says. "To not see Black or Latina women as famous in my industry [meaning the plus size model industry] is crazy! I have to talk about it. I want to give those women kudos because they are the ones who paved the way for me," she said.[684]

The glass is always half empty with social justice warriors. Even when things are good, they're not good enough, and when a fat woman has a successful modeling

---

[682] Los Angeles Times "Valentina Sampaio makes history as first transgender Victoria's Secret model" by Christi Carras (August 5th 2019)

[683] New York Post "Abercrombie tries to redeem its body-shaming past with inclusive ad campaign" by Melkorka Licea (February 6th 2020)

[684] The Cut "Now, This Is a Supermodel. Ashley Graham isn't a sample size. Which is exactly why she's become the face of a movement" by Jada Yuan (August 6th 2017)

career she can't be happy about that either, because she's worried that her success is due to "White privilege."

There are also calls for the NFL to start using plus-sized cheerleaders, and the league is under fire from feminists because the cheerleaders must abide by various strict rules, including maintaining their "ideal weight." There are even calls to ban cheerleaders altogether because it's "demeaning to women."[685]

In 2016 toy maker Mattel released a "curvy" Barbie to celebrate "body diversity." An executive at the company said, "These new dolls (are) more reflective of the world girls see around them—the variety in body type, skin tones and style allows girls to find a doll that speaks to them."[686]

Sofie Hagen, a fat "comedian" who got triggered by billboards warning about the link between obesity and cancer, is also hoping Disney will soon feature a princess in one of their cartoons who is fat. She tweeted, "I cannot stress how much we need a fat Disney princess. We need it now. Shut up. We fucking do."[687] (No, she's not joking, and on a side note, she blocked me on Twitter for laughing at her).

Feminists are often fat, ugly, angry women, as you know, so the AMC television network aired a dark comedy series called *Dietland* where a morbidly obese woman fed up with "society's beauty standards" decides to start killing men who contribute to the "objectification of women," like fashion photographers. It was basically a

---

[685] USA Today "NFL cheerleading is demeaning to women. It's time to end this nonsense" by Tom Krattenmaker (August 9th 2018)

[686] New York Daily News "Mattel remakes Barbie dolls to include a curvy body type" by Nicole Lyn Pesce (January 28th 2016)

[687] https://twitter.com/sofiehagen/status/903706367646687232

fat chick revenge fantasy. Only in Hollywood would someone come up with the idea of the protagonist being a fat woman who kills people who hurt her feelings!

The Four Waves

Feminism is like an old tool that has outlived its usefulness, but instead of discarding it and appreciating what it accomplished during the time it was needed, feminists have continued trying to "advance" the movement in our modern era.

Feminism has gone through four different phases, or waves as they're called, since its first incarnation in the early 1900s when women banded together to demand the right to vote (women's suffrage). In the 1960s and 70s the second wave rose up to fight against the lack of women in political positions, and they were very successful in popularizing birth control pills and legalizing abortion, but for some power-hungry feminists there was more work to be done to dismantle "the Patriarchy."

They continued pushing forward in the 1990s (the third wave) where they worked to get more women into leadership positions in the government and corporations, often simultaneously complaining about men continuing to "objectify women" while doing everything they could to artificially boost their sex appeal and use it to their advantage in every possible situation.

Then came the fourth wave of feminism which is completely unrecognizable from the first two waves which actually had a legitimate purpose and goals. Around 2012, not coincidentally coinciding with social media becoming a fixture of most peoples' lives, the fourth wave of feminism hit the Internet like a tsunami of insanity. Through social media, crazies from across the country were able to connect with each other and affirm one another's bizarre ideas about their abnormal lifestyles and celebrate their mental illnesses. They now come up with new "causes" to fight for online like "free-bleeding" (not wearing tampons or pads during their period) in order to "raise awareness" for periods (as if we're not already painfully aware of them), and "smashing the scale" (celebrating obesity).

The most radical feminists (the ones with blue or purple hair) eventually turn into cat ladies. Single, childless, alone, and filled with regret and hate. As their looks fade, so does their ability to attract new mates, thus leading them to the inevitable downward spiral of despair which is then used as fuel to reaffirm their beliefs that men have ruined the world and their lives.

The LGBT Agenda

Gays are only approximately one or maybe one and a half percent of the population.[688] But because of the bombardment of LGBT propaganda, many Americans falsely believe ten or even *twenty percent* of people are homosexual.[689] And liberals want everyone to think that there is no more of a difference between someone who is straight or gay than there is between someone who is left-handed or right-handed.

Homosexuality used to be officially classified as a mental illness by the American Psychiatric Association until 1973 when they gave in to intense pressure by LGBT groups and had it removed from their Diagnostic and Statistical Manual (DSM).[690] Now they just call it a "sexual orientation."

Gays used to deny there was a "gay agenda" and claimed that they weren't *promoting* homosexuality; all they wanted was to not be "attacked" or "discriminated against"—but those claims, like almost everything that

---

[688] The Atlantic "Americans Have No Idea How Few Gay People There Are" by Garance Franke-Ruta May 31st 2012)

[689] Gallup "Americans Still Greatly Overestimate U.S. Gay Population" by Justin McCarthy (June 27th 2019)

[690] Psychology Today "When Homosexuality Stopped Being a Mental Disorder" by Neel Burton (September 18th 2015)

comes out of liberals' mouths, turned out to be a massive lie.

Today it's not even about LGBT "rights" to them, it's about LGBT *privilege*. They get *extra* rights. They're *special*. And any criticism about their behavior or lifestyle is deemed "hate speech" and "harassment" no matter how mild or reasonable. These days anyone who doesn't celebrate them is considered an enemy. You must put them on a pedestal and marvel at their "awesome" sexuality, or you're a Nazi!

The reason gays and transgenders went from being widely viewed as strange, to being "privileged" and "special" people over the course of a single generation is the result of a massive propaganda campaign the likes of which the world had never seen.

In 1987 *Gay Community News*, a popular LGBT publication at the time, admitted the "gay revolution" would require the use of entertainment in order to be achieved, saying, "We shall sodomize your songs, emblems of your feeble masculinity, of your shallow dreams and vulgar lies. We shall seduce them [children] in your schools...in your youth groups, in your movie theater bathrooms...wherever men are men together. Your sons will become our minions and do our bidding. They will be recast in our image. They will come to crave and adore us."[691]

In 1989 two gay activists published a book titled *After the Ball: How America Will Conquer its Fear and Hatred of Gays in the 90s* which detailed their goals to have Hollywood produce propaganda that portrayed gays as "victims of circumstance and oppression, not as

---

[691] Gay Community News "Gay Revolutionary" by Michael Swift (February 15th 1987)

aggressive challengers." Their idea was that, "Gays must be portrayed as victims in need of protection so that straights will be inclined by reflex, to assume the role of protector."[692]

Their plan worked perfectly, as Joe Biden admitted when giving a speech for Jewish American Heritage Month, where he said, "It wasn't anything we legislatively did. It was 'Will and Grace,' it was the social media. Literally. That's what changed peoples' attitudes. That's why I was so certain that the vast majority of people would embrace and rapidly embrace [gay marriage]. Think behind all that, I bet you 85 percent of those changes, whether it's in Hollywood or social media are a consequence of Jewish leaders in the industry. The influence is immense, the influence is immense."[693]

All gays wanted was to be able to get "married" they said, but within just a few short years after the Supreme Court ruling made it legal nationwide (in 2015) we saw the proliferation of dozens of different "genders," pre-teen child drag queens and "Drag Queen Story Hour" events popping up at public libraries across the country. In numerous cases the drag queens who were reading books to children at the events have been found to be convicted pedophiles.[694] What a surprise!

---

692 *After the Ball: How America Will Conquer its Fear and Hatred of Gays in the 90s* by Marshall Kirk and Hunter Madsen (1989 Doubleday)

693 Washington Post "Biden: Jewish leaders helped gay marriage succeed" by Rachel Weiner (May 22nd 2013)

694 Newsweek "Sex Offender Busted as Drag Queen Who Read Books To Children in City Library" by Scott McDonald (March 16th 2019)

An LGBT website called *Pink News* ran a headline titled, "Republican Lawmakers Want to Make Child Drag Shows Illegal," expressing their anger that a U.S. Representative proposed a bill that would prohibit anyone under the age of eighteen from participating in drag shows.[695]

And now LGBT activists harass Christian owned businesses like Chick-Fil-A for not supporting gay "marriage."[696] I put gay "marriage" in quotes when referring to gay "marriage" because a marriage is between a man and a woman—I don't care what the Supreme Court says, and I refuse to acknowledge it. Chick-Fil-A restaurants have been banned from opening in airports and on college campuses, and new locations often face boycotts wherever they are. How much longer until the LGBT extremists start trying to run churches out of town and harass parishioners as they come to worship on Sundays?

Ellen DeGeneres, the Trailblazer

Ellen DeGeneres is considered a pioneer in the television industry for normalizing gay people after her sitcom *Ellen* decided to depict her character as a lesbian when she came out in real life in 1997. *Will and Grace* then picked up the baton in 1998 with a sitcom about a woman (Debra Messing) and her gay roommate. "Will and Grace was the first time you saw characters on television that made gay normal, you wanted to be friends

---

[695] Pink News "Republican Lawmakers Want to Make Child Drag Shows Illegal" by PinkNews Staff Writer (April 22nd 2019)

[696] New York Times "Chick-fil-A Thrust Back Into Spotlight on Gay Rights" by Kim Severson (July 25th 2012)

with them," said Lance Bass from the boy band NSYNC.[697]

Sean Hayes, the actor who played Will's boyfriend on *Will and Grace,* said, "The best feeling I get is when people come up and say thank you for all you do for the gay community and thank you for playing that part and that show and you feel so fortunate to have been part of something so great."[698]

Since then, the world has been flooded with countless shows and movies where homosexuality is at the center of the plot. Films like *Brokeback Mountain* (2005) about two gay cowboys; *Milk* (2008) about Harvey Milk, the first openly gay politician to be elected to public office; *Call Me by Your Name* (2017) about an adult male who falls in "love" with a teenage boy; and many others which have been made for the sole purpose of promoting "gay rights" no matter how little success they'll have commercially.

But that's not enough. They want gays and transgenders in every TV show and movie. In 2018, a transgender "woman" was included in the Miss Universe Pageant, a move, as you expect by now, was praised as a "historic first."[699] Two years later *Sports Illustrated* included a transgender "woman" in their famous swimsuit edition.[700] And throughout this chapter you'll see they're

---

[697] In CNN's "The Nineties" miniseries in episode 1 "The One About TV Part 2"

[698] Ibid.

[699] NBC News "In a first, transgender woman competes in Miss Universe competition" by Tim Frizsimons (December 17th 2018)

[700] CNN "Valentina Sampaio becomes Sports Illustrated's first trans model" by Kiely Westhoff (July 13th 2020)

trying to "gay up" everything from Star Wars to Sesame Street.

When producers of the HBO vampire series *True Blood* decided they wanted to depict a character as bisexual and have him do soft-core porn sex scenes with other men (since it's HBO and shows regularly include nudity), the actor Luke Grimes, who played the character, quit the show.[701] He was immediately denounced by the media and his castmates as "homophobic."[702]

NBC launched a sitcom in the Spring of 2019 called *Abby's* about a bisexual woman who runs a bar—a move that was celebrated as the first sitcom on network television to feature a bisexual as the lead character. For extra diversity she is also a Cuban-American, and the show was promoted as a "multicultural comedy."[703] It was canceled after just one season.

Congresswoman Alexandria Ocasio-Cortez was recently a guest host on *RuPaul's Drag Race*, a reality show where drag queens compete to see who is the "best." When the drag queens thanked her for being so "brave" for standing up against Republicans, she responded by lavishing praise on them for being on the forefront of changing the culture and the laws. "People think Congress and government is all about leading people, but ultimately, a lot of our politics is about following the public will. And the people who change the

[701] BuzzFeed "Luke Grimes Left 'True Blood' Because He Refused To Play Gay" by Louis Peitzman (June 25th 2015)

[702] New York Daily News "'True Blood' star Nelsan Ellis on Luke Grimes quitting show because he didn't want to play gay: 'I'm over him'" by Kirthana Ramisetti (July 24th 2014)

[703] NBC News "'Abby's,' 2nd network sitcom with a bisexual lead, premieres" by Gwen Aviles (March 28th 2019)

way people think are artists and drag queens."[704]   She went on to call the contestants "patriots" and gushed about how proud she was of them.

Gay Superheroes

In 2011 Marvel released *Captain America: The First Avenger* which was a huge success, and when a sequel was released in 2014 (*Captain America: Winter Soldier*), many liberals were upset that Captain America and his best friend Bucky weren't in a gay relationship together. *Vanity Fair* gave the film great reviews, but said it had one "flaw," writing, "So while Marvel was likely never going to make the homoerotic subtext of Cap and Bucky into text, would it really have hurt to keep their relationship more ambiguous?"[705]

It went on, "As if to put the nail in the coffin of speculation, Bucky and Cap paused for a moment in the middle of snowy Siberia to reminisce about their days chasing skirts in pre-War Brooklyn. It's a sweet, human bonding moment but one that also bristles with heterosexual virility. If Disney isn't inclined to give audiences a gay superhero, couldn't they have at least left us the dream of Bucky and Cap?"[706]

The critic was literally upset they reminisced about chasing women in the previous film, which normal guys do, but LGBT extremists were projecting their own

[704] Washington Examiner "AOC backs drag queen 'patriots' to 'push society forward'" by Spencer Neale (April 11th 2020)

[705] Vanity Fair "Is this the one flaw in the otherwise great Captain America: Civil War?" by Joanna Robinson (May 9th 2016)

[706] Ibid.

thoughts onto the characters and hoping that they would be just like them.   When the much-anticipated *Black Panther* film came out in 2018, the first superhero film starring a Black man, some people were upset because it didn't include any gay characters.[707]

GLAAD, the gay lobbying organization, was upset after the first *Wonder Woman* film was released because there weren't any gay or lesbian characters, saying "On screen, record-breaking films like *Black Panther* and *Wonder Woman* prove that not only does inclusion make for great stories—inclusion is good for the bottom line. It is time for lesbian, gay, bisexual, transgender, and queer (LGBTQ) stories to be included in this conversation and this movement."[708]

Wonder Woman was turned into a bisexual later in the comics, and the LGBT extremists clamored for her to be explicitly bisexual in *Wonder Woman 1984*, the sequel to the 2017 film.   When the trailer was released, Gal Gadot (Wonder Woman), teased that it may involve a potential romance between her and the villain, "The Cheetah" played by Barbara Ann Minerva.[709] *The Eternals* includes a gay superhero named Phastos and is Marvel's first film to feature an on-screen gay kiss which takes place

[707] The Washington Times "'Black Panther' packed with action, diversity -- but no gays" by Bradford Richardson (February 20th 2018)

[708] Washington Times "GLAAD report condemns Hollywood for decline in LGBT representation on big screen" by Bradford Richardson (May 23rd 2018)

[709] The Daily Mail "'The sexual tension is always there': Gal Gadot teases potential romance between her character and Kristen Wiig's villain Cheetah in Wonder Woman 1984" by Roxy Simons (May 30th 2020)

between him and his "husband."[710]   As soon as the new year rang in for 2020, the president of Marvel Studios announced that the franchise would also be introducing a transgender character.[711]

Marvel's *Thor: Love and Thunder* (scheduled to be released in February 2022) will feature a lesbian superhero called Valkyrie.[712]   And the trend continues. The CW television network's *Batwoman* series depicts the superhero as a lesbian.[713]   In the first season she was played by actress Ruby Rose, who is herself a lesbian in real life, and throughout much of the series "Kate Kane" (the character whose alter ego is Batwoman) makes it abundantly clear she's "very gay."

In one episode after a college student tearfully tells Batwoman that her parents hate her because they found out she's gay, Batwoman "outs" herself and is then shown on the cover of *CatCo* (a fictional magazine in the DC Comics universe) with the headline "Batwoman Reveals Herself as a Lesbian."[714]   It was hailed as a "historic

710 Entertainment Weekly "*The Eternals* will feature Marvel's first onscreen LGBTQ kiss: 'It's a beautiful, very moving kiss'" by Sydney Bucksbaum (February 15th 2020)

711 NBC News "Transgender character coming to Marvel Cinematic Universe, studio president suggests" by Gwen Aviles (January 2nd 2020)

712 NBC News "Tessa Thompson's Valkyrie to become Marvel Studios' first LGBTQ superhero" by Alexander Kacala (July 22nd 2019)

713 The Hollywood Reporter "Ruby Rose to Play Lesbian Superhero Batwoman for The CW" by Lesley Goldberg (August 7th 2018)

714 Newsweek "'Batwoman' Officially Comes Out on the CW Show: Ruby Rose 'Cried' While Reading the Script" by Samuel Spencer 1-20-2020)

reveal" and celebrated that the character is now an "openly gay superhero."[715]

Even back in the late 1990s, director Joel Schumacher (who is gay) tried to depict Batman and Robin as gay. When asked about the seemingly gay innuendo between Batman (played by George Clooney) and Robin (played by Chris O'Donnell) in the 1997 *Batman & Robin*, O'Donnell admitted, "going back and looking and seeing some of the pictures, it was very unusual."[716] George Clooney later said he played a "gay" Batman.[717] In 2012, DC Comics relaunched the Green Lantern as a gay man.[718] A few years after that they also decided to turn Catwoman into a bisexual.[719]

There are growing calls to depict Spider-Man as gay now too. The character has been played by numerous actors over the years in various incarnations, and now one of them (Tom Holland) who currently portrays the character, is lobbying Marvel Studios to depict Spider-Man as gay or bisexual.[720]

Sources close to the franchise say the character will be depicted as bisexual or have a boyfriend in a future

---

[715] The Hollywood Reporter "'Batwoman' Boss Goes Inside That Historic Reveal"by Shannon O'Connor (January 19th 2020)

[716] Shadows of the Bat: The Cinematic Saga of the Dark Knight Part 6-Batman Unbound (2005) Warner Home Video

[717] ABC - Barbara Walters Interview (2006)

[718] New York Post "DC Comics Green Lantern relaunched as gay superhero" by Dareh Gregorian (June 1st 2012)

[719] The Washington Times "Catwoman comes out as bisexual in new DC comic" by Jessica Chasmar (March 1st 2015)

[720] The Sun "SASSY SPIDEY Tom Holland hints there will be a gay Spider Man in the next few years" by Carl Greenwood (June 30th 2019)

film.[721] Andrew Garfield, who played the character in *The Amazing Spider-Man* (2012), said, "Why can't we discover that Peter is exploring his sexuality? It's hardly even groundbreaking!...So why can't he be gay? Why can't he be into boys?"[722]

Star Wars Isn't Gay Enough

When the new *Star Wars* film *The Force Awakens* was about to be released in 2015, activists said they wanted Luke Skywalker to be gay. Mark Hamill who plays the character said fans kept asking him, "Could Luke be gay?" and instead of telling them they're insane, he gave them hope, saying, "If you think Luke is gay, of course he is. You should not be ashamed of it."[723]

If you're a fan of the franchise you may recall that before Luke learned of his true identity (and that of his twin sister) both he and Han Solo had a crush on Princess Leia.

After *Star Wars: The Last Jedi* was released in 2017, LGBT extremists were upset that characters Finn and Poe weren't in a gay relationship. *BuzzFeed* wasn't happy

[721] We Got This Covered "Sony Reportedly Wants To Introduce A Bisexual Spider-Man" by Christian Bone (February 11th 2020)

[722] Entertainment Weekly "Andrew Garfield on Spider-Man's sexuality: 'Why can't he be gay?'" by Sara Vilkomerson (July 10th 2013)

[723] Vanity Fair "'Of Course' Luke Skywalker Is Gay, Confirms Mark Hamill, Echoing Thousands of Fan-Fiction Prayers" by Charles Bramesco (March 5th 2016)

either because they hoped the two men might have a "romance" as part of the plot.[724]

Oscar Issac who plays Poe Dameron, "expressed regret that the 'natural chemistry' between Poe and Finn in *The Force Awakens* was not explored in an overtly romantic way in 'Star Wars: The Last Jedi'—and wouldn't be in 'The Rise of Skywalker.'"[725]

"Personally," he said, "I kind of hoped and wished that maybe that would've been taken further in the other films, but I don't have control. It seemed like a natural progression, but sadly enough it's a time when people are too afraid, I think, of... I don't know what."[726]

John Boyega, who plays Finn (the Black former Stormtrooper), agreed, saying, "They've always had a quite loving and open relationship in which it wouldn't be too weird if it went beyond it."[727] LGBT websites seized the news with one declaring, "Oscar Isaac wishes Star Wars' Poe and Finn were in a gay relationship but 'people are too afraid.'"[728]

Trying to appease the criticism, director J.J. Abrams included a scene showing two lesbians kissing at the end when everyone was celebrating that the First Order had been defeated. It was hailed as "making history" for the

---

[724] BuzzFeed "Why LGBT Representation Didn't Make It Into 'The Last Jedi'" by Adam B. Vary (December 18th 2017)

[725] Ibid.

[726] Ibid.

[727] Ibid.

[728] Pink News "Oscar Isaac wishes Star Wars' Poe and Finn were in a gay relationship but 'people are too afraid'" by Emma Powys Maurice (December 4th 2019)

first same-sex kiss in a *Star Wars* movie, but that wasn't good enough—nothing ever is.[729]

Just a few years ago all they wanted was for gay "marriage" to be legal, they said. And now they're furious that leading male characters in *Star Wars* aren't having sex with each other. They just want to be "accepted" for who they are, they said, and then once they were, they began demanding everyone embrace them and celebrate them. But it's not just gays and lesbians. Now it's transgenders too, and the "gender non-conforming" people, and even child drag queens.

Disney Goes Gay

Even what was once the most family friendly entertainment brand in the world has gone gay, and is adding an increasing number of LGBT characters and storylines. In 2014 the Disney Channel's most popular comedy at the time, *Good Luck Charlie,* included a lesbian couple in the show.[730] They tried to make it funny by depicting two parents confused about the name of the mother of their daughter's friend.

Each one of them had met the "mom," but one thought her name was Susan, and the other swore it was Cheryl. Then there's a knock on the door and they open it to reveal their daughter's friend has two "moms." The media celebrated Disney for being "brave" and said it was "about time," and once the LGBT foot was in the door

---

[729] New York Post "'Star Wars: The Rise of Skywalker' has a same-sex kiss – but not the one fans hoped for" by Eric Hegedus (December 19th 2019)

[730] E! News "Disney Channel Introduces Its First Lesbian Couple on Good Luck Charlie" by Alyssa Toomey (January 28th 2014)

activists started pressuring the network to include a gay teenager in one of their shows.[731]

The following year on the Disney-Owned ABC Family Channel [which has since been renamed "Freeform"] they included a gay kiss in a show called *The Fosters* between two thirteen-year-old boys.[732] The executive producer Peter Paige (who is a homosexual) was proud to have depicted the "youngest same-sex kiss in US television history."[733]

When Disney's *Beauty and the Beast* was made into a live-action film in 2017, it included a brief scene of a same-sex couple dancing, which was hailed as the "first exclusively gay moment" in a Disney movie.[734] That same year they included a "male princess" in their animated series *Star vs. The Forces of Evil.*[735]

The *Huffington Post* called it a "beautiful message" for kids.[736] The show also depicted Disney's "first same-

[731] New York Times "Waiting for Disney's First Gay Teenager" By KJ Dell'Antonia (February 27, 2014)

[732] Breitbart "ABC Family's 'The Fosters' Airs Youngest-Ever Gay Kiss Between Two 13-Year-Old Boys" by Kipp Jones (March 4th 2015)

[733] BuzzFeed "This May Be The Youngest Ever Same-Sex Kiss On US TV" by Lane Sainty (March 2nd 2005)

[734] The Guardian "Beauty and the Beast to feature first 'exclusively gay moment' in a Disney movie" by Catherine Shoard (March 1st 2017)

[735] Entertainment Weekly "Disney XD gets a male princess in Star vs. the Forces of Evil" by Nick Romano (November 22nd 2017)

[736] Huffington Post "Disney Sends Beautiful Message With First 'Boy Princess,' Complete With Chest Hair" by Noah Michelson (November 22nd 2017)

sex cartoon kiss," another move which thrilled the liberal media.[737]

Toy Story 4 (2019) had a brief scene where a child is dropped off at school by "two moms," something that LGBT activists were happy about. "It's a small scene, sure, and it's certainly not the major representation that queer people have been waiting for, but it's still important," wrote the *Gay Times*.[738]

In Disney's *The Jungle Cruise* (2020) starring Dwayne Johnson, one of the characters (played by Jack Whitehall) comes out as gay, which is the first-ever openly gay character to have a role in a Disney movie.[739]

Disney then announced that a character in an upcoming animated movie called *Onward* would be a lesbian. "It's been a long wait, but a Disney heroine finally has a girlfriend," gloated *Yahoo News* when it was revealed that Officer Specter, which is voiced by a lesbian actress named Lena Waithe, would also be a lesbian in the movie.[740]

The idea was praised as "making history" for being the first LGBTQ character in a Disney animation film, but as expected, critics complained that the character only appears in one scene.

---

[737] Teen Vogue "Disney Just Aired its First Same-Sex Cartoon Kiss" by Brittney McNamara (February 27th 2017)

[738] Gay Times "Toy Story 4 has a small but important moment of LGBTQ representation" by Daniel Megarry (June 26th 2019)

[739] Newsweek "Comedian Jack Whitehall to Play Disney's First-Ever Openly Gay Character in 'Jungle Cruise' by Dory Jackson (August 13th 2018)

[740] Yahoo! "'Onward' introduces the first LGBTQ character in Disney animation history" by Ethan Alter (February 21st 2020)

Then a few months later Disney released an animated film on their streaming service Disney+ called *Out* about a kid who was nervous about moving in with his boyfriend because he hasn't told his parents that he's gay. The parents then come to find that his roommate is actually his boyfriend, but instead of being horrified, to his surprise, they're happy for him. It was hailed as Disney/Pixar's "first gay main character."[741] Then they introduced their first bisexual character who stars in another animated series on Disney+ called *The Owl House*.[742] The character, a 14-year-old girl, had previously been interested in boys, but after the show's creator, Dana Terrace (who is bisexual herself), lobbied the network to turn the character bisexual just like her, they complied.[743] Soon they'll probably make Mickey Mouse or Donald Duck gay.

More Gay Characters for Kids

Ever since 2017, *Sesame Street's* official social media accounts have been posting annual "Happy Pride Month" messages along with pictures of rainbows and various characters from the show celebrating it.[744] In 2018 a former writer for *Sesame Street* claimed that Bert and

---

[741] NBC News "New short film 'Out' features Pixar's first gay main character" by Gwen Aviles (May 22nd 2020)

[742] CNN "Disney confirms its first bisexual lead character, who is also multi-cultural" by Adrianne Morales (August 15th 2020)

[743] New York Post "'The Owl House' becomes Disney's first show with bisexual lead character " by Lee Brown (August 16th 2020)

[744] Hornet "'Sesame Street' Celebrates Pride Month, But How LGBTQ-Friendly Is the Show?" by Daniel Villarreal (June 27th 2017)

Ernie are gay.[745] That man himself is a homosexual (what a surprise) and really just wished they were gay.

The next day the show's producer issued a statement rebuking the former writer's claim, saying, "As we have always said, Bert and Ernie are best friends. They were created to teach preschoolers that people can be good friends with those who are very different from themselves. Even though they are identified as male characters and possess many human traits and characteristics (as most Sesame Street Muppets do), they remain puppets, and do not have a sexual orientation." [746] But PBS would soon cave in to the gay agenda completely.

The following year (in 2019) their cartoon *Arthur* included a gay "wedding" in the season premiere where they revealed that one of the teachers in the show, Mr. Ratburn, is gay. The episode is titled "Mr. Ratburn and the Special Someone" and his students all attend the wedding expecting he's going to marry another character in the show, Patty, but it's revealed that she's actually his sister, and then his new "husband" is introduced to everyone.[747]

The year after that (in 2020) PBS included a lesbian couple in their animated series *Clifford the Big Red Dog*,

[745] NBC News "Bert and Ernie are indeed a gay couple, 'Sesame Street' writer claims" by Kalhan Rosenblatt (September 18th 2018)

[746] The Washington Post "'They remain puppets': 'Sesame Street,' once again, shuts down speculation over Bert and Ernie's sexual orientation" by Elahe Izadi (September 19th 2018)

[747] Entertainment Weekly "*Arthur* season premiere reveals Mr. Ratburn is gay" by Tyler Aquilina (May 13th 2019)

based on the popular children's book series that follows the adventures of an 8-year-old and her dog.[748]

The official Twitter account for Nickelodeon and the Cartoon Network now post messages celebrating "Pride Month," as well as "International Transgender Visibility Day," which is another made-up "holiday" by the Left used to promote transgenderism.[749]

Old Comedies "Transphobic"

Mrs. Doubtfire, a 1993 comedy starring Robin Williams, has come under attack recently for being "transphobic" after it was revealed that a musical adaptation would hit the stage at a theater in Seattle, and then later on Broadway. In the film, Robin Williams loses custody of his kids after a divorce and in order to remain in their lives poses as an elderly woman who successfully applies for a job working as the kids' nanny.

It was well-received at the time, but the culture has shifted so far Left that when word of the musical was announced, activists started a petition on Change.org calling for it to be canceled because the plot uses "tired, transphobic tropes" and "strengthens the assumptions and misjudgments that continue to harm trans women in implicit, pervasive ways."[750]

---

[748] CBN News "'Clifford the Big Red Dog' Becomes Second PBS Kid Series to Feature LGBT Character" by Steve Warren (February 28th 2020)

[749] The Daily Caller "Kids' Networks Celebrate Transgender People Through #TransDayOfVisibility" by Mary Margaret Olohan (March 31st 2020)

[750] Seattle Times "Does 'Mrs. Doubtfire' at The 5th Ave transcend the original's problematic elements?" by Seattle Times Staff (December 20th 2019)

Jim Carrey's 1994 comedy *Ace Ventura: Pet Detective* has now been deemed "transphobic" because the pet thief who kidnapped the Miami Dolphins' mascot is found to be a transsexual, now living as a woman. When Jim Carrey realizes this, he runs to the bathroom and starts vomiting, burns his clothes, and jumps in the shower, because earlier in the film "she" came onto him and they made out.[751]

Silence of the Lambs (1991) is also now considered "transphobic" since the serial killer Jodie Foster is trying to hunt down (Buffalo Bill) has gender dysphoria. As part of the plot he murders women so he can make a "woman suit" out of their skin to complete his "transformation." *Variety* magazine recently denounced the film for "depicting the criminal's transgender identification as part of his mental illness."[752] GLAAD complained that the killer is "a walking, talking gay stereotype."[753]

What's next? Older classics like *Some Like it Hot* or *Tootsie?*, or more modern shows like Tyler Perry's "Madea" character or Martin Lawrence's "Shanaynay?" Jimmy Fallon also used to have a regular segment on the *Tonight Show* called "Ew" where he would dress up as a

---

[751] BuzzFeed "25 Years Of Transphobia In Comedy" by Meredith Talusan (February 27th 2016)

[752] This quote was included in the original article published by Variety titled "10 Problematic Films That Could Use Warning Labels" by Tim Gray (June 17th 2020) but was later removed because it insinuates that transgenderism is a mental illness. The Internet Archive Wayback Machine has the original article saved and can be viewed at https://web.archive.org/web/20200618004648/https://variety.com/2020/film/news/gone-with-the-wind-problem-films-forrest-gump-1234640666/

[753] Slate "When Gays Decried *Silence of the Lambs*, Jonathan Demme Became an Early Student of Modern Backlash" by Jeffrey Bloomer (April 28th 2017)

woman, but he hasn't done it in quite some time, and it probably won't be much longer until he apologizes for it.

Soon it will probably be considered a slur to call a transgender person "transgender," and making any distinction between them being born the opposite sex from which they currently identify will be considered an invasion of their privacy, much like releasing someone's medical records. To call a transgender "woman" a "transgender woman" will be considered "dehumanizing" and "hateful," and no distinctions will be allowed.

LGBTQ extremists claim people are "assigned" a gender at birth, much like they are given a name—and maintain that the "assignment" of one's gender is just as arbitrary and is used to confine the "gender expression" of people to correspond with their biological sex. They won't say that a transgender "woman" was born a male, they say "she" was "assigned" the male gender at birth, as if it was just a coin toss.

The animated comedy series *Family Guy* announced in early 2019 that they were going to stop making jokes about gay people and transgenders. The series, which has been on air for over 20-years, is known for its no holds barred comedy about typically taboo subjects, but now offending LGBTQ people is too much even for them. The executive producers said, "Some of the things we felt comfortable saying and joking about back then [earlier in the series], we now understand is not acceptable...The climate is different, the culture is different and our views are different."[754]

---

[754] CNN "'Family Guy' phasing out gay jokes" by Lisa Respers (January 2019)

Drag Queen Story Hour and "Drag Kids"

One of the three strikes on Alex Jones' YouTube channel that led to him being banned from the platform was a rant about a local drag queen festival that included children giving dollar bills to the drag queens as they engaged in simulated strip teases. He called it a "freak show" and an "abomination" in a segment for his show and YouTube considered that to be "hate speech."[755]

In my previous book *The Liberal Media Industrial Complex* I detail the "unpersoning" of Alex Jones and the censorship of conservatives on social media, which I encourage you to read if you haven't already so you can grasp just how big the ramifications are for speaking out against this degeneracy.

At one of the Drag Queen Story Hour events in New York, a drag queen asked the children, "Who wants to be a drag queen when they grow up?"[756] At another, one of them taught the children how to "twerk," asking them, "Does anybody in this room know how to twerk?" Nobody spoke up, and the drag queen continues, "All you need to do is you just need to stand with your feet sort of shoulder-width apart like so…and then you crouch down in this sort of position, so you're bum's sticking out. And

---

[755] Politifact "Why Infowars' Alex Jones was banned from Apple, Facebook, Youtube and Spotify" by Manuela Tobias (August 7th 2018)

[756] Associated Press "NY Library Brings Drag Queens to Kids Story Hour" Video posted on official AP Archive YouTube channel (May 21st 2017)

then you just move your bum up and down like that [as he does it]. And that's twerking."[757]

Equally disturbing is the recent phenomena of young pre-teen boys being dressed in drag by their parents and paraded around at drag queen festivals in hopes they'll become social media stars. One such "drag kid" who goes by the name "Desmond is Amazing" was even featured on *Good Morning America*.[758]

"Desmond is Amazing" certainly isn't one of a kind. Other child drag queens like "E! the Dragnificent" and "Lactacia" (who started doing drag at eight-years-old) are building up their social media followings, all trying to be the next YouTube or TikTok star.[759]

YouTube even hosts a documentary film called *Drag Kids* which follows a group of pre-teen kids as they travel around the country participating in child drag shows.[760] The documentary's purpose isn't to raise the alarm about this horrific practice, it's to show how "cool" the kids are.

Netflix has a reality series called *AJ and the Queen* where a 10-year-old child travels across the country with RuPaul as he performs drag shows in gay bars. The sexual things the drag queens say about the child are too disgusting to include here because they'll make you

---

[757] Lifesite News "WATCH: Drag queen teaches kids to 'twerk' at library story hour" by Calvin Freiburger (August 7th 2019)

[758] Media Research Center "Good Morning America Devotes a Whole Segment to a Child Drag Queen" by Ferlon Webster Jr. (November 19th 2018)

[759] The Advocate "Meet 8-Year-Old Drag Queen Lactatia" by Neal Boverman (May 6th 2017)

[760] HuffPost "Meet The 'Drag Kids' Who Want To Slay The World And Then Some" by Curtis M. Wong (October 24th 2019)

physically ill as they did me when I first read about it.[761] Another Netflix original series called *Dancing Queen* follows the life of a drag queen who teaches dance lessons to kids.[762]

In 2015, TLC premiered *I Am Jazz*, a reality show following the life of Jazz Jennings, a transgender teenager, who at the time was one of the youngest people in the world to identify as transgender. "Jazz Jennings" is a pseudonym, and unlike every other public figure on the planet who uses one, "her" birth name is not allowed to be mentioned on Wikipedia because of the special protections given to transgender people.

Similarly, "Lavern" Cox's birth name (Roderick) is not allowed to be mentioned either. In fact, simply mentioning a transgender person's birth name or legal name is considered a violation of the terms of service on Facebook and Twitter.[763]

TLC was originally called "The Learning Channel" and aired educational programming about science, history, and nature, but slowly morphed into another reality TV network (just like the History Channel has), and now instead of featuring anything remotely educational, TLC is known for mind-numbing trash like *Here Comes Honey Boo Boo*, and *Toddlers & Tiaras*.

---

[761] Newsbusters "Sick: RuPaul's New Drag Queen Dramedy Sexualizes 10-Year-Old Child as a 'Top'" by Elise Ehrhard (January 13th 2020)

[762] NPR "'Dancing Queen': Alyssa Edwards Doesn't Let Dance Moms Drag Her Down" by Glen Weldon (October 11th 2018)

[763] The Verge "Twitter has banned misgendering or 'deadnaming' transgender people" by Adi Robertson (November 27th 2018)

Celebrities Raising Kids Trans

Celebrities love to adopt children from Africa as a novelty and to show how much they "care" about Black people, and since transgenderism has become the coolest new fad in Hollywood, many celebrities seem to be inspired to raise their kids as the opposite gender to defy cultural norms. Charlize Theron adopted two Black kids, one boy and one girl, and then later was spotted around town with the kids both wearing dresses and now insists she has "two beautiful daughters."[764]

Brad Pitt and Angelina Jolie (who are now divorced) adopted several children, but their first biological child was daughter Shiloh who they started dressing in boy's clothes, causing many to speculate whether she is a tomboy or actually identifies as a boy.[765]

Megan Fox (now divorced from Brian Austin Green) dresses her six-year-old son in girls' clothes. "He likes to wear dresses sometimes and I send him to a really liberal, hippy school, but even there—here in California—he still has little boys going, 'Boys don't wear dresses' or 'Boys don't wear pink.' And so, we're going through that now, where I'm trying to teach him to be confident, no matter what anyone else says."[766] Megan and her son were once

---

[764] E! News "Why Charlize Theron Decided to Speak Out About Raising Two Daughters" by Jess Cohen (December 17th 2019)

[765] OK Magazine "Shiloh Jolie-Pitt 'Only Wears Boys' Clothes' After Questioning Gender Identity To Brad & Angelina" (August 4th 2016)

[766] Today "Megan Fox opens up about letting her 6-year-old son wear dresses" by Ree Hines (September 20th 2019)

spotted by paparazzi when he was dressed up as Elsa from Disney's *Frozen*.[767] Singer Adele also dresses her son up as Disney princesses, which the liberal media has hailed as "a triumph for us believers in gender-neutral parenting."[768] Actor Liev Schreiber brought his eight-year-old son to Comic-Con dressed as Harley Quinn, the Joker's girlfriend from *Suicide Squad*.[769]

When Mario Lopez appeared on Candace Owen's podcast and the subject of parents raising their children transgender came up, he said he didn't think it was right to be deciding that a 3-year-old kid should start being treated as the opposite gender.[770] But he was immediately attacked for being "transphobic" and soon apologized. That wasn't enough, however. The LGBT fascists demanded that he become an "advocate" for transgender kids.

Commercials Go Gay

It's not just movies and television shows that have been filled with LGBT people, now even many commercials feature them as well. Homosexual couples

---

[767] Teen Vogue "Megan Fox's Son Wore a *Frozen* Dress Again in Spite of Critics" by Alyssa Hardy (October 5th 2017)

[768] The Independent "Adele letting her son dress as Disney princess Anna is a triumph for us believers in gender-neutral parenting" by Siobhan Freegard (February 19th 2016)

[769] HuffPost "Liev Schreiber's Son Dressed As Harley Quinn, And the Internet Inevitably Reacted" by Isabelle Khoo (July 25th 2017)

[770] NBC News "Mario Lopez's comments about transgender kids aren't just dumb. They're dangerous." by Chase Strangio (August 1st 2019)

are now regularly included in commercials for major brands from IKEA and Chevrolet, to Target and Tide laundry detergent.[771] Each time another one jumps on the bandwagon, their allies in the media always write an article about it celebrating how "great" it is, encouraging more.[772]

For example, Campbell's Soup created a commercial in 2015 showing two gay "dads" feeding "their son" because the company wanted to show the "diverse mix" of American families. The *Huffington Post* said it, "will melt your heart."[773]

In 2017, the Dove soap company released an ad featuring "real moms" with their babies and praised the "diversity" in how each of them were raising their children, saying there was "no one right way." Included with the "moms" was a transgender woman who is the biological father of one of the babies, along with the actual mother who gave birth to the poor child.

"We are both his biological parents," the transgender says. "You get people that are like, 'What do you mean you're the mom?' We're like, 'Yep! We're both gonna be moms.'"[774]

Gillette razors released a commercial in 2019 featuring a transgender "boy" being taught how to shave by "his" dad for the first time as part of their campaign to

[771] LGBTQ Nation "The new normal: Gay couple featured in Tide TV commercial" (December 14th 2014)

[772] Huff Post "J.C. Penney and Gap's Gay-Themed Ads Seek Profit With Progress" by Ron Dicker (May 17th 2012)

[773] Huffington Post "This Campbell's Soup Ad Featuring Gay Dads Will Melt Your Heart" by Curtis M. Wong (10-6-2015)

[774] NewsBusters "Dove Ad Features Transgender Mom: 'No One Right Way'" by Sarah Stites (April 12th 2017)

"redefine masculinity."[775]   Starbucks released a commercial in support of people's "preferred pronouns" showing a teenage girl with a butch haircut named Jemma who appears to be uncomfortable every time someone says her name as she goes about her day until she walks into a Starbucks and is asked what it is so the barista can write it on the cup, which is customary.

She proudly answers "James" and is revealed to be transitioning to a boy.   The commercial was part of Starbuck's announcement that they were partnering with a charity that supports transgender children.[776]

Coca-Cola's 2018 Super Bowl ad featured a lesbian and a "non-binary" person.[777] In another commercial for Diet Coke released the following year a blue-haired woman drives around in an Uber picking up all kinds of different people while enjoying her Diet Coke all night. At one point her passengers are shown to be two gay men, one White and one Black for extra "diversity," who are kissing in the back seat. The camera then cuts back to the driver who has a big smile on her face.[778]

Smirnoff vodka now features transgender actress Lavern Cox in their commercials.[779] Other alcohol brands

---

[775] CBS News "New Gillette ad shows dad teaching transgender son how to shave" by Aimee Picchi (May 29th 2019)

[776] Daily Caller "Starbucks Partners With Trans Children Charity, Releases Ad On Calling Transgender Youth By Preferred Pronouns" by Marty Margaret Olohan (February 5th 2020)

[777] Daily Beast "Why Coke's Non-Binary Super Bowl Moment Mattered" by Samantha Allen (February 5th 2018)

[778] The commercial is titled "Late-Night Driver" and can be seen on YouTube and elsewhere.

[779] Forbes "Behind The Scenes Of Smirnoff's New 'Hang Out From Home For America' Campaign With Laverne Cox" by Emily Price (April 24th 2020)

like Absolut, Effen, Bud Light, and Barefoot Wine, all release special edition "Gay Pride" bottles for the month of June every year featuring rainbows on them.[780]

Most major food brands now release special "Pride" themed packages for gay pride month each year, and on social media change their avatars to pictures that include rainbows. All major retailers celebrate it too, from Walmart and Target, to Kohl's and Old Navy. All tweeting about it and posting on Facebook and Instagram how important LGBT people are to them and issuing press releases alerting the media how they're going to be "celebrating Pride month."[781]

Sprite even released a commercial for "Pride" month in 2019 showing a bunch of transgender people transitioning; including a man having makeup put on him by another transgender "woman," and a girl engaging in "breast binding" with her friend as they joyfully wrap her breasts tightly to her chest so she can "pass" as a male.[782]

Gay Sexual Predators Swept Under the Rug

In the "Me Too" era, Harvey Weinstein has become the symbol of sexual degeneracy in Hollywood, but most of the women who accused him of sexual "assault" willingly had sex with him in order to further their own careers, and they weren't forcibly raped. Years later they

---

[780] Newsweek "These 50+ Brands Are Celebrating Pride by Giving Back to the LGBT Community" by Daniel Avery (June 3rd 2019)

[781] USA Today "How retailers have turned Pride month into a marketing, sales bonanza" by Verena Dobnik via Associated Press (June 23rd 2019)

[782] PJ Media "Creepy New Sprite Commercial Sells Transgenderism and Breast Binding, Not Soda" by Megan Fox (November 18th 2019)

just jumped on the bandwagon to cash-in once they saw the opportunity, and in hindsight regretted they had sex with such a pig for a chance to be a star.

That's not to say he didn't make some of them feel extremely uncomfortable by blatantly propositioning them for sex—and he's undoubtedly a sexual predator—but powerful men using the "casting couch" to entice women into having sex with them isn't Hollywood's dirtiest secret.

One of the things nobody wants to talk about (aside from the industry's pedophilia problem which is actually the *biggest* secret and covered in the next chapter) is the fact that gay men are basically allowed to sexually harass (and assault) other men with impunity because daring to say that a gay man has done anything sexually inappropriate amounts to blasphemy.

Surprisingly, actor Terry Crews developed the courage to come forward in 2017 to admit that he was once sexually assaulted by his agent, who grabbed his genitals while making sexual advances toward him.[783] James Van Der Beek, star of the teen drama *Dawson's Creek*, later came forward as well to reveal that he was sexually harassed (and groped) by "older, powerful men" in Hollywood.[784]

Others including Brendan Fraser, *Bill & Ted's Excellent Adventure* star Alex Winter, and *Star Trek: Discovery* actor Anthony Rapp, have also come forward with allegations of being sexually harassed by gay men in

---

[783] The Guardian "Actor Terry Crews: I was sexually assaulted by Hollywood executive" by Gwilym Mumford (October 11th 2017)

[784] Vanity Fair "James Van Der Beek Reveals His Own Experience of Sexual Harassment" by Hilary Weaver (October 12th 2017)

Hollywood.[785] Their stories were just a blip on the radar however, and then the issue was swept under the rug.

Undoubtedly the same thing has happened to many others who are afraid to come forward out of embarrassment or because they don't want to make waves out of fear it may derail their career. In fact, after Terry Crews revealed he was assaulted, others in the entertainment industry including D.L Hughley and 50 Cent mocked him.[786]

During a 2011 interview, Rapper Fat Joe admitted that he believes a "gay mafia" controls the music industry, saying, "The hip hop industry is most likely owned by gays. I happen to think there's a gay mafia in hip hop. Not rappers—the editorial presidents of magazines, the [program directors] at radio stations, the people who give you awards at award shows. This is a fuckin' gay mafia, my man, and they are in power."[787]

It's not just in the entertainment industry that gay sexual predators are mostly ignored. The same thing is happening in the U.S. military, especially after Barack Obama lifted the ban on them enrolling.[788] According to the Department of Defense statistics, more men than

[785] Vanity Fair "'I Was Terrified, and I Was Humiliated': #MeToo's Male Accusers, One Year Later" by Laura Bradley (October 4th 2018)

[786] Newsweek "Terry Crews Threatens to 'Slap' D.L. Hughley for Mocking His Sexual Assault Allegation" by Dory Jackson (January 28th 2019)

[787] VLADTV "Fat Joe thinks the Gay Mafia Controls Hip-Hop" (November 7th 2011)

[788] Washington Times "'Gay' rape in military underreported by Pentagon" by Rowan Scarborough (November 3rd 2015)

women are victims of sexual assault in the military.[789] You won't hear that on the news because it's another uncomfortable fact that shows the liberal agenda is severely flawed.

When gay couples adopt small children and molest them, those stories are just reported in local outlets and never make the national news.[790] Few people want to even comment on such abuse out of concerns they'll be branded "homophobic." Reports of gay couples sexually abusing their adopted or foster children can be found around the world.[791]

In some cases the couples force the children into sex trafficking and sell them to other pedophiles.[792] But just mentioning those cases is enough to anger LGBT activists who may then target you to be "canceled."

Same sex couples adopting children was the real issue at hand regarding legalizing gay "marriage," but very few conservatives or even Christians dared talk about it. When gays are allowed to adopt children it's no longer about what "two consenting adults" are doing "in the privacy of their own bedroom," it's about an innocent third party, and no child should be held prisoner in such an environment.

---

[789] U.S Army S.H.A.R.P (Sexual Harassment / Assault Response & Prevention report "What We Know About Sexual Assault of Military Men"

[790] Sky News "Adopted Boy Sexually Abused by Gay Fathers" (July 3rd 2013)

[791] The Telegraph "Gay couple arrested for abusing foster children" by Paul Stokes (June 24th 2006)

[792] Australian Broadcast Network "Australian paedophile Peter Truong jailed for 30 years in US after trafficking adopted son to Boy Lovers Network" (December 9th 2013)

Like many gay people, CNN's Anderson Cooper became a father (at the age of 52) after he bought an egg from a fertility clinic and then hired a surrogate—and had the egg artificially inseminated with his sperm.[793] The woman carried the child to term and then turned it over to Anderson Cooper to be raised by him and his boyfriend.

The kid will most likely never know his mother due to privacy shields regarding egg donors, nor even have the surrogate in his life either, and instead will be raised by two homosexual men in their fifties, only to someday have to be told the horrible truth about how he came to exist.

What Causes It?

In 2019, a massive study conducted by over 30 organizations including Harvard and Cambridge Universities was released after scientists analyzed the DNA of almost 500,000 people and ruled out any supposed "gay gene" that caused people to be born homosexual.[794] They cited "the environment" for being 75% responsible for people's sexual preference.[795]

"Obviously, there are environmental causes of sexual orientation. We knew that before this study," said Michael Bailey, a psychologist at Northwestern

---

[793] USA Today "Anderson Cooper proudly announces the birth of his son Wyatt: 'I am a dad. I have a son'" by Cydney Henderson (April 30th 2020)

[794] CBS News "Is there a 'gay gene'? Major new study says no" by Dennis Thompson (August 29th 2019)

[795] The Telegraph "'Gay gene' ruled out as huge study shows environment is major factor in homosexuality." by Sarah Knapton (August 29th 2019)

University who has researched the causes of sexual preferences.[796] The same may be true of transgenderism as well.

In other words, if an infant boy not yet knowing the difference between men and women, sees mommy putting on makeup—and for a moment wants to be like mommy and do what she does—and if the mother doesn't teach him the distinctions between boys and girls, he'll obviously grow up extremely confused and have a difficult time knowing which behaviors are normal for a man and which are not. The boy might start "identifying" with the mother if he is not brought up to understand the biological and sociological differences between boys and girls, possibly leading to gender dysphoria and transgenderism later in life.

Some psychologists believe that "Rapid Onset Gender Dysphoria" is a form of social contagion or mass psychosis sparked by teens being bombarded with depictions of transgender people on social media portrayed in a positive light, and as a result see *themselves* as transgender in order to be a part of this "in" group of "cool" people as a coping mechanism for other underlying psychological disorders.[797]

YouTube as a company promotes and glorifies transgender YouTubers like "Gigi Gorgeous" as well as gender-bending male makeup artists like Jeffrey Star and James Charles who identify as men but wear women's makeup and clothes, which is fueling this phenomenon.

---

[796] PBS "There is no 'gay gene.' There is no 'straight gene.' Sexuality is just complex, study confirms" (August 29th 2019)

[797] Psychology Today "Why Is Transgender Identity on the Rise Among Teens?" by Samuel Paul Veissiere Ph.D. (November 28th 2018)

They have created an extremely confusing environment for children, who as you know, are so impressionable they can be convinced that a fat bearded man in a red suit flies around the country every Christmas to bring them presents.

Today, with so many of them being raised by social media personalities instead of their parents they have no idea what kinds of behaviors are conducive or detrimental to a happy, fulfilling life.

Freud believed homosexuality is a mental disorder that develops from a disruption in the Oedipal phase of children's psychosexual development.[798] It's possible that it could also be a birth defect resulting in a certain region of the brain being wired backwards, so to speak, during gestation while the fetus is developing.[799] Transgender people could be born with the brain of the opposite sex due to the same reason.

If, as some scientists believe, prenatal abnormalities in the womb due to a hormone imbalance or other external forces are causing these issues, then scientists just admitting that homosexuality and transgenderism are birth defects is considered "hate speech" today.[800] To admit that they have a "defect" would be to admit that they're not normal—and that's "hateful." Searching for a cure that would prevent the prenatal changes to a fetus that

---

[798] *Basic Freud: Psychoanalytic Thought for the 21st Century* by Michael Kahn, Ph.D page 77 - on the negative resolution of the Oedipus complex (2002 Basic Books)

[799] Sci Tech Daily "Homosexuality Might Develop in the Womb Due to Epigenetic Changes" (December 12th 2012)

[800] Science Magazine "Homosexuality may be caused by chemical modifications to DNA" by Michael Balter (October 8th 2015)

cause such things is tantamount to eugenics, and equally opposed by the liberal ideologues.

Another theory is that homosexuality arose as a maladaptive behavior due to a mutation in the gene pool as a result of the decline of the pressures of natural selection, because in our modern age humans don't have to complete for mates to pass on their genes as if it were a life or death situation for the species since there are already billions of us, often crammed in large cities literally living on top of one another.

Today large groups of "free-riders" exist because of economic abundance, modern conveniences, and social safety nets, so the urge to become financially successful and physically fit in hopes of attracting a beautiful female mate is drastically diminished for many males.

Conversely, because of our economic abundant society, many females don't feel the need to attract a male to provide protection and resources for them like our ancestors did for tens of thousands of years, since modern society offers those luxuries instead. This would explain the explosion of florescent-haired lesbians and socially dysfunctional people who identify as dozens of different genders whose sole purpose in life seems to be ruining it for everyone else.

Under this school of thought, because the evolutionary pressures for men and women to find mates have been lifted, many are no longer conforming to the social framework and norms our species has known since the beginning of time, and their behaviors are "mutating." But instead of being content as "free-riders" whose survival is protected through modern-day conveniences and social programs, these changes are causing the rise of what some scientists call "spiteful mutants" who hold hostile views towards those who are normal (i.e. people who continue heterosexual traditions, behaviors, and gender roles; and those who work hard in their careers and take care of their health).[801]

The end result of these "spiteful mutants," according to the theory, is the collapse of the social structure of the entire group of organisms (humans in this case) because the non-affected group (heterosexual and cis gender people) who do not suffer from the same mutations are still severely impacted due to the disruption of the entire social fabric of the species by those with the mutation.[802]

People who are molested as children tend to later *become* child molesters themselves. So it appears that pedophilia may in some cases be a psychological condition that is induced from an experience rather than something someone is born with.[803] The same may be true of homosexuality and gender-bending. Is it a birth defect, or a psychological disorder exacerbated by the celebration of sexual deviancy and other abnormal lifestyles in the media and on the Internet? Just asking this question is considered "hate speech," and few scientists will dare risk their career by publicly doubting

---

[801] Evolutionary Psychology Science (2017) "Social Epistasis Amplifies the Fitness Costs of Deleterious Mutations, Engendering Rapid Fitness Decline Among Modernized Populations" by Michael A. Woodley, Matthew A Sarraf, Radomir Pestow, and Heitor B.F. Fernandes

[802] Of Mice and Men: Empirical Support for the Population-Based Social Epistasis Amplification Model by Matthew Alexander Sarraf and Michael Anthony Woodley (National Institute of Health 2017)

[803] The Journal of Offender Rehabilitation "The Genesis of Pedophilia" by J. Paul Fedoraff and Shara Pinkus pages 85-101 (Volume 23, 1996)

the new liberal orthodoxy regarding gender identity and sexuality.

Once a crazy idea takes hold in a culture it becomes reinforced through social policing, and anyone who begins to doubt the practice is ostracized, reprimanded, or in some cases physically punished. Others who may quietly have the same concerns about the current practice are thus afraid to voice those concerns, which helps to maintain the hegemony, no matter how irrational, abusive, or dangerous it is.

Imagine living in Central America and speaking up when your fellow villagers were getting ready to cut out someone's beating heart to appease the Aztec "gods," or telling the tribal elders in Africa that slicing your bottom lip and stretching it out by sticking a large plate in there is ridiculous. It's extremely difficult to break cultural traditions once they have taken root.

"Homophobia" is a Hoax

Anyone who doesn't celebrate this onslaught of homosexuality, bisexuality, and gender-bending is branded "homophobic," "transphobic," or a basic "hateful bigot," but those are just more lies from the Left. A phobia is an irrational fear of something.[804] People who are sick of seeing drag queens and homosexuals celebrated in the media aren't *afraid* of them, they're repulsed by them. The same way normal people are when they hear their parents or grandparents talking about having sex with each other. What they do behind closed

---

[804] Dictionary.com definition of "phobia": a persistent, irrational fear of a specific object, activity, or situation that leads to a compelling desire to avoid it. (2020)

doors in the privacy of their own home is their business, but the rest of us don't want to hear about it, much less see depictions of it.

Unfortunately, today you can't avoid having gender benders and other LGBT people shoved in your face every time your turn on the TV or scroll through a news feed on social media. And you must not criticize them. You must *celebrate* them, or you are a "Nazi!" A few years before this cultural Marxism infected the country, comedian Adam Carolla joked that he believed in the future, kids would get bullied for *not* being gay.[805] It's sad how right he was.

---

[805] Adam Carolla - *In 50 Years We'll All Be Chicks* page 12 (Crown Archetype 2012)

Sexual Deviants

In the 1950s sitcom *I Love Lucy,* the couple Ricky and Lucy had to each sleep in their own twin bed for a few seasons because the network was concerned about the show being "too sexual" if they were seen lying in the same bed together.   Back then it was considered too suggestive to depict a couple in bed on network television even if they were married.[806]   *The Brady Bunch* (1969-1974) didn't even have a toilet in the bathroom of their house because executives thought it would be too disgusting to show one on TV during scenes when the cast was brushing their teeth or doing their hair.[807]

Fast forward a few decades and Charlie Sheen would become Hollywood's darling and the highest paid sitcom actor in history.[808]   An HIV-infected scumbag who smoked crack and regularly used hookers became the industry's favorite star!   Hollywood once celebrated wholesome characters and families but now embraces the biggest degenerates as creative "geniuses" who can't help being a little "eccentric."

The media raved over *Fifty Shades of Grey,* the sadomasochistic film series based on the bestselling novel, and "The Weeknd" performed a song from the soundtrack at the 2016 Grammys as they attempted to

---

[806] TVtropes.org "Sleeping Single"

[807] Mental Floss "16 Things You Might Not Know About The Brady Bunch" by Kara Kovalchik (February 25th 2016)

[808] Forbes "Hollywood's Highest-Paid TV Actors" by Dorothy Pomerantz (October 11th 2011)

mainstream this once-fringe lifestyle. Target even sold *50 Shades of Grey* sex toys.[809]

Skip Chasey, the vice president of Endeavor (formerly known as the William Morris Endeavor) one of the largest management firms in Hollywood, accidentally killed a man in his sex dungeon in 2017, but no charges were filed, not even for negligent homicide.[810] He also kept his job at the agency.[811]

Lady Gaga tried to revive R. Kelly's career at the 2014 American Music Awards by doing a live performance with him, despite the allegations of him being a child predator making headlines for well over a decade at the time.[812] She also put him in her video "Do What You Want" which was directed by the infamous Terry Richardson, who has been accused of sexually exploiting models for years.[813]

Then a couple years later at the 2016 Grammys, she performed her song "Till It Happens To You" and was hailed as a hero for "raising awareness" about sexual

---

[809] CNN "'Fifty Shades of Grey sex toys hit stores like Target" by Katie Lobosco (February 3rd 2015)

[810] Hollywood Reporter "Death in a Hollywood Sex Dungeon: How a Top Agency Executive's 'Mummification' Ritual Ended in Tragedy" by Seth Abramovitch (June 29th 2018)

[811] Page Six "S&M-loving Hollywood exec keeps job after man dies in his sex dungeon" by Richard Johnson (June 29th 2018)

[812] New York Times "R. Kelly's Two-Decade Trail of Sexual Abuse Accusations" by Jacey Fortin (May 10th 2018)

[813] The Guardian "Fashion photographer Terry Richardson accused of sexually exploiting models" by Caroline Davies (March 19th 2010)

assault and everyone forgot that just a few years earlier she single-handedly put R. Kelly back in the spotlight.[814]

Ellen DeGeneres once introduced two little girls aged six and eight to rapper Nicki Minaj because she was their favorite pop star.[815] Ellen had Nicki surprise them on stage live on her show and the audience couldn't have been any happier. No adult should be letting their children listen to Nicki Minaj's music because it's filled with sexually explicit and vulgar lyrics, but that didn't stop Ellen DeGeneres from introducing the adult entertainer to the little girls.

Perversion apparently runs in Nicki Minaj's family because her 25-year-old brother was convicted of raping an 11-year-old and sentenced to 25 years in prison.[816]

Hulk Hogan's infamous sex tape was the result of him sleeping with his best friend's wife (with his permission) as he hung out in another room of the house after inviting Hulk over to have his way with her. At one point during the escapade the husband even came into the bedroom to see how they were doing.[817]

Celebrities often have dysfunctional lifestyles, becoming jaded and numb from overindulgence due to an endless supply of money and an inner circle of yes men who will never doubt their desires out of fear that they

---

814 MTV "Lady Gaga Gives a Lesson On 'Chemistry' with R. Kelly in 'Do What U Want' Video" by Jocelyn Vena (November 11th 2013)

815 Hollywood Reporter "Nicki Minaj Performs 'Super Bass' With YouTube Star Sophia Grace" by Erika Ramirez (October 12th 2011)

816 USA Today "Nicki Minaj's brother Jelani Maraj sentenced to 25 years to life for raping 11-year-old" by Cydney Henderson (January 27th 2020)

817 New York Post "Husband cheered on Hogan during sex-tape romps with wife" by Kathianne Boniello and Laura Italiano (March 20th 2016)

may be cut off from the cash cow they have attached themselves to. Their carnal appetite can never be satisfied, causing them to obsessively try to fill the emptiness in their souls with worldly pleasures. Instead of the media acknowledging these kinds of decisions lead to a disastrous downward spiral, they are celebrated and encouraged.

HGTV's popular series *House Hunters* follows a couple around town as they search for a new home, and they make sure to regularly include LGBT couples in the show for "diversity," but that wasn't enough so they recently included a "throuple," a group of three people in a polyamorous relationship.

"The past four years, I have been living in Lori and Brian's house, so buying a house together as a 'throuple' will signify our next big step as a family of five rather than all four of them plus me," said one of the three.[818] The "throuple" is also raising two children because for some reason child protective services doesn't think the kids are in a toxic and abusive household. Imagine trying to explain to the children who the third person is that's living with them.

Democrat Congresswoman Katie Hill was also in such a relationship before she resigned when it was revealed the third wheel was one of her staffers.[819]

In ABC's sitcom *Single Parents* they introduced a "throuple" that consists of two men and a woman, one of

---

[818] Deadline "HGTV's House Hunters Breaks New Ground With Its First Throuple Exploration" by Bruce Haring (February 13th 2020)

[819] New York Post "Rep. Katie Hill resigns amid snowballing 'throuple' scandal" by Marisa Schultz and Kenneth Garger (October 27th 2019)

whom is a public school teacher.[820]   When they explain their "relationship" to their friends, instead of being taken aback by the weirdness, one of them gets excited and pulls out her phone to download the same app the "throuple" used to find each other.

We're even seeing incest promoted on network television and in films.[821]   Nick Cassavetes, the director of *The Notebook,* endorsed incest while promoting his film *Yellow* (2012) which features the main character having an incestuous relationship with her brother, saying, "If you're not having kids—who gives a damn?   Love who you want.   Isn't that what we say?   Gay marriage— love who you want?…you're not hurting anybody, except every single person who freaks out because you're in love with one another."[822]

Other films like *Close My Eyes* (1991), *The Cement Garden* (1993), *Lovers of the Arctic Circle* (1998), *Delta* (2008), *Beautiful Kate* (2009), and *Illegitimate* (2016) all have incest as the central plot.   Some websites have even compiled lists of what they call the "20 Best Incest Movies of All Time,"[823] and the "13 Steamiest Incestuous Relationships In Film."[824]

---

[820] Newsbusters "Now Even Network Sitcoms Have 'Throuples:' ABC Comedy on Polyamory: 'It Just Works!'" by Elise Ehrhard (January 15th 2020)

[821] Newsbusters "Gay Psychiatrist on 'New Amsterdam' Pushes Incest" by Karen Townsend (February 26th 2020)

[822] Fox News "'The Notebook' director Nick Cassavetes says of incest: 'Who gives a damn?'" (September 10th 2012)

[823] The Cinemaholic "20 Best Incest Movies of All Time" by Vishnu Warrior (August 16th 2018)

[824] Ranker "13 Steamiest Incestuous Relationships In Film" by Roger Nackerman (June 8th 2020)

Actress Mackenzie Phillips, best known for her role in *American Graffiti* and more recently working on the Disney Channel's *So Weird,* wrote in her memoir that when she was 19-years-old she began having sex with her biological father and continued the incestuous relationship for *ten years* until she was almost thirty! She described the relationship as "consensual" and once had an abortion after becoming pregnant because she figured he was the father.[825]

In recent years we have been seeing more stories approving of people engaging in incest.[826] *Cosmopolitan* magazine published a story about how "great" it was with the headline, "Girl describes what it was like to have sex with her dad." In the article the woman is quoted as saying, "The sexual intensity was nothing like I'd ever felt before. It was like being loved by a parent you never had, and the partner you always wanted, at once."[827] They did a similar article about a brother and sister who were separated at birth but entered into a sexual relationship with each other when they were reunited as adults.[828]

Scientists believe that when parents are reunited with their adult children after giving them up for adoption when they were born, they sometimes develop a strong

---

[825] ABC News "Mackenzie Phillips Confesses to 10-Year Consensual Sexual Relationship With Father" by Russell Goldman, Eileen Murphy, and Lindsay Goldwert (September 22nd 2009)

[826] Fox News "North Carolina father-daughter couple arrested for incest after having love child" (February 4th 2018)

[827] Cosmopolitan "Girl describes what it was like to have sex with her dad" (February 19th 2015)

[828] Cosmopolitan "This is what it's like to fall in love with your brother" by Asher Fogle (October 30th 2015)

sexual attraction for each other, called GSA (Genetic Sexual Attraction).[829]   The same phenomena can happen to adult siblings when they meet for the first time.[830]

Soon liberals will likely welcome incest into the LGBT community and declare it no more abnormal than homosexuality.   In fact, there are already a growing number of blogs, Tumblr accounts, and YouTube videos dedicated to legalizing "consensual incest."[831]

As everyone knows, it's common for Hollywood-types to date people a decade or two younger than them, but some in the industry like partners so young it's utterly disgusting, and in some cases illegal.   Billionaire music mogul David Geffen has a well-known reputation of dating men who are over 40 years younger than him.[832] When he was in his *seventies* he was "dating" a 20-year-old former college football player.[833]

The famous pianist Liberace had a 16-year-old boyfriend when he was fifty-seven years old.[834]   75-year-old actress Holland Taylor, who played Charlie Sheen's

[829] The Guardian "Genetic sexual attraction" (May 16th 2003)

[830] The Telegraph "Disgusted by incest? Genetic Sexual Attraction is real and on the rise" by Charlie Gill (September 9th 2016)

[831] https://marriage-equality.blogspot.com/p/genetic-sexual-attraction.html

[832] Daily Mail "Billionaire David Geffen, 69, splits from toyboy lover 41 years his junior after six years together" by Daniel Bates (February 21st 2012)

[833] Daily Mail "David Geffen takes out restraining order against his '20-year-old former college football player ex after ending affair'" by James Nye (December 29th 2014)

[834] Daily Mail "Liberace's ex-lover who wrote memoir 'Behind the Candelabra' is back behind bars after violating his probation and testing positive for meth in random drug test" by Ashley Collman (September 6th 2013)

mother on *Two and a Half Men,* has a 35-year old girlfriend.[835] David Bowie is alleged to have had sex with a 14-year-old groupie at the height of his career.[836] Jerry Seinfeld dated a 17-year-old when he was thirty-nine years old.[837] And these are just a few of the most well-known instances.

Writer, director, and actor Woody Allen is considered a "treasure of the cinema" (having won four Academy Awards and nominated 24 times), but nobody in the industry seems to care that he began a sexual relationship with his girlfriend Mia Farrow's adopted 21-year-old daughter when he was fifty-six.[838]

Such people would be shunned in most professions, but for decades Hollywood has welcomed those who engage in the most bizarre behaviors and nothing is too taboo. The "MeToo" movement really originated in Hollywood from actresses who finally grew tired of the predatory environment that was pervasive in the industry. A long list of big-named actors have been accused of sexual harassment and other predatory behavior as the "MeToo" movement gained momentum in 2017.

But it seems everyone in the industry was very well aware of what was happening and who the perpetrators were. It took the fall of Harvey Weinstein to finally open

---

[835] Page Six "Sarah Paulson defends 32-year age gap with girlfriend Holland Taylor" by Francesca Bacardi (May 22nd 2018)

[836] The Guardian "'I wouldn't want this for anybody's daughter': will #MeToo kill off the rock'n'roll groupie?" by Thea De Gallier (March 15th 2018)

[837] Seinfeld FAQ: Everything Left to Know About the Show About by Nicholas Nigro Nothing (2015 Applause Theatre and Cinema Books)

[838] New York Times "Woody Allen, Mia Farrow, Soon-Yi Previn, Dylan Farrow: A Timeline" by Sopan Deb and Deborah Leiderman (January 31st 2018)

the floodgates and admit the entertainment industry had a massive sexual predator problem. But sleazebags in Hollywood who prey on young actresses are just the tip of the deviance iceberg that runs rampant in the industry. And even worse, what they're doing is being exported to the rest of society.

Celebrity Selfies

Selfies are a symptom of our narcissistic culture, with people obsessing over posting pretty pictures of themselves on social media in order to feel validated. It's a sickness that has infected large portions of our society and celebrities like Rihanna, Miley Cyrus, and Kim Kardashian have normalized posting nude pictures online, something that just a few years ago would have been unthinkable for most girls.[839]

Some experts have even said that celebrities like Kim Kardashian are making children vulnerable to predators online because so many of them mimic their scantily clad selfies in hopes of attracting the attention of complete strangers who "like" and comment on their posts.[840] Kim even had her 4-year-old daughter (at the time) take a topless photo of her and posted it on Instagram.[841]

---

[839] Time "Study Finds Most Teens Sext Before They're 18" by Randye Hoder (July 3rd 2014)

[840] Daily Mail "Children 'at risk of abuse' because they're copying Kim's sexy selfies: Trend for imitating explicit images posted online by celebrities leaves young girls vulnerable to predators, experts warn" by Laura Cox (November 14th 2014)

[841] People "Kim Kardashian Posts Topless Photo Taken by Daughter North West" by Brittany Talarico (February 8th 2018)

You could see little North (her daughter) in a mirror holding the phone, taking the picture. Kim Kardashian even captioned it "By North." Teaching 4-year-old girls to take topless photos and post them online—that's Hollywood today.

Kim Kardashian, perhaps more than any other celebrity has normalized sex tapes. Without hers being "leaked" in 2007 showing her with her then-boyfriend pop singer Ray J, she would be just another spoiled rich girl in Los Angeles, but her sex tape made her a star. The same thing with Paris Hilton's.

When her sex tape was leaked in 2003 she became a star overnight only to be later overshadowed by Kim Kardashian as the "queen" of pop culture. Some wannabe reality stars have even leaked their own sex tapes hoping to follow in these footsteps thinking they too will become famous.

Mainstreaming of Porn

People who regularly watch porn have their brains physically altered through the creation of new neural pathways, causing them to become less aroused by actual women during real sexual encounters over time.[842] These neurological changes are similar to the tolerance level of drug addicts which cause them to need more of the drug to achieve the same high they once got the longer they use it.

People who develop porn habits often find themselves in need of more hardcore porn to get aroused, even leading them to watch bizarre fetish videos hoping to get

---

[842] The Telegraph "How porn is rewiring our brains" by Nisha Lilia Diu (November 15th 2013)

off since they don't experience enough gratification from "regular" porn, let alone actual sexual partners.[843]

The Internet has mainstreamed porn since people had to once drive to seedy adult video stores to get VHS tapes of it, but now millions of videos are just a few clicks away. Twitter even allows porn stars (and aspiring porn "actresses") to have accounts where they can post sexually explicit content in their feed which can easily be accessed by children.[844]

A site called PornHub is basically YouTube for porn, where anyone can upload hardcore pornographic videos and they are then instantly published for the world to see. Due to the lack of oversight that traditional pornography producers follow, like verifying the identity, age, and consent of the parties involved, PornHub has hosted numerous videos of underage girls and even rape videos, including one of a 14-year-old girl from Ohio who was kidnapped and gang raped while being recorded by the assailants.[845]

The video was uploaded to PornHub several times with titles like "Teen Crying and Getting Slapped Around," "Teen Getting Destroyed," and "Passed out Teen." One upload had over 400,000 views.[846] The victim later emailed the website, explaining she was raped (which was clear by the video and the titles) but the video remained online.

---

[843] Ibid.

[844] Vice "Porn Is Still Allowed On Twitter" by Samantha Cole (November 3rd 2017)

[845] BBC "'I was raped at 14, and the video ended up on a porn site'" by Megha Mohan (February 10th 2020).

[846] Ibid.

A 30-year-old man in Florida uploaded over 50 different videos of him sexually abusing a 15-year-old girl after she went missing before he was finally arrested.[847] Breitbart pointed out, "Pornhub apparently has no idea whatsoever who is uploading content. Pornhub also has no idea and apparently doesn't bother to verify the age of the performers in the videos, or if they consented to have sex, to be filmed, or to have the video commercialized and made public."[848]

There's now a social media company called OnlyFans that caters to girls who want to start selling their own amateur nude photos and porn videos. OnlyFans is basically like Instagram, but people have to pay a monthly fee to see what others are posting, and the website has no rules about nudity other than the users have to supposedly be 18 years old.

When unemployment levels skyrocketed because of the stay-at-home orders during the Coronavirus Pandemic of 2020, many young girls flocked to OnlyFans hoping to make some easy money. Once they're signed up they use Instagram and Twitter to promote their accounts by leaving the link to their OnlyFans page in their bio and then post content using trending hashtags hoping to get guys' attention and drive traffic there.

Previously if a girl wanted to get into porn she would have to go to work for a company that had the infrastructure to host the videos and charge customers' credit cards, but now OnlyFans has given the ability to

---

[847] Newsweek "Florida Man Arrested After 58 Porn Videos, Photos Link Him To Missing Underage Teen Girl" by Scott McDonald (October 23rd 2019)

[848] Breitbart "Nolte: Pornhub Under Fire for Allegedly Hosting Rape, Child Porn Videos" by John Nolte (February 10th 2020)

anyone to become a "porn star" within just a few minutes. It's well known that many aspiring actresses who move to Los Angeles hoping to become stars end up working in porn out of desperation to pay their bills (or to afford their drug habits). Some even resort to prostitution.

Teen Vogue magazine even published an article in 2019 titled "Sex Work is Real Work," encouraging girls to become prostitutes and demanding that it become legalized around the world.[849]

Many psychologists are warning that porn and video game addiction is actually causing a masculinity crisis among young men. A study by researchers at Stanford University looked into how excessive gaming and use of pornography is causing many young men to be extremely isolated and preventing them from developing the social skills needed to form relationships with girls, which only fuels more isolation.[850]

Pedophiles in Hollywood

Sexual harassment and pornography aren't Hollywood's worst problems however, as child actor Corey Feldman said, "the number one problem in Hollywood was, is, and always will be, pedophilia. That's the biggest problem for children in this industry...It's the

---

[849] Teen Vogue "Sex Work is Real Work" by Dr. Tlaleng Mofokeng (April 26th 2019)

[850] The Independent "Porn and video game addiction leading to 'masculinity crisis', says Stanford psychologist" by Doug Bolton (March 10th 2015)

big secret."[851]   He made the claim in 2011 on ABC's *Nightlight*, but his concerns largely fell on deaf ears.

A few years later in 2013 when he was a guest on *The View* the topic came up again.   "I'm saying there are people that were the people that did this to both me and Corey [Haim] that are still working, they're still out there, and that are some of the richest most powerful people in this business. And they do not want me saying what I am saying right now," he told the hosts.[852]

Barbara Walters responded, "Are you saying that they are pedophiles and that they are still in this business?"

"Yes," Corey replied, going on to warn parents who are thinking about getting their children involved in acting.

"You're damaging an entire industry," Barbara responds, looking disappointed in him.

Feldman said that his best friend Corey Haim, who he costarred with in numerous movies, told him that Charlie Sheen raped Haim in 1986 on the set of a movie (*Lucas*) they were filming together.[853] Sheen allegedly told Haim, "it was perfectly normal for older men and younger boys in the business" and "it was what all the guys do."[854] Sheen denies the allegation.

---

[851] ABC News Nightline "Actor Corey Feldman Says Pedophilia No. 1 Problem for Child Stars, Contributed to Demise of Corey Haim" By Steven Baker and David Wright (August 10, 2011)

[852] Fox News "Corey Feldman's tense Barbara Walters interview recirculates amid Harvey Weinstein scandal" (October 17th 2017)

[853] Entertainment Weekly "Corey Feldman accuses Charlie Sheen of sexually abusing Corey Haim in *(My) Truth* documentary" by Rosy Cordero (March 10th 2020)

[854] Ibid.

"It's all connected to a bigger, darker power," Feldman later said. "I don't know how high up the chain that power goes, but I know that it probably is outside of the film industry too. It's probably in government; it's probably throughout the world in different dark aspects."[855]

Elijah Wood, who was a child actor in various films before hitting it big by playing Frodo in the *Lord of the Rings* trilogy, once made some comments during an interview about the issue, saying, "Clearly something major was going on in Hollywood. It was all organized. There are a lot of vipers in this industry, people who only have their own interests in mind. There is darkness in the underbelly. What bums me about these situations is that the victims can't speak as loudly as the people in power. That's the tragedy of attempting to reveal what is happening to innocent people: they can be squashed, but their lives have been irreparably damaged."[856]

He later "clarified" his statements, claiming that his interview was supposed to be about his latest film but "became about something else entirely" and said he had "no first-hand experience or observation of the topic" and that he just heard about such things from a documentary he had seen (most likely *An Open Secret*, which had come out a year earlier).[857]

[855] Vanity Fair "Corey Feldman on Abuse Allegations: 'It's All Connected to a Bigger, Darker Power'" by Yohana Desta (November 10th 2017)

[856] Vanity Fair "Elijah Wood Says Hollywood Has a Pedophilia Problem" by Alex Stedman (May 23rd 2016)

[857] CNN "Elijah Wood clarifies comments on pedophilia and Hollywood" by Lisa Respers (May 24th 2016)

An Open Secret

In 2014, a film maker named Amy Berg investigated Corey Feldman's claims of pedophiles in Hollywood in a documentary titled *An Open Secret*. Previously she had been nominated for an Oscar for another documentary she made called *Deliver Us From Evil* about sexual abuse in the Catholic Church, so it was a subject she was quite familiar with.

An Open Secret alleges that pedophile producers have held parties where they enticed young child actors with drugs and alcohol in order to take advantage of them.[858] It details the alleged activities surrounding an Internet media company called Digital Entertainment Network that was founded in the late-1990s by Marc Collins-Rector [a convicted sex offender], and his boyfriend Chad Shackley.[859] The company is alleged to have held pool parties at their 12,000-square foot mansion that were used to entice underage teenage boys into having sex with adult men.[860]

Leonardo DiCaprio's former talent agent was convicted of molesting a 13-year-old boy in 2005 and sentenced to eight years in prison.[861] The Los Angeles

---

[858] The Hollywood Reporter "Hollywood Sex Abuse Film Revealed: Explosive Claims, New Figures Named (Exclusive)" by Gregg Kilday (November 12th 2014)

[859] The Atlantic "Nobody Is Going to Believe You" by Alex French and Maximillian Potter (March 2019 Issue)

[860] The Hollywood Reporter "Bryan Singer Sex Abuse Case: The Troubling History Behind the Accusations" by Kim Masters and Jonathan Handel (April 30th 2014)

[861] Los Angeles Times "Child sexual abuse cases in Hollywood attract attention" by Dawn C. Chmielewski (January 08, 2012)

county deputy district attorney said, "People like this are predators who prey on little kids who want to be the next Justin Bieber—and they're told, 'That's what's done, this is all normal in the industry.'"[862] *The Los Angeles Times* noted that, "At least a dozen child molestation and child pornography prosecutions since [the year] 2000 have involved actors, managers, production assistants and others in the entertainment industry."[863]

One of those was a talent agent named Martin Weiss who managed kids that had roles on Nickelodeon, the Disney Channel, and in numerous films like *Parenthood* and *The Muppets Movie*. He was charged with several counts of child molestation and faced up to 80-years in prison, but was given just one.[864]

Director Bryan Singer, whose credits include *X-Men, Superman Returns, Valkyrie*, and many others, has been accused by numerous men who say he made sexual advances towards them when they were boys.[865] Singer, who denies the allegations, has also claimed journalists who were investigating him were just "homophobic."[866]

Singer is also alleged to have been in attendance at some of the parties held by the Digital Entertainment Network, and is well known in Hollywood for hosting his own pool parties filled with what many have described as

---

[862] Ibid

[863] Ibid

[864] Ibid

[865] People "Bohemian Rhapsody Director Bryan Singer Accused of Sexually Assaulting Four Underage Boys" by Ale Russian (January 23rd 2019)

[866] Variety "Bryan Singer Hit With Fresh Allegations of Sex With Underage Boys" by Gene Maddaus (January 23rd 2019)

"kids."[867]   He has been followed by sexual predator accusations for decades.   As far back as 1997 several child actors accused him of asking them to film a nude scene when they were working on one of his movies, yet his career has continued almost unscathed.[868]

Infamous pedophile Jeffrey Epstein also had numerous ties with Hollywood A-listers, some of which had flown on his private jet to his island in the Caribbean, dubbed "Pedo Island."[869] Epstein operated with impunity for years and is believed by many to have worked as an intelligence operative for Mossad (Israel's CIA) to get dirt on powerful people, including many politicians, so they could be blackmailed.[870]

For decades Hollywood hasn't seemed to care about child abuse, and in fact many defend it and give awards to the abusers.   Director Roman Polanski fled the United States in the 1970s after he was convicted of drugging and raping a 13-year-old girl, but continued to make films in Europe where he could avoid being extradited by U.S. authorities.[871]   Not only did he continue to make films, but Hollywood continued to give him awards.

---

[867] The Federalist "A Timeline of the Many Sexual Assault Accusations Against Director Bryan Singer" by Paulina Enck (June 25th 2020)

[868] Chicago Tribune "Bryan Singer Allegations Part of Upcoming Sex Abuse Documentary" by Ramin Setoodeh (April 18th 2014)

[869] New York Magazine "Jeffrey Epstein's Rolodex: A Guide to His Famous Friends and Acquaintances" by Adam K. Raymond and Matt Stieb (July 10th 2019)

[870] Fox News "Jeffrey Epstein's alleged 'spy' ties under fresh scrutiny in new book" by Hollie McKay (June 18th 2020)

[871] Daily Mail "French government drops support for director Roman Polanski as he faces extradition to the U.S." by Peter Allen (October 1st 2009)

In 2002 he was given the Oscar for Best Director for his film *The Pianist*. When he was announced as the winner, the audience gave him a roaring applause and a standing ovation by many, including Martin Scorsese and Meryl Streep.[872] Harrison Ford, who was presenting the winner that year, looked out at the crowd astonished, knowing very well why Polanski wasn't there to accept his award. After the applause died down he said, "The Academy congratulates Roman Polanski, and accepts this award on his behalf."[873]

Not only did his peers give him a standing ovation at the Oscars, but many in Hollywood defend Polanski, still to this day. Whoopi Goldberg said that things were "different" in the 1970s, and it wasn't "rape-rape" and thinks Polanski should be left alone and not extradited to the United States to serve the prison time he has been avoiding for over 40 years.[874]

In an interview on the Howard Stern Show director Quentin Tarantino defended Polanski. Howard interrupted him, saying, "Wait a minute. If you have sex with a 13-year-old girl and you're a grown man, you know that that's wrong."[875]

Howard's cohost Robin Quivers was stunned and pointed out that Polanski had also given her alcohol and

---

[872] Snopes "Did Meryl Streep Applaud Roman Polanski at the Academy Awards?" Rating: True (January 9th 2017)

[873] CBS News "An Oscar Out Of Reach For Polanski" via the Associated Press (Marcy 24th 2003)

[874] The Guardian "Polanski was not guilty of 'rape-rape', says Whoopi Goldberg" by MaevKennedy (September 29th 2009)

[875] Time "Quentin Tarantino Defends Roman Polanski in Resurfaced Interview: 13-Year-Old Victim 'Wanted to Have It' by Cady Lang (February 7th 2018)

Quaaludes to which Tarantino responded, "She wanted to have it…And by the way, we're talking about America's morals, not talking about the morals in Europe and everything…Look, she was down with this."[876]

In 2009, Harvey Weinstein wrote an op-ed in *The Independent* titled "Polanski has served his time and must be freed."[877] Over one hundred Hollywood celebrities and directors including Natalie Portman, Penelope Cruz, David Lynch, and Martin Scorsese, signed a petition that year to show their support for Polanski, demanding his release after he was taken into custody in Switzerland since he was facing extradition back to the U.S.[878]

Switzerland later decided against extraditing him and let him go free. Virtually an entire industry rallied behind a man who drugged and raped a 13-year-old girl and then fled the country to avoid going to prison. That's Hollywood!

After a documentary called *Leaving Neverland* investigated some of the allegations surrounding Michael Jackson, singer Barbra Streisand said she believed boys were molested by Jackson, but, "they were thrilled to be there" and "his sexual needs were his sexual needs," adding, "They [the alleged victims] both married and they both have children, so it didn't kill them."[879]

[876] Ibid.

[877] The Independent "Polanski has served his time and must be freed" by Harvey Weinstein (September 28th 2009)

[878] Indy Wire "Over 100 In Film Community Sign Polanski Petition" by Peter Knegt (September 29th 2009)

[879] Rolling Stone "Barbra Streisand Draws Criticism for Stance on Michael Jackson's 'Leaving Neverland' Accusers" by Daniel Kreps (March 23rd 2019)

In 2017, Stephen King's *It* was remade into a feature film due to the wildly popular TV miniseries in 1990, but what people who hadn't read the 1987 novel don't know is that Stephen King depicted the kids all having an orgy after they finally defeated the "It" creature in the sewer. Out of the blue Beverly Marsh, the only girl in the group, tells the boys "I have an idea," and then they all got naked and she has sex with all six of them.[880]

In the book she's depicted as eleven-years-old (and twelve in the 1990 TV miniseries). Once the boys are all done having sex with her, they magically remember which way to go in order to get out of the sewer and finally escape. Stephen King literally wrote an entire scene about an eleven-year-old girl getting gang banged and nobody seems to care.[881]

Actress Annette O'Toole, who played Beverly Marsh in the 1990 television version, was upset that the orgy scene wasn't allowed in the film. "This was their greatest attachment to one another—she thought they were all going to die, and this was a gift she was giving to each one of them, and I thought it was the most beautiful, generous love-filled gift, and it tied them all together in such an amazing way."[882]

In 2017 after Kevin Spacey was accused of trying to engage in a sexual relationship with a 14-year-old child actor back in 1986, he announced for the first time that he

---

[880] The Independent "It movie: How the book's infamous orgy scene is handled and why Stephen King wrote the scene" by Jack Shepherd (September 10th 2017)

[881] The Telegraph "Why the It movie left out Stephen King's Losers' Club sewer orgy" by Adam White (September 8th 2017)

[882] SciFiNow Annual "Stephen King's It: 25th Anniversary" (Vol. 2. 2015) pages 160–163

was gay. That deflected much of the media criticism away from the allegations and he was celebrated for his "emotional" admission.

ABC News ran a story with the headline, "'I choose now to live as a gay man,' Kevin Spacey comes out in emotional tweet," but later changed it due to the backlash from people who on social media were shocked ABC sanitized the story with such a pleasant headline.[883]

The CEO of entertainment giant Allied Artists, Kim Richards, said of Spacey, "If true, acting on impulse while inebriated speaks to over-indulgence, not predatory behavior. You're good & decent, deserving forgiveness."[884]

Years earlier Seth McFarlane's *Family Guy* animated comedy series included a brief scene of a character (Stewie) running naked through a shopping mall screaming "Help! I've escaped from Kevin Spacey's basement!"[885] McFarlane had previously called out Harvey Weinstein in 2013, years before the MeToo movement and the widespread reports about Weinstein. When he read off the names of the nominees for Best Supporting Actress for the Oscars, he followed up by

---

[883] Mediaite "ABC News Changes Headline About Kevin Spacey After Spinning His 'Emotional' Coming Out" by Joseph A. Wulfsohn (October 30th 2017)

[884] News.com.au "'Over-indulgence, not predatory behaviour': Hollywood CEO says Kevin Spacey deserves forgiveness" by Frank Chung (October 31st 2017)

[885] Entertainment Weekly "Family Guy producers finally explain origin of 2005 Kevin Spacey joke" by Dan Snierson (January 4th 2018)

saying, "Congratulations, you five ladies no longer have to pretend to be attracted to Harvey Weinstein."[886]

McFarlane knew of the rumors about Weinstein but at the time outsiders just though it was a joke. Many wondered if he also heard rumors about Kevin Spacey's secrets as well, resulting in him adding the bizarre scene in *Family Guy*. Others came forward with similar allegations as well. Spacey was soon fired from his Netflix series *House of Cards*, and went into hiding.

But on Christmas Eve of 2019 he posted a bizarre video on YouTube speaking in the tone of his evil *House of Cards* character Frank Underwood while sitting in front of a fireplace. "You didn't really think I was going to miss the opportunity to wish you a Merry Christmas, did you?" he began. "I know what you're thinking, 'Can he be serious?' I'm dead serious. The next time someone does something you don't like, you can go on the attack. But you can also hold your fire and do the unexpected. You can…kill them with kindness."[887] He smiled menacingly at the camera and the video ends.

Even more disturbing is that one of his accusers had died just a few months earlier.[888] He seemed to be alluding that he had killed him. The very next day, on Christmas, *another* one of his accusers died from a

---

[886] Hollywood Reporter "Seth MacFarlane Explains 2013 Oscars Jab at 'Abhorrent, Indefensible' Harvey Weinstein" by Ashley Lee (October 11th 2017)

[887] USA Today "Kevin Spacey posts bizarre video suggesting you 'kill people with kindness'" by Maria Puente (December 24th 2019)

[888] Hollywood Reporter "Kevin Spacey Accuser Dies in Midst of Sexual Assault Lawsuit" by Eriq Gardner (September 18th 2019)

purported suicide.[889]   That person's estate then dropped
the lawsuit against Spacey which had been pending.

---

[889] CBS News "Kevin Spacey accuser and writer Ari Behn dies by
suicide" via Associated Press (December 26th 2019)

Crimes Inspired by Hollywood

While it's not entirely accurate to say that violence depicted in movies *causes* real world violence, it can be said that sometimes it's a catalyst, and in numerous cases mass murderers, bombings, bank robberies, and other crimes have been inspired by popular movies. Extensive news coverage of mass shootings is actually correlated with *more* mass shootings because it seems to plant the seeds in other lunatics' minds.[890]   The same is true of news reports about suicide, a phenomenon called suicide contagion.[891]

The FBI and Department of Homeland Security were concerned that *Joker* (2019) may inspire mass shootings at theaters, so police presence was increased during the film's opening weekend and some even inserted undercover agents inside as a precaution.[892]   The fears arose from a lunatic dressed as the Joker opening fire inside a theater during a showing of *The Dark Knight*

---

[890] NBC News "Mass shootings: Experts say violence is contagious, and 24/7 news cycle doesn't help" by Dennis Romero (August 5th 2019)

[891] Time "Suicide Deaths Are Often 'Contagious.' This May Help Explain Why" by Jamie Ducharme (April 18th 2019)

[892] Washington Post "Undercover police officers in theaters as Warner Bros.' 'Joker' opens" by Steven Zetchik (October 4th 2019)

Rises in 2012, killing a dozen people and injuring many more.

The *New York Post* reported that, "It's reasonable to ask if 'Joker' will inspire would-be killers."[893] Some of the victims' families of *The Dark Knight Rises* shooting wrote a letter to Warner Brothers, the studio that produced *Joker*, expressing their concern that the movie gave the character a "sympathetic origin story."[894] It's not a typical superhero film, nor is it cartoonish in any way like many of the previous Batman movies. Instead, *Joker* is a depressing "character study" showing a man descend into madness and morph into a mass murderer, but because a portion of the population are severely mentally ill, many saw the Joker as a hero.

The 1976 film *Taxi Driver* starring Robert De Niro (which was largely the inspiration for *Joker*) is said to have triggered John Hinckley Jr.'s murderous fantasy that resulted in him attempting to assassinate President Ronald Reagan in 1981. In *Taxi Driver,* Robert De Niro's character plots the assassination of a presidential candidate he becomes fixated on, which gave John Hinkley Jr. the idea to do the same thing to Ronald Reagan. He later shot Reagan outside the Washington Hilton Hotel.[895]

In the 1995 film *Basketball Diaries* starring Leonardo DiCaprio, his character has a dream sequence where he

---

[893] The New York Post "It's reasonable to ask if 'Joker' will inspire would-be killers" by Sara Stewart (September 24th 2019)

[894] NBC News "'Joker' backlash: Aurora shooting victims' families express concerns to Warner Bros." by Daniel Arkin (September 24th 2019)

[895] Washington Post "Hinckley, Jury Watch 'Taxi Driver' Film" by Laura A. Kiernan (May 29th 1982)

walks into his high school wearing a black trench coat and starts blowing away his fellow classmates with a shotgun. Three years later in 1998, two students in Colorado carried out the infamous Columbine High School shooting, causing the very name "Columbine" to become synonymous with a school shooting.

The killers wore black trench coats on the day of the massacre just like Leonardo DiCaprio. Some parents of the victims filed lawsuits against the producers of *The Basketball Diaries* for inspiring the attack. The Columbine massacre itself has inspired dozens of copycats from more unhinged high school students who see the killers as heroes.[896]

Oliver Stone's 1994 black comedy *Natural Born Killers* is believed to have inspired over a dozen copycat murders and mass shootings by teenagers in the 1990s and early 2000s.[897] In the film, a murderous couple (Mickey and Mallory) go on a drug-fueled killing spree and become television news sensations. Oliver Stone says he meant the film to be a critique of how the media sensationalizes violence and murders, but some unhinged viewers actually saw Mickey and Mallory as true heroes and wanted to become famous mass murderers just like them.

After actor Robin Williams committed suicide in 2014, researchers believed it caused suicide rates to spike almost 10% from copycats. "Although we cannot determine with certainty that these deaths are attributable

---

[896] The Hill "Investigation shows more than 100 copycat shooters inspired by Columbine since 1999" by Rachel Frazin (April 17th 2019)

[897] The Guardian "Natural Born Copycats" by Xan Brooks (December 19th 2002)

to the death of Robin Williams, we found both a rapid increase in suicides in August 2014, and specifically suffocation suicides, that paralleled the time and method of Williams' death," said a report compiled by researchers at Columbia University.[898]   NBC News admitted, "It has been known for decades that media reports about suicides, especially celebrity suicides, lead to an increase of suicide deaths."[899]

The Netflix teen drama 13 Reasons Why is about a girl who commits suicide after being bullied and gossiped about at her high school. She left behind a box of cassette tapes where she recorded the "13 reasons why" she killed herself, which forms the basis of the show, and many researchers believe that the series actually increased the rate of teenage suicide.[900]   Studies show that suicide is "contagious" and the more widely it is portrayed in the media, the more people get inspired to follow the same path in hopes of putting an end to their own personal struggles.[901]

At the University of Illinois, a student was arrested for sexually assaulting a woman he tied up in his dorm room in order to re-create a scene from Fifty Shades of Grey, the popular sadomasochism film based on the bestselling novel.[902]   The lead actor in the film, Jamie Dornan, later

---

[898] NBC News "Robin Williams' death followed by rise in suicides" by Maggie Fox (February 7th 2018)

[899] Ibid.

[900] NPR "Teen Suicide Spiked After Debut Of Netflix's '13 Reasons Why,' Study Says" by Matthew S. Schwartz (April 30th 2019)

[901] New York Times "The Science Behind Suicide Contagion" by Margot Sanger-Katz (August 13th 2014)

[902] Time "Fifty Shades of Grey Inspired Student's Sexual Assault, Prosecutors Say" by Kevin McSpadden (February 24th 2015)

admitted that he feared a crazy obsessed fan would actually murder him like John Lennon.[903]

Ben Affleck's 2010 film *The Town* was the admitted inspiration behind a pair of Brooklyn crooks who, like the characters in the film, dressed up as cops to rob a local check-cashing business.[904] Another robbery at a bank in Chicago is also believed to have been inspired by *The Town*, where the perpetrators copied a different scene from the film in which the characters dressed as nuns for their disguise when they robbed one of the banks.[905]

A teenager in New York City was inspired by *Fight Club* to bomb a Starbucks which thankfully didn't cause any injuries because it was closed.[906] In the 1999 film, the underground fight club started by Brad Pitt and Edward Norton escalates into a terrorist organization with the launch of "Project Mayhem," beginning with a series of attacks on symbols of corporate America. One of those attacks was on a "corporate piece of art" consisting of a gigantic metal ball which is knocked off its foundation and rolls into a nearby coffee shop, clearly designed to look like a Starbucks, destroying it.

There is also speculation that a serial bomber in Austin, Texas who ultimately blew himself up after being pulled over by police may have been inspired by a recent

---

[903] New York Daily News "Jamie Dornan says he's scared of 'Fifty Shades of Grey' fans: 'I fear I'll get murdered like John Lennon'" by Kirthana Ramisetti (January 8th 2015)

[904] Daily Mail "Revealed: How black robbers copied Ben Affleck film 'The Town' by disguising themselves as white cops with latex masks to snatch $200,000 from check-cashing store" (July 31st 2013)

[905] ABC News "Thieves Dressed Like Nuns Rob Chicago Bank in Scene out of 'The Town'" by Russell Goldman (May 31st 2011)

[906] NBC New York "Teen Pleads Guilty to 'Fight Club'-Inspired Starbucks Bombing" by Colleen Long (September 17th 2010)

television series about Ted Kaczynski, the "Unabomber."[907] The perpetrator had sent five package bombs in the Austin area, killing two people and injuring five others during a three week period in March 2018.

On Halloween night in 2018 police in France arrested over 100 masked people for rioting and threatening locals after word spread through social media calling for a "Purge," referring to the 2013 horror film of the same name which depicts the American government allowing all crimes, including murder, to be perfectly legal for one night a year. [908]

Similar "Purge" threats have gone viral through social media in the United States claiming such uprisings would occur in various communities on specific dates, thankfully turning out to be hoaxes posted by troublesome teenagers.[909] But the inspiration for the threats of indiscriminate killing for "fun" were obviously inspired by the film.

Following the 1996 release of *Scream* there were also numerous murders and attempted murders by people inspired by the teen slasher film, several of which actually involved the famous Ghostface mask that the killer used in the movie.[910] Two days after watching *Interview with the Vampire* when it first came out in 1994, a man told his

---

[907] Inside Edition "Was Suspect in Austin Explosions Inspired by Unabomber Miniseries?" (March 20th 2018)

[908] Reuters "French police arrest over 100 after Halloween 'Purge' night riots" by Michael Roseand Catherine Lagrange (November 1st 2018)

[909] USA Today "Social media 'Purge' campaigns spark fear of bloody copycats" by Nindsay Deutsch, Kelsey Pape and Ryan Haarer (August 19th 2014)

[910] The Irish Times "Student charged with murder amid concerns in France over violent films" (June 6th 2002)

girlfriend "I'm going to kill you and drink your blood," and proceeded to stab her seven times and did indeed drink her blood. She miraculously survived, and when he was arrested the "vampire" admitted to police he was inspired by the film starring Tom Cruise and Brad Pitt.[911]

Rap Videos

Nothing promotes violence and crime more than rap music. Listeners internalize the lyrics which are presented from a first-person perspective, putting them in the proverbial driver's seat of countless drive-by shootings and other mayhem which is portrayed as exciting and fun.

It would be impossible to know how many seeds have been planted in the minds of thugs who become accustomed to crime and whose music choices reflect back to them a distorted world where they are a hero for the lifestyle they chose. Many former gang members have admitted that the music helped to "brainwash" them.[912] And numerous studies have connected rap music to real world violence.[913]

It's common for rappers to include a line in their songs about doing a "187 on a cop," which is a police code for murder. Countless rappers from Snoop Dogg and NWA, to Eminem and Tekashi 6ix9ine have entire songs about murdering people. Just two weeks after the

---

[911] Orlando Sentinel "Inspired by Vampire Film, Man Stabs His Girlfriend" (November 30th 1994)

[912] Chicago Tribune "Ex-gang member talks about rap music's influence" by Dawn M. Turner (November 5th 2015)

[913] NPR "Study: Rap Music Linked to Alcohol, Violence" (May 8th 2006)

Sandy Hook Elementary School massacre, where twenty children and six adults were gunned down by 20-year-old lunatic Adam Lanza, stunning the entire country, a popular rapper who goes by "The Game" released a song titled "Dead People" which is about him stalking and murdering people for fun.[914]

A 17-year-old acting out the music video "Bustin' At 'Em" from rapper Waka Flocka Flame accidentally shot and killed his friend while he was waving a gun around.[915] The lyrics go "Shoot first ask questions last. That's how these so called gangstas last. Bitch I'm bustin' at 'em (shooting). Ain't no talkin' homie I'm just bustin' at 'em. Bitch I'm bustin' at 'em." In the music video Waka Flocka Flame and his thug friends are waving guns around shooting them in all directions the entire time.

After a man in Hawaii shot and killed his landlord, he claimed he was possessed by rapper Jay Z and said that *he* should be the one who goes to prison.[916] In a certain sense the man *was* possessed by Jay Z, since the rapper's murderous lyrics filled his head. In his mind he just did what he thought Jay Z would have done. Jay Z has called for George Zimmerman, the man who shot Trayvon Martin in self-defense, to be killed, and has numerous songs about murdering people.[917]

---

[914] "Dead People" by The Game on the album "Jesus Piece" (2012)

[915] USA Today "Sheriff: Man acting out rap song fatally shoots friend" by J.D. Gallop via Florida Today (January 28th 2015)

[916] Hawaii Tribune Herald "Nanawale murder suspect says Jay Z possessed his body" by John Burnett (October 10th 2015)

[917] Spin "Jay-Z Asks Why XXXTentacion Died While George Zimmerman Lives on Drake's 'Talk Up'" by Israel Daramola (June 29th 2018)

Thousands of years ago philosophers like Plato, Aristotle, and Socrates understood the influence that music has on its listeners. Aristotle recognized that music can even shape people's character, saying, "Music directly represents the passions of the soul. If one listens to the wrong kind of music, he will become the wrong kind of person."[918]

Bobo Doll Experiment

A famous study conducted in the early 1960s known as the Bobo Doll Experiment demonstrated how children often mimic violent behaviors they see others engaging in. Researchers monitored the children in a playroom filled with a variety of toys including a bobo doll, a sort of inflatable punching bag with a weighted bottom that stands on the ground—and when punched, returns to its upright position.

Even though the bobo doll was in the room and available for the children to play with, they mostly ignored it at first, but after witnessing an adult punching the toy, they began doing the same thing, imitating their actions shortly after they had left the room.[919] The experiment clearly demonstrates the fundamentals of social learning theory and observational learning because the children's behavior immediately changed from simply witnessing the adults interact with the doll in a "violent" manner, or as the saying goes—monkey see, monkey do.

---

[918] *A Concise Survey of Music Philosophy* by Donald A Hodges page 111 (Routledge 2016)

[919] Simple Psychology "Bobo Doll Experiment" by Sean McLeod (February 5th 2014)

And just like children mimicked the actions they saw against the bobo doll, they also mimic behaviors they see in the media. A Senate Committee was formed in 1999 to investigate the influence of media violence on children and concluded that one of the primary catalysts of youth violence *is* media violence.[920]

The word *cause* may be too strong of a word, and to more accurately describe the relationship between viewing violence and engaging in violent acts, media effects researchers often use the word *prime*, instead— meaning viewing violence primes people to potentially act out similar behaviors.[921]

One popular textbook, *The Fundamentals of Media Effects*, explains, "Media message content triggers concepts, thoughts, learning, or knowledge acquired in the past that are related to the message content. In this way, message content is connected, associated, or *reinforced* by related thoughts and concepts that it brings to mind."[922]

There are numerous variables that function as catalysts for priming aggressive or violent behaviors in viewers, such as the extent they identify with a character engaging in violence, the consequences the character

---

[920] CHILDREN, VIOLENCE, AND THE MEDIA: A Report for Parents and Policy Makers Senate Committee on the Judiciary, Senator Orrin G. Hatch, Utah, Chairman, Committee on the Judiciary, Prepared by Majority Staff Senate Committee on the Judiciary (September 14, 1999)

[921] Fundamentals of Media Effects - Second Edition by Jennings Bryant, Susan Thompson, and Bruce W. Finklea page 74 (Waveland Press Inc. 2013)

[922] Fundamentals of Media Effects - Second Edition by Jennings Bryant, Susan Thompson, and Bruce W. Finklea pages 78-81 (Waveland Press Inc. 2013)

faces for such behavior, and the perceived justification for it, or meaning of the violence.[923]

Media mogul Ted Turner knew this, as do most people with common sense. Best known for founding CNN in 1980, he once noted, "You know that everything we're exposed to, influences us...those violent films influence us, and the TV programs we see influence us. The weaker your family is, the more they influence you. The problems with families in our societies are catastrophic, but when you put violent programs before people who haven't had a lot of love in their lives, who are angry anyway, it is like pouring gasoline on the fire."[924]

---

[923] Fundamentals of Media Effects - Second Edition by Jennings Bryant, Susan Thompson, and Bruce W. Finklea page 79 (Waveland Press Inc. 2013)

[924] Los Angeles Times "We're Listening, Ted" by Jane Hall (April 03, 1994)

Author's Note: Once you finish this book, please take a moment to rate and review it on Amazon.com, or wherever you purchased it from if you're reading the e-book, to let others know what you think. This also helps to offset the trolls who keep giving my books fake one-star reviews when they haven't even read them.

Trolls often target books on Amazon written by people they don't like and flood them with fake one-star reviews in order to tank the ratings and hope to dissuade people from reading them. It's a dirty tactic they've used on my other books. If you look close, you can see that practically none of the one-star reviews are from actual verified purchases which is a clear indication they are fraudulent.

Also, please spread the word about this book by posting a link to the Amazon listing on your social media accounts, or order a few extra copies for family and friends. I don't have a large publisher behind me to promote the book since I self published it; all I have is word of mouth, social media, and you.

Thank you!

Conclusion

There's a famous quote attributed to Eleanor Roosevelt that says, "Great minds discuss ideas; average minds discuss events; small minds discuss people." The moronic masses are concerned about who their favorite celebrities are dating, which rappers are having a new beef, or the latest actor found to have said something "racist" years (or decades) ago, while life is passing them by. It's a circus, and as media analyst Neil Postman noted, people are amusing themselves to death.[925]

Everything is backwards and upside down in Los Angeles, even the city's name. "Los Angeles" is Spanish for the *City of Angels,* when it's really a city of demons. Hollywood is the "city of dreams" they say, but it's really the city of *broken* dreams. Cute girls from across the country move to LA thinking they're going to be the next Kim Kardashian or Jennifer Lawrence only to realize that they're just one of tens of thousands of other girls equally as beautiful who are all competing for the same prize.

After a string of dead end auditions or maybe landing a few bit parts in b-movies that are never released in theaters, most girls eventually give up or turn to drugs hoping to numb the increasing depression they feel from not seeing their dreams materialize as they are faced with the harsh reality of the entertainment industry.

---

[925] *Amusing Ourselves to Death* is the title of his famous book on the media, first released in 1985. The subtitle is "Public Discourse in the Age of Show Business"

The supposed sunny blue skies of Los Angeles are filled with toxic smog from the overcrowded freeways. Many of the people driving fancy cars and renting nice houses are often living paycheck to paycheck and have no money saved for retirement and spend most of what they earn trying to portray an image of a person they're not, living further beyond their means every day.

Almost everything is fake in Los Angeles. The LA River is made of concrete. The city's basketball team is called the *Lakers,* but most of the lakes are man-made. Most people think the Hollywood Walk of Fame is a beautiful place symbolic of the glitz and glam they see on the award shows, but in reality it's a dirty street filled with homeless people and beggars.

Los Angeles is widely considered to be one of the loneliest cities in America because so many people living there have few (or no) close friends they can confide in or trust. Many residents don't even make eye contact with their neighbors when out to check the mail, they just ignore them and pretend they don't exist. It's a strange and sad city.

Unfortunately, much of our country is now afflicted with the same kinds of sentiments. The American empire will most likely collapse someday just as ancient Rome did. The United States has too much debt, there is no sense of community throughout much of the country anymore, national pride has been undermined by floods of immigrants who won't assimilate and are openly hostile to our culture, customs, and history—and now even many millions of native-born Americans hate our country as a result of the Marxist indoctrination they've been inundated with.

Open hatred of America by enemies within has never been more widespread, and they are determined to overthrow our Republic and put an end to our Constitutionally protected freedoms.

Child drag queens are being celebrated by major media outlets, celebrities are bragging about their abortions, work ethic is dwindling, calls for socialism are spreading, and people can't decide which one of the fifty-eight different "genders" they are. The angry and ignorant masses want to seize financial assets through force from those who have worked hard and saved their money for decades instead of steadily pissing it away on things they don't need.

But we do need entertainment (in moderation). It's important to relax your mind at the end of the day or get a little distracted after a long week, so what should we do? What can you show your kids without having them indoctrinated with the idiocy and enemy propaganda that surrounds us? Fortunately, there *are* limitless choices of quality entertainment if you just take the time to look.

There are science shows, cooking shows, how-to videos, and plenty of family friendly entertainment available—not to mention good old-fashioned books like the one in your hands. Aside from quality non-fiction books that can educate while they entertain, there are also countless literarily classics that will take your mind on a journey to faraway lands, all from the comfort of your own home.

But it's critical to do a regular digital detox, especially on the weekends, and tune out the endless distractions competing for your attention on television and smartphones. Spend time with family and friends, having face to face interactions, not artificial ones by "liking" their Facebook posts or communicating through social media.

It's important to limit social media consumption because by design it's addictive due to the endless feedback and dopamine boosts people get from "likes" retweets, comments, and follows. Stories on social media are hard to resist because they personalize incidents that happen across the country in cities and states you'll never step foot in, but the viral videos and photos open a window to an artificial world you have no business being in.

It's also dangerous because lies spread through social media at the speed of light, racking up tens of thousands of retweets and "shares" within minutes. By censoring opposing voices, manipulating trending topics, and major celebrities constantly jumping on the bandwagon for liberal causes, the Big Tech companies create the false appearance of a consensus around issues. Many are afraid to stand up against it out of concern they may catch the attention of the angry online mobs who will harass them, dox them, and do everything in their power to destroy them.

All of this leads many to wonder—what is wrong with liberals? Why do they always seem like they have no sense of right and wrong, almost like they have no soul? Researchers at Virginia Tech discovered that people can be identified as either liberal or conservative by a simple fMRI (Functional MRI) scan of their brain.

They found that when they show people images of disgusting things like a dead animal or food covered with maggots, they could predict with a 95% accuracy rate whether the person was a liberal or a conservative based solely on brain scans which showed how people's brain activity reacted to seeing such things.[926]

How is this possible? What they found was that the brains of liberals don't show the same signals of being disgusted when shown the disgusting images. It was a discovery made by accident, but it has an enormous significance. What it means is, the further Left someone is on the political spectrum, the higher their tolerance is for abnormal (and horrifying) things. It makes perfect sense when put into perspective.

They're the ones who accept and embrace the most bizarre, unhealthy, and disgusting behaviors and lifestyles. So when shown images of disgusting things, their brain scans show little reaction, when a normal person should be repulsed. The researchers who conducted the experiments appear to be afraid to explain *why* liberals aren't disgusted by disgusting things, but the answer is clear. The Bible calls this the reprobate mind.[927]

The Bible also predicted, "There will be terrible times in the last days. People will be lovers of themselves, lovers of money, boastful, proud, abusive, disobedient to their parents, ungrateful, unholy, without love, unforgiving, slanderous, without self-control, brutal, not lovers of the good, treacherous, rash, conceited, lovers of pleasure rather than lovers of God—having a form of godliness but denying its power. Have nothing to do with such people."[928]

---

926 New Scientist "Left or right-wing? Brain's disgust response tells all" by Dan Jones (October 30th 2014)

927 Romans 1:28

928 2 Timothy 3:1-5

The fact that you read this book shows where your heart and mind is, and while we may be a minority, there are many millions of us who see the principalities and powers that oppose us and refuse to go along with their agenda or submit to their demands. We know the truth, and the truth has set us free!

Made in the USA
Middletown, DE
05 November 2020